European
Farmers' Markets Cookbook

By
Dr. Ann M. Crowley

Penfield
BOOKS

Publisher: Penfield Books, 215 Brown Street, Iowa City, Iowa 52245
Edited by Mary Sharp, Penfield Books
Layout and graphic by Molly Cook, MACook Design
Cover design by Susan DeSmet
Photography by Ann M. Crowley
All recipes developed and tested for home production by Ann M. Crowley

Publisher's Cataloging-in-Publication data

Crowley, Ann M.
    European Farmers' Markets Cookbook covers the history, stories and recipes of markets in Europe.
    Written and photographed by Ann M. Crowley
    p. 198 cm. 21.59 x 27.94
    Includes index.
    ISBN-13: 9781572160743 (paperback)
    1. European farmers' markets. 2. Stories. 3. History. 4. Recipes.
    Title: European Farmers' Markets Cookbook

Library of Congress Control Number: 2013949757

Preface

The markets in Europe have been in existence for centuries. A brief history of each market is found at the beginning of the chapters of this book with the recipes on the following pages. The countries with similar climates, geography, crops and cuisines are grouped under the headings of: British Isles (England, Scotland and Ireland), Scandinavian countries (Sweden, Norway and Finland), Iberian Peninsula (Spain and Portugal), and Eastern European countries (Germany, Poland, Hungary, Czech Republic and Austria). Italy, Russia, France and Greece have separate chapters.

Although there are hundreds of farmers' markets in Europe, the limited space in the book allowed the inclusion of only a few markets from each country. This was difficult because each market I visited was unique, fascinating and interesting. I visited all of the markets included in the book and photographed the vendors, shoppers and foods.

A complete index of all the recipes in the book begins on page 189. Recipes are listed alphabetically under the food category such as: appetizers, fruits, meats, salads, etc. Many are cross-referenced. For example, a fruit salad would be included in both the fruits category and in the listing of salads. Substitutions are given for ingredients that might be difficult to purchase in the United States, such as whale meat or horse meat.

Each of the recipes has been developed, tested and photographed for inclusion in *European Farmers' Markets Cookbook.* In developing the book, I tested and included some recipes for the traditional dishes of each country. They provide a taste of the favorite dishes of Spain, France, Greece and the other fourteen countries. Most of the recipes in the book are simple and easy to prepare. They are planned for four, six or eight servings.

The book has taken me years to research and develop and has been a very enjoyable experience. I hope the readers will marvel at the history of the markets and delight in the recipes.

European Farmers' Markets Cookbook
Table of Contents

Dedication

To my husband, John, and our son, John Jr.

Thanks

A very special thanks to Susan DeSmet, who was the architect of the book.
Her help was invaluable.
A big thanks to Miriam Canter for her assistance
in reviewing the material in the book.
And sincere thanks to friends and relatives who sent me pictures
and gave me encouragement.

European Farmers' Markets Cookbook

Introduction

My travels have taken me to thirty foreign countries. In each I sought the farmers' markets in small villages and large cities. Some had only a few ladies selling their products and others had well-established markets with large pavilions and attractive huge open buildings filled to overflowing with an endless assortment of foods and kitchen equipment. In writing the stories of more than one hundred markets and developing recipes for each, the book grew and expanded to where it became three books; *European Farmers' Markets Cookbook, Asian Farmers' Market Cookbook* and *American Farmers' Markets Cookbook.* This is the *Cookbook of the European Markets* from seventeen countries and thirty-three farmers' markets. The chapters include the clusters of countries with similar cuisines such as the Scandinavian countries of Norway, Sweden and Finland, and the British Isles with England, Scotland and Ireland. The colorful pictures taken at and in the markets of the vendors, the shoppers and the food make the markets come alive.

Markets have been around since the beginning of mankind. The barter, trade or exchange of food products were the first types of a market. The Egyptians had established trade with neighboring countries at the time of Cleopatra. As early as 2000 B.C. they were trading their foods with Italy, Greece and other ports along the Mediterranean Sea. In Europe the market has been in existence for centuries. The Campo di Fiori Market in Rome was up and running at the time of Caesar. In Ireland in the ninth century it was impossible to have a road built to a village unless it could prove that it had a market. Many of the European markets grew up around the land owner's castle. The gathering became a village when enough people were involved in the market. A square or plaza was always incorporated for a market in the plans for a town.

Marco Polo is credited for creating the trade route from the Orient bringing exotic spices and tea as well as silk to Europe as early as the thirteenth century. Markets grew up all along the road. With the discovery of the "New World" by Columbus, the markets in Portugal and Spain expanded to serve all of Europe. The conquistadors brought back food stocks of more value over the years than all the gold and silver they acquired.

From the earliest times, markets have been governed by local, regional or country administrations. They must be licensed, or certified to operate. A group or committee was appointed to oversee the operations. Stories have been written of corruption by the officials assigned to collect the dues or fees and those who issue the permits.

The markets are much more than just a place to trade, barter or buy food. They are a cultural and social center for the community. It is a gathering place for old and new friends, relatives and neighbors. Sometimes markets are called fairs because of the entertaining of music, dancing, horse racing, ball games, athletic events, children games and magicians' demonstrations.

There was a time, and still is in some countries, when the market was the main social gathering for the neighborhood or community. Marriages were arranged; quarrels were settled or started at the market. Arrangements for the harvesting or help with construction of a building were made on market day. Women particularly looked forward to the opportunity to visit with other women. They welcomed the exchange of health tips, child-rearing advice or the use of a new food product found in the market.

Each market is unique. The culture, the economic conditions of the community and the social status can be seen in the quantity and quality of the food for sale. The atmosphere of the market and, indeed, the community can be seen in the attitude of the vendors and customers. Some markets are happy places with laughter and noisy barter between seller and buyer while other markets are very sober. The economic condition of the community is reflected in the appearance of the market. When the vendors and customers are poorly dressed and few in number, it may well reflect a local economic depression. A severe drought in the area will reflect in the produce the farmers have for sale, both in quantity and quality.

Markets come in all sizes, shapes, organizations, structures and philosophies. They look different, and they even seem to have their own aroma. Each has something different of interest to me. It might be the food for sale that I find fascinating. I was surprised to see whale meat for sale at the Fisketorget Fish Market in Bergen, Norway, or the tubs of live snails at the Mercado in Seville, Spain, and the giant octopus with tentacles six feet long spread over the entire counter in the fish pavilion at Dimotiki Agora Market in Athens, Greece. Another characteristic that makes each market different is the variety of the products they sell. At the permanent large market in Vienna, I saw a large bin of small red pomegranate seeds, and in London I was served a delicate fresh scallop still in its pink shell.

The Billingsgate Fish Market in London displays and sells tons of fresh and frozen fish every morning, and the fishermen at the seaside market near Lagos, Portugal, sell their morning catch from the shore near their boats.

The personality of the vendors, as well as the culture of the market, will vary. I enjoyed listening to the exchange between a cheerful, friendly vendor at the Hotorget Market in Stockholm and the smartly dressed lady who was attempting to get a reduced price on the fresh strawberries. He was enthusiastically telling her that he could not reduce the price or his children would go without shoes. A less enjoyable experience was at the Kuzneckny Market in Saint Petersburg, Russia. The stoical vendors refused to smile or even recognize me when I complimented them on how fresh the food looked that they were selling.

The vendors were generally anxious to tell me about their products. I was told, "The fish was caught this morning," and it was not unusual to learn that the tomatoes for sale came from a small garden that had been in the family for generations.

This is a cookbook with more than one hundred seventy recipes. I developed and tested several recipes for each market using the products that I saw there. If the recipe calls for a product that is difficult to find or unavailable in the market in the United States, I suggested a substitute, such as tuna for whale steak. The final prepared product was photographed so each recipe in the book has a picture of the finished dish.

I attempted to develop some recipes for each country that are traditional dishes such as Irish soda bread for Ireland, flatbread for Finland, borscht for Russia and sauerbraten for Germany. The recipes for the variety of products cover all categories from appetizers to vegetables.

The interest in natural and organic food products in Europe has grown and facilitated the growth of farmers' markets. This trend was obvious in European markets. The European Union has been helpful in promoting organic farming by supplying financial aid to farmers who convert to raising organic products. In many of the European countries, the conversion to organic farming was simple because many of the farms were of small acreages and frequently were free of chemicals. In Spain and Portugal, the olive orchards often met the standards for organic crops. The markets are constantly changing and today the movement is influenced by organic foods, the Slow Food Movement and the impact of tourism.

The joy of wandering through a farmers' market is unmatched. The aroma, the sights, the sounds all add to an exhilarating experience. I believe food at the market provides a wonderful art show in all the colors, textures, shapes, sizes and diversity. Farmers' markets provide us with a way of keeping in touch with the people who produce the food we eat. It is a rewarding experience to talk with the person who has raised or caught the food you have the privilege of buying and serving to your family. This is the freshest food you can purchase.

I hope you enjoy preparing the market recipes and eating the array of delicious foods. I find the stories and pictures of the European markets fascinating, and I hope you do, too.

British Isles Markets

The British Isles, England, Scotland, Wales, and Ireland, comprise two islands. Markets and fairs and barter have been a way of life in the islands for as long as they have been populated. In the early times in the British Isles, the exchange of products between the producer and the consumer was in the form of barter. In 43 A.D. the Romans occupied the islands and brought with them currency representing value. This brought about markets for the trade of food and useful items for the home. The markets soon held products from Italy such as wine, olive oil, pottery and papyrus. Rome received lead, iron, tin and woolen products in exchange.

By the fifth century, with the arrival of Saint Patrick and Christianity, the countries were mostly rural. With the spread of Christianity, monasteries were established. These became the centers of interest and soon communities were established around or near them. Farmers would gather at or near the monastery to sell their goods. The church held control of the market and granted the right to hold the market in the church yard. It was the market location that brought about the development of a village or hamlet. For a road to be built to a town, it had to qualify as a market town. The landlord often had a castle where the market would be held. The Edinburgh Castle in Scotland was the

site for the farmers' market for centuries. Throughout the time, either the English or the Scottish occupied the castle, and the market adjusted to the demands of the ruling king. From the 1600s on, the king granted the right to hold a market to the landowner or to the village.

In the seventh and eighth centuries, the Vikings made their imprint on the British Isles. They established ports and created trade. The Vikings took home corn, wool, iron, coal and looted treasures from the monasteries, and their long ships returned with herring and timber.

Markets and fairs were common. The fairs were larger and held less frequently.

They were a time of celebration with music, dancing, horse racing, boxing, food and drink. Markets were becoming specialized, with grain markets selling wheat, oats, rye and barley. The grain market was called the Corn Market.

Beer was brewed from grain and an alcoholic drink called mead made with honey were sold at the markets in Ireland, England and Scotland. The local farmers' wives brought produce, honey, butter and live poultry to the markets. Because fuel was expensive and difficult for city dwellers to acquire, the farm women would make bread and sell the loaves at the market or deliver them to the homes.

Livestock on the hoof were driven to market from nearby farms and in some markets slaughtered on site. The wild and bewildered cattle, pigs, sheep and goats caused a loud disturbance at the market.

These were known as Livestock Markets. There were sanitary and health concerns. Inspectors watched for rotten meat, poultry and fish. Disposing of animals' offal, blood and entrails was a special problem. The shoppers found the sights, sounds and odors offensive.

Markets throughout the British Isles have changed greatly with the times. The large pavilions and market buildings have high sanitary standards. Refrigerated cases and crushed ice help to control safe temperatures for the products. The gist is to provide a place for local farmers and fisherfolks to sell their products. The governing bodies for the markets have established the rules. The products must be raised, caught or produced within a prescribed radius of the market. All items for sale must be produced by the stall holder, who must be present at the market.

The administrators of the farmers' markets have allowed for "guest traders," who are not registered but who provide essential products for the customers. This allows for the market to sell items not raised in the local countryside. These stalls will have fruits, vegetables, wines, oils and seafood from other countries.

There are approximately five hundred registered farmers' markets in England today. However, there are many more markets that are not included in those reported as registered farmers' markets. The number of farmers' markets in Ireland has declined to an approximately one hundred thirty-seven registered markets.

Chelsea Market | London, England

An unusually warm day in late May with a temperature of 76 degrees brought forth shoppers to the Chelsea Farmers Market located in Chelsea on Kings Road and Sloane in Duke of York Square. Kings Road was named for King Charles II, who used this road as his private lane from St. James Palace to his home on Fulham Road. The area around the Square has always been a popular location for the wealthy and in 1694 was described as "a village of palaces." However, there was still land for market gardens that served the population of the area and of London. This trade continued until the nineteenth century when the expansion of building took over the land. Another popular market business was the selling of Chelsea buns made with long strips of twisted dough with currants inside the strips and the tops sprinkled generously with sugar. These were popular with the workers and shoppers at the Chelsea Porcelain Factory that operated near the area until 1759.

Every Saturday, the Chelsea Market is held in the Square next to the statue of the Duke of York. I saw approximately twenty-five stalls arranged along the walkway. Some were tented and some were well-stocked open tables. The butcher stall had the meat enclosed in a glass counter as were the confectioneries at the chocolate stall.

The first Market stand that I saw as I entered the Market was McManus Oysters. The fresh oysters in their shells and the fish were on a bed of crushed ice. For immediate consumption oysters were shucked and placed on the open half shell. The price of six oysters for five pounds was displayed on a chalk board. I noted that fresh fish heads were for sale at the stand.

The fresh produce stands featured large, thick stalks of green asparagus. Both red and yellow large tomatoes and the smaller cherry tomatoes were perfectly shaped without a single blemish. The greens included spicy arugula, spinach and leaf lettuce. At Robert's produce stall, I saw the longest shallots I have ever seen. They were at least six inches long. The shallots were in a plastic tub next to cauliflower that was labeled "KukkaKaali." To me the vegetable looked like a small cauliflower about the size of a baseball.

The portobello mushrooms provided me with a Kodak moment. The four white mushrooms were arranged in a wooden basket. The basket was framed with green watercress, alfalfa sprouts and an English cucumber.

I had to take a picture of two happy shoppers. Rick and Rose live in Denver, Colorado, and were on a holiday in England.

Several stalls were busy selling a variety of cheeses. I asked a young lady selling cheese where the cheese came from. She pointed to the Partridges' store located just behind her table of cheeses. I said,

"No, I wonder where the cheese is produced." She said she did not know. I then realized the cheese stand is owned and run by the Partridges' grocery store. The selection of cheeses was extensive. I found some of the cheese names fascinating, such as Stinky Bishop.

Bread and rolls were sold at two stands and a table sold decorated cupcakes and brownies made by Betty. Betty told me she started decorating the cupcakes at 4 a.m. this morning.

Several stands were selling prepared foods that could be taken home or eaten at one of the tables arranged in the square for

service. One stand featured Brazilian stew with red and black beans that smelled delicious. Timothy was selling meat pies made with venison meat. He offered a sample of the meat pie that I enthusiastically accepted. The texture was not runny with gravy but more like a thick porridge. The stall selling prepared pasta offered several varieties available from warm chafing pans.

The stall I could not resist sold candies in dark chocolate, milk chocolate and white chocolate. These were well protected in a glass-enclosed case.

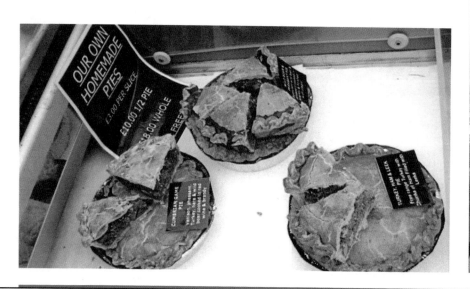

Borough Market | London, England

As early as the Roman occupation of London, a market has existed on the banks of the Thames River near the site of the present London Bridge. The farmers and traders brought their wares: grain, vegetables, livestock, fish, metal weapons, animal skins and utensils by boat or on carts across the wooden bridge to sell at the market. In 1276, the market moved to what is now Borough High Street. This area was outside the jurisdiction of the City of London. The area soon became congested and attracted undesirable inhabitants. Prisons and brothels were found throughout the section adjacent to the market.

The city of London received a royal charter vested by Edward VI in 1550 to control all markets in Southwark, including Borough Market. Charles II confirmed the charter in 1671. The Market grew and expanded until it was cramped and crowded. This caused a problem of traffic congestion with reports of mile-long lines to get into the city and blocking the only southern exit from the city. An act was passed by Parliament to allow the local residents to pay six thousand English pounds to buy a plot of 4.5 acres on Rochester Yard known as "the triangle" for a site for the new market.

The twentieth century saw the Market transformed again, this time as a result of its successes and expansion as a wholesale market. It was estimated that during the year 1933 there were 1,750,000 bushels of vegetables, 250,000 boxes of fruit and 500,000 pecks of loose fruit sold at the Market. By the late 1960s the wholesale Market held at night was doing well but the retail sales had declined to where the Market was nearly empty of stalls during the daytime. It was time for another transformation.

It took thirty years and today the Borough Market is the showplace of all the markets in London. The Market is administered by sixteen trustees who must live in the community. They oversee the vendors and the quality and sanitation of the products sold at the wholesale and retail Market. The Market features foods from around the world as well as locally produced products. The 130 stalls provide a wide variety of foods and beverages. There are stalls selling olive oils from Italy, cheeses from France, tomatoes from the Isle of Wight, teas from the East, pies from Leicestershire, hams from Spain, fresh produce from Lincolnshire and Highland beef from Preston.

A large fruit and vegetable area was called "Turnips." The produce was locally grown as well as shipped in from around the world. Pineapple from South

America, grapes from Spain, papaya from Africa and dates and figs from Asia were at several stalls. Most of the vegetables for sale were grown in England but others, such as artichokes and truffles, were imported. A large selection of organically raised vegetables and fruit was identified and available. One of the produce stalls had fresh basil, parsley, cilantro and oregano in cardboard boxes for the customers to select the herbs they desired. Fresh, locally grown gooseberries were for sale. I had not seen them at other markets in England. The home-grown English strawberries were in season. They were in plastic containers, but it was possible to see the perfectly shaped, very large, bright red berries.

Another section was devoted to the sale of beverages: beer, wine and cider. The beverages were promoted as being organic and locally produced. The stall-owner was a fairly young man with a full beard and well-trimmed hair. He was very knowledgeable about the wine-making process and stressed the need to

pick only the best and healthiest grapes. I enjoyed talking with him.

Close by the wine stand were several tables loaded with extra virgin olive oils and vinegars. Some of the vinegars were flavored, such as lemon, basil and garlic.

Fresh fish and seafood were sold from three large stalls and a fourth, slightly enclosed stall was a short distance from the other vendors. The selection of fish was endless. I saw eel, several kinds of shrimp, crab, clams, mussels, and oysters. I did not see squid or octopus. The

fishmongers were interacting with the customers and offered samples of their catch. At one of the fish shops, a young, tall, attractive and enthusiastic man was shucking scallops for samples. He would open the delicate, pink shell and hand the scallop in the shell to the customer to taste. The creamy white scallops were not large, just bite size. My sample was delicious and certainly the freshest scallop I had ever eaten. I noted that when I left the market several hours later he was still shucking scallops and handing out samples.

The butcher shops in the Market advertised the meat and chicken as "organic." When I asked the butcher at a busy stall if all the meat he sold was organic, he told me that the customers were very particular about the food they buy and most prefer the organic meats. He pointed to a plaque on the wall and said the people do use the information. The plaque stated: "The information on the breeding,

feeding and butchering of our meat products is available for customers who are interested in this information."

In the meat section of the Market, I saw several kinds of sausages on display. One fresh meat vendor sold ostrich and game meat.

Several bakery stalls had a variety of sizes and shapes of bread piled high on the counter. The artisan Bakers DeGustibus Shop has been in the Market for decades. The assortment of tarts and pastries made one's mouth water. The displays were colorful and the aroma divine.

Cheese was available at several stands. These were not refrigerated. Most of the cheeses were in large, round wheels or irregular chunks. The shoppers would indicate the size of the piece they desired, and the salesperson would slice it from the large wheel. One stand sold only

sheep milk cheese, and another had a glass-front refrigerator filled with soft goat cheese for sale.

A tea stand sold a variety of loose tea, no tea bags. The middle-aged Asian lady in a black kimono was serving tea to the prospective buyers. If a customer was interested in a certain type of tea, the lady would prepare a sample of that tea for tasting before buying. She also sold glass and China teapots and porcelain tea cups.

Many of the vendors provided samples of their products. While I was at the Market, I tasted scallops, cheese, bread, olive oil, wine, cider, olives, tea, salmon and sausage. Prepared foods were also available. Some stands that I saw were selling bouillabaisse, pot pies, beef steak and onion pie, roast pork, chicken with apricot stuffing, Cornish pasties, a variety of prepared sandwiches and fried

chicken. These could be eaten at tables near the shops or taken home.

Each hour on the hour a vendor would give a demonstration on a stage in an area where the visitors could sit and watch. The stage had good amplifiers for clear sound. I watched Anna from Sweden prepare gravlax, a marinated salmon. And the lady who was selling tea gave a demonstration on how to marinate and prepare fish with tea using a Thai recipe.

Borough Market is a very busy place with local shoppers and tourists. I noted people of all ages at the Market: mothers with babies, families with both parents and children, young and middle-aged singles, older women with shopping carts and bags. I was impressed with the friendly, pleasant, kind attitude of the vendors. It was an enjoyable experience to visit the Market.

Billingsgate Fish Market | London, England

Billingsgate Fish Market was once the largest fish market in the world. Today it is still the largest inland fish market in the United Kingdom. Its name comes from the ward southeast of the city of London called Billingsgate.

In the sixteenth and seventeenth centuries, the Billingsgate Wharf, close to the River Thames, was a busy fish market. The fishermen delivered their catch to the fishmongers. On market days the street was crowded and noisy. The fishmongers shouted the value of their fish in loud and rough language. In fact, the word "Billingsgate" became a reference for crude and vulgar language. One of the earliest uses can be seen in a 1577 chronicle by Raphael Holinshed, where the writer makes references to the foul tongues of Billingsgate oyster-wives.

In 1699 the Act of Parliament officially established the Billingsgate Fish Market. It remained an open-air, street market until 1849 when it was moved off the street into its own riverside building. Twenty-five years later the building was demolished and replaced by an arcaded market hall designed by the city architect Sir Horace Jones. The fish market grew and became the source of fresh fish and shellfish for retail and wholesale trade in London. Vans and lorries from grocery markets, schools, hospitals and large institutions arrived for purchase of large orders of fish. They competed with the foot traffic for the best products available. The area became congested and unable to function efficiently. Also, the land had become very valuable for business buildings and real estate. In 1982, the fish market was relocated in a new thirteen-acre, 159,000-square-foot building close to Canary Wharf in Docklands.

The New Billingsgate Fish Market comes alive around midnight when vans and refrigerated lorries loaded with fish from the fishing boats start to arrive. The stall owners and their staff in clean white lab

coats and water-proof aprons meet the delivery on the loading dock. Each company has its own location in the Market. Immediately the fish are transferred to the stand where they are arranged in crushed ice in Styrofoam boxes about 12 inches by 20 inches and about 12 inches deep. The larger fish end up in much larger boxes or are simply laid on beds of crushed ice on the counters.

By 2 a.m. each vendor knows what he has for sale and orders start coming in by phone. These orders can be filled but

...pply of wild salmon has been depleted. ...e salmon caught off the coast of Chile ...e been infected with a parasite and are ...the market, adding to the shortage. ...ole, flat flounder were at a couple of ...s, and another smaller version of this ..."plaice," was available. The plaice fish ...ut 12 to 15 inches long and flat. I ...ed that the young fish has an eye on ...ide of the head and as it matures ...comes a flat fish, the underneath ...ves around the head to join the eye ...top side of the fish.

was effectively displayed with labels as to the type of each fish.

The buyers park their trucks and vans in the loading dock and fill them with their early morning purchases. By 8 a.m., the Market becomes quiet and the selling is pretty much over except for some local individuals who are buying fish for the family dinner. The cleanup begins. The need for sanitation is vital. All of the unsold fish are packed with ice and hauled off to the cold storage area. The counters and floors are washed to assure there is no debris or waste left from the fish products.

There are two small restaurants, one on each end of the building, that serve the workers and visitors. It is a spot for the workers to gather after working since midnight to have a meal before they go home. It is a time of camaraderie and enjoyment for the people who have so much in common. The menu lists kippers and scrambled eggs and smoked haddock with poached eggs. I enjoyed the haddock for breakfast.

...of various sizes and colors ...d in tubs and large bins. ...s and crabs are packed ...One vendor had bundles ...hat looked exactly like ...vigs and as fat as a man's ...r had a box of tiny, dark ...le, simply called winkle. ...atly enclosed in mesh ...n to look like enlarged ...vere fresh, silvery sar- ...and large, sea bass and ...lled red. Smoked fish

...e loads of crushed ice weigh more than one hundred pounds and each day tons of ice are moved through the aisles to the stalls.

Walking through the Market, I saw almost every species of fish and shellfish found in the ocean, rivers and lakes. Whole, large halibut were wrestled onto scales. Salmon from the North Sea east of England are farm-raised because the

Newgate Market | York, England

The Newgate Market in the town of York is a traditional market located in the square with a web of narrow roads leading to its center. The market is as old as the city of York and probably the catalyst for the founding of the town in 71 A.D. during the reign of the Roman Emperor Vespasian.

In the early fourteenth century, the English King Edward II signed a royal charter granting the town of York the right to hold a market. Through time, additional charters for a market in York were granted by King Henry IV, King Henry VII, Queen Elizabeth I, King Charles II, and King James. The Market sprang up adjacent to the beautiful Cathedral that was built more than one hundred years in the fifteenth and sixteenth centuries. The church is the second largest church in England next to Westminster. It was common practice for a market to be built next to a church

The city grew, and the market prospered. The land around the walled city produced fruits, vegetables and grains for the expanding population. The market

also provided household items, clothing, leather goods and hardware as arms implements.

The Newgate Market is certified by the national association that established criteria for farmers' markets in the United Kingdom in 1997. The local farmers, growers or producers bring their products to market from within a radius of forty miles of the market. All goods that are sold at the Newgate Market have either been grown, reared, caught, brewed, picked, baked, smoked or processed by the stallholder. Guest traders are granted permission to bring products that are not available in the area to the Market.

On the day I visited the Newgate Market, some of the stalls were closed although the Market is open seven days a week. My introduction to the Market was the flower stands along a busy passage. The cut flowers were grown locally and also brought from London's nurseries. Potted plants and seedlings were sold for the home gardens.

The Market stands were out of doors, and the vendors had tents over their stalls. The two produce stalls were quite large. The wooden tables used to hold the fruits and vegetables were each about twenty feet in length. A good variety of produce was beautifully displayed.

Gordon and Jane's stall had one section with a wide variety of fresh greens in all shades. Jane, an enthusiastic middle-aged lady, and her husband are owners of the stand and have been coming to the Market for twenty years. She introduced me to new greens that looked like miniature or baby watercress. I learned it is called "cress" not watercress. At the second stand, a display of watercress next to cress showed the difference. The English leeks and the asparagus for sale at Jane's stand were larger, fatter than most I had seen. The beets, listed as beetroots, were fresh from the ground that day.

The second produce stand adjacent to Gordon and Jane's is owned by the Shlilas family and has been selling produce at the Market for many years. Their sign reads "high class fruits and fresh vegetables." They had a selection of fruit including: Belgium pears, Italian golden plums, American red delicious apples, pineapples, blueberries, Spanish cherries, Italian kiwis, oranges, lemons and limes. When I asked how they could have all the fruit from different countries and still be considered a farmers' market, the stout man running the stand said, "We have permission to sell the fruit because it helps the Market, and the stand is considered a "guest stall."

This stall also had a wide selection of vegetables. Several cardboard boxes held small baseball-sized cauliflowers. The snow white cauliflowers were encased in their green stalks and leaves, making an attractive display. Boxes held cherry tomatoes that were bright red and of uniform size and shape. The vendor, a rather large man with a close-shaved head, was busy conversing with the shoppers and packaging their orders.

The well-stocked cheese stall looked enticing and had a wonderful aroma. English Stilton and a combination of Stilton and cheddar took center stage. Several kinds of goat cheese and cheese made from ewe's milk were featured at the stall.

At the end of a small table were stacks of eggs in cartons. The eggs were from free, range-chickens, and eggs with both white and brown shells were displayed.

The butcher shop displayed the meat and poultry of various cuts of beef, pork and lamb in a refrigerated glass front counter.

Pork belly, fresh leg of pork, pork fillets as well as ham and rashers were available. The well-trimmed beef roasts and steaks were arranged in trays. Lamb chops, legs of lamb and lamb steaks took up one end of the display. The butcher shop in the Market has an interesting history. In the medieval times, the live livestock and poultry were brought to the market to butchers who were located along a narrow lane next to the present market. The animals were slaughtered along the cobblestone path called Shambles. This roadway slopes down a small decline that allowed the blood from the animals to flow away from the butcher's workshop. There is one shop along Shambles Street that still has the meat hooks along the overhang where the animal carcasses were displayed after slaughter.

Westmorland County Fair
County Food Fest | Westmorland, England

Incorporating the former Westmorland Food Lovers Festival with the County Food Fest gave a real taste of the North England Lake District. This is a celebration of the quality and diversity of the superb independent food and drink producers and suppliers that abound in Cumbria and the northwest of England. The second annual two-day Food Festival sponsored by the Westmorland County Agricultural Society was held in a field outside Kendal on the last weekend in May 2010. I felt very fortunate to be there on the right date.

Large tents were set up for exhibits and for the food and beverage shops.

This was truly a farmers' market and a county fair. All the food stands were manned by the producers of the products being sold. Like most fairs, entertainment went on all day. There was music and dance by the Scottish Country Dance Group, the Kendal Concert band, maypole dancing and a ballet performance by the Regency Bank Ballet School. The outdoor demonstrations were of birds of prey, terrier dog racing, carriage driving, Fell pony and zero gravity presentations.

At noon, Sean Wilson of the Saddleworth Cheese Company whipped up a cheese soufflé all the while talking about the Lancashire cheese he had developed. He stated, "the aim is to start with specially formulated cultures to create a cheese that tastes like cheese used to taste. With traditional cutting,, we are preserving the all-important body and character of the curd, which really does make all the difference when it comes down to true taste." He believes food should be fun and has given his cheeses names that he feels fits the taste of each type.

Muldoons Picnic (a Lancashire term given to a room full of screaming kids)

is a crumbly creamy cheese that has won many awards.

How's Yer Father cheese is a smooth, velvety creamy Lancashire cheese.

Mouth Almighty has a mouthy tang that opens up to a full flavor and unfolds into the mouth with a creaminess not unlike the **How's Yer Father.**

Smelly Apeth (a child covered with muck after a day's play in smelly apeth) is a beautiful blue-veined cheese. It is a medium soft cheese with a mild, sweet nuttiness.

Sean served samples of his cheeses to all sixty spectators at his demonstration and asked us to evaluate each.

Outside and adjacent to the exhibit tent, Ben had set up his stand of smoked fish. He had one smoker loaded with rows of hanging fish fillets actually being smoked and another smoker that had just completed the process. Ben, who appeared to be about twenty years old, told me he had been in the business of smoking fish and other foods for twenty years. He buys his herring and other fish from fishermen on

the coasts. He has both dried and smoked kippers for sale.

Inside the large food tent were at least fifty stalls selling fresh and prepared foods. The products at each stand were produced by the person behind the counter or table.

Several cheese stands, including the Lancashire, were selling both soft and hard cheeses. The samples were snatched up very quickly. The St. James Cheese Company featured ewe's milk cheese, both the soft and semi-soft types. Margaret, the neatly dressed shop owner, informed me that they have a flock of fifty sheep to produce the milk for their cheese.

The selection of bread at the stands was in piles for everyone to see and check. The choice included various grains, sourdough, and dark bread with treacle (a kind of molasses) and multigrain breads. The breads of different sizes and shapes made for a beautiful display.

The Ginger Shop sold cakes and cookies (called biscuits) with a ginger flavor. They

also had sheets of gingerbread. Wendy Ash was selling the most attractively decorated cupcakes. The cutest were in the shape of pink pigs.

Several meat stands had a variety of cuts of meat for sale from their counters. The roasts, called joints, were often rolled. Lamb was available in steaks, chops, roasts and chopped. One stall was selling veal.

Wild boar and venison were also for sale at several stands. The deer and wild boar were raised on estates in the north of England. One seller told me he contracted for the boar meat with an estate not far away so he knew its quality. The estate has about forty wild boars at one time. Hamburgers made with wild boar meat were being prepared and sold at several café stands. Venison is also quite popular in this area.

The Knipey stand was selling free-range chickens and the fresh eggs they laid. The chickens were large, weighing five or more pounds. Each chicken was dressed and neatly wrapped in a plastic cover.

Two stands were selling prepared baked meat pies. The variety of meats used in the pies was impressive. Wild boar, turkey, pheasant, venison, hare, and mixtures of pork, veal and beef were used. Chicken pot pies were also for sale. At Grub's shop, I found roasts in interesting shapes: boneless duck leg medallions stuffed with cranberry, apple and pork sausage meat, as well as a chicken crown stuffed with venison sausage meat, onions and peppers.

A lady, whose name was Sarah, was selling jars of relishes. She had an unlimited

selection of every kind you could imagine, including beetroot relish. She prepares all relishes in her home kitchen. Right next to Sarah was a stand with large bowls of olives, pimientos, pickles and nuts. The stand was operated by two young men. I asked if I could take their picture and they said, "If you take our picture, will we become famous?"

Several types of beverages that are produced in this area were presented by the producers. A product named "Brew" was brewed and sold by the young entrepreneurs. They were having a good time visiting with the customers and were happy to talk with me. They told me that they had been making Brew for two years. A shop of spirits by the Spencerfield Spirit Company had a tasty Scotch whiskey called Sheep Dip. A brewer of beer also had some shockingly interesting names for his products such as "Cat Piss" and "Old Fart."

If you were interested, you could learn how to make beer by watching the demonstration and presentation of beer-making in the separate beer tent. Of course, you could also enjoy a glass of beer while there.

The Festival was well attended by all ages. Families were enjoying this outing even on a gray, rainy day.

Edinburgh Farmers' Market | Scotland

The Edinburgh Farmers' Market is situated on the plaza of the historic Edinburgh Castle on the top of the Royal Mile at the west end of Edinburgh. Since the twelth century there has been a royal castle atop the volcanic Castle Rock. The rocky cliffs to the south, west and north, rearing up two hundred and sixtyfeet from the surrounding landscape, made the castle secure from attack. The only accessible road to the castle is the eastern approach where the ridge slopes more gently. This has been the passageway for food and supplies to reach the castle for generations.

The history of the Edinburgh Castle is very colorful and relates to the rise and fall of Scotland as an independent country. Over the centuries, England captured the Castle several times only to have it taken back by the Scottish. The Edinburgh Castle is now run and administrated by Historic Scotland, an executive agency of the Scottish government. It is responsible for operating the Castle as a commercial tourist attraction while maintaining and conserving the castle as a historic monument. This is no easy job for management in that 1.2 million visitors toured the castle in 2009.

The Farmers' Market in the shadow of the Edinburgh Castle in the Castle Plaza welcomes shoppers and visitors every Saturday when the Market is open. The sixty or more vendors bring to the Market a variety of fresh products that they have grown or produced. Many of the stallholders belong to the Scottish Association of Farmers' Markets. The association has established rules and guidelines for members to assure the best and freshest quality of products. According to their bylaws, "the Scottish Farmers' Market is defined as a Market in which farmers, growers and producers from throughout Scotland sell their produce direct to the public. All food products sold should have been grown, reared, caught, brewed, pickled, baked, smoked or made/prepared by the producer." The association also indicates to the members the standards for sanitation, food safety, legal resources, environmental considerations and other services available.

At the Edinburgh Market, I found several purveyors of fresh, smoked, cured and prepared meats. In fact, nearly one-quarter of the stalls in the Market sell meat products. The Carmichael Meats and Border County stalls sold organic beef, pork, lamb, veal and fresh cuts of venison and buffalo.

The Carmichael Estate Farm is one of the oldest single-estate farming businesses in Scotland, established in 1292. It struck me that was two hundred years before Columbus discover Americas. The Puddledub meat shop was established in 2005 and has been selling fresh cuts of buffalo, as well as barbequed buffalo, at the markets for several years. Other wild game, such as boar, pheasant, elk and ostrich, can occasionally be found at the Market. I learned there are farms that raise boar, deer and ostrich just outside of Edinburgh. The Fletchers of Auchtermuchty sell fresh venison and products made with venison such as homemade sausage.

A popular sausage in Northern England and Scotland is the Cumberland sausage that is, of course, chopped pork and spices. The recipe is said to be five hundred years old and was created when the spices black pepper, ginger, white pepper and nutmeg became available in the region. Molasses, cane sugar and rum became available at the same time and found their way into the Cumberland sausage.

At the Edinburgh Farmers' Market, there is a stall with the unique name "Well Hung and Tender." The vendor sells beef of Aberdeen Angus cattle that are grass-fed in the fertile Scottish borders for the most flavor and high levels of omega-3-fatty acid. According to its booklet, "All the beef is hung on the bone to mature for at least four weeks. The hanging process allows enzymes longer to tenderize the meat and reduce moisture content, concentrating the flavor and preventing shrinkage during cooking."

Hugh Grierson, owner and stallholder, sells organic, grass-fed Aberdeen beef that has matured in the traditional manner and hung for three weeks. Organic Berkshire rare breed pork, home-bred lamb and free-range organic chickens are vacuum-packed in convenient size cuts. Hugh Grierson has raised Aberdeen cattle for thirty-five years and obtained organic status in October 2002.

Yet another unique stall is Hog Roast, owned by Adam Marshall and Sandy Pate. They began specializing in hog roast in the year 2000 and brought their fresh roast pork to the farmers' market

in Edinburgh in 2001 and have attended every single Saturday since. I found they were happy to cater a whole roast pig for celebrations or other events with up to five hundred guests.

Creelers and S & D Patterson are the two main stalls selling seafood. At the Patterson stall, I found the bright red crayfish. They are scary to look at but delightful to eat. Edinburgh is close to the sea so the seafood at the Market is the freshest.

Organic-raised vegetables and fruits were featured at the Market. An outstanding example was the Phantassie Farm. The farm is on the edge of East Linton just twenty-five miles from Edinburgh. The original growing area of a one-acre,

walled garden has been raising produce for one hundred and fifty years. The two large polytunnels and greenhouses enable them to supply the Market all year long. Patricia Stephen will explain the use of nature compost and manure, comfrey and seaweed. Using crop rotation, green manuring and companion planting aids the strength and fertility of the soil.

Patricia Stephen is the owner of the Earth Food Market, where she sells and delivers fresh organic produce from orders placed by her list of customers.

Mushrooms are present in the stalls from spring through late fall. Early dryad's saddle mushrooms are on the Market tables by May. In the summer there is a plethora of oyster, chanterelle, hedgehog, saffron milkcap, smooth white button and St. George mushrooms. Gypsy and

chicken of the woods, or hen mushrooms, are plentiful from late August through October. The gypsy mushrooms are a special delicacy raised in Southern Scotland. Trooping funnel mushrooms are abundant in Southern Scotland in October and November. However, they are fragile and are available in the Market for only a short period of time.

The Brewster Farm sells organic eggs. These large brown and white eggs are collected from the free-range chickens on the morning of the Market. The shoppers report they are the very best eggs available in all of Scotland.

Not all farmers' markets have stands selling beverages, and even fewer allow the sale of alcoholic beverages. At the Edinburgh Farmers' Market, I was excited to see the Spencerfield Spirit Company. Their two Scotch whiskeys have names that would discourage a committed drinker of whiskey: Pig's Nose, a blended Scotch, and Sheep Dip, a blended Scottish whiskey. However, I understand both Scotch whiskeys are selling well.

Alex Nicol, owner of Spencerfield Spirit Company, has expanded his line to include Edinburgh Gin.

"In 1777, there were eight licensed distilleries and almost four hundred illegal

stills in Edinburgh and Port of Leith. As gin rose to become a fashionable spirit, Edinburgh distillers, like their London counterparts, produced gin from locally sourced ingredients. The juniper berries, spices and citrus fruits arrived daily in Leith from all over the world. These exotic botanicals were redistilled or rectified together with the finest Scottish grain spirit in the time-honored fashion."

Mr. Nicol states, "Edinburgh gin is a reminder of the days when Edinburgh was the center of the distilling expertise.

We distill small batches in 'jenny' a much treasured Scottish copper pot still, using traditional gin botanicals. Then we add extra Scottish juniper as well as heather, Scot pine and milk thistle."

The recipe and production methods for Edinburgh Gin used by the Spencerfield Spirit Company were created in Edinburgh two hundred and fifty years ago.

Not only did the market have whiskey for sale, but Sara Barton was at her stall, the Brewster's Brewing Company, with an assortment of beers and ales.

Brewster's has been used as the Old English word for female brewers. In medieval times, women brewed and sold most of the ale. With the introduction of hops, beer lasted longer and could be distributed to distant markets. The trade became dominated by male brewers who began to brew beer with hops on an industrial scale.

Sara Barton established her brewery in 1998 with the aim of becoming an all-around craft brewery producing an array of beer styles. Today, she has regular beers and two ranges of development beers, Whimsicale with 4 percent (alcohol by volume) and Wicked Women with 4.8 percent abv. The unpasteurized beer also includes Porter and Pale Ale.

St. George's Market | Belfast, Ireland

The enclosed St. George's Market built of red brick and sandstone opened for business on June 20, 1890. By 1980, St. George's Market was nearly one hundred years old and badly in need of an update and modernization to meet health regulations. In restoring the building, an effort was made to maintain the building's original features. Special bricks were produced in England to match the original unusual sized bricks. In 2006, the Market was voted as one of the UK's top five markets by the National Association of British Market Authorities.

I visited the Market early on a Saturday morning in June and was impressed with the building. The entrance has a tall arch with beautiful iron spokes in a fan shape over the iron entrance gate. Above the arch are the words St. George's Market and above that in a pointed steeple is the Belfast Coat of Arms. The bricks were a bright orange color in the morning sun.

The Market is a long, open area with black metal rails along the sides and ceiling. The shops are along the walls and also down the center of the facility.

The first stalls I encountered as I entered were the fish markets spaced all along the front wall of the Market. The fish were in plastic tubs and baskets. The fishmongers would select a fish from the tub, pick it up by the tail, slap it on the long, stainless steel table and proceed to chop off the head and gut the fish. Several men dressed in blue jackets and plastic aprons were working behind the counter. On the wall behind the fish counter was a beautiful painted mural titled *Fish Galore*. It depicts a red boat with a red-bearded fisherman riding on white waves over an ocean of fish.

The C. & O. Milligans, known as "the fish people," were selling not only the dressed salmon, halibut, sea bream and mullet but also had trays of crab, clams, mussels and shrimp. Another stall had the whole shrimp with head and shells still on spread over the stainless steel

were in season. James Murdoch, a tall, heavy-set, handsome man, has had a produce stand in the Market for many years. He also was selling other fruits, such as pineapple, bananas, and citrus, that were imported from Africa and Spain.

A rather large stand selling an assortment of olives had products in woven baskets. The vendor, Patrick, told me his olives sold well in Belfast. He encouraged me to taste several. I found the black olives with orange zest and sections to be delightful.

The butcher shop had most of its meat in glass, refrigerated cases. All types of local meats were available, and I even saw venison and pheasant for sale. The butchers were proud of the beef from Amagh. The smoked bacon in large slabs and the smoked sausages were on a wooden counter close to the shoppers. Michael McWhinney owns the stall selling sausages of all types. I asked about black

counter. The fish and seafood were the freshest, having been caught in the nearby cold waters of the Irish Sea and Atlantic Ocean. Alan Comfy's fish stall was also along the wall, as was the Something Fishy stand. It had round, flat fish like a flounder on ice in a container in front of the stall.

Numerous stalls along the hall were selling produce: tomatoes, lettuce, watercress, green onions, cauliflower, spinach, cucumbers, beets, carrots and turnips. The carrots and beets were laid on the counter with their long, green stems draped over the back of the table. Most of the produce stands also had fresh fruit. The locally grown cherries and berries

pudding sausage, made with blood, and Michael pointed to the meat case and showed me the sausage.

One very busy stand was selling curry products. It was possible to buy a dish of curry over rice already prepared. The aroma from this stand was enticing. Another stand that was selling prepared food was Belfast Pasta, owned by Justin Nichall. Preparing the pasta from scratch, he then cooked it as ordered by the shoppers. Fortunately, there were tables and chairs for them to sit and enjoy their meal. Another cooked delicacy was Pig

on a Stick. Alan Park roasts the whole pig on a rotisserie spit and brings it to the Market on the spit.

Anne-Marie Mullan from the Mullan Organic Farm was selling organic eggs from the free-range chickens. She had both white and brown eggs in different sizes. Free-range eggs were also available at Limavady's stall.

Ireland has some of the best cheeses in the world. Some of the cheeses I saw at the Market were: Fermoy, Glebe Brethan, Mount Callan, Coeragh, Porter, with a brown burgundy color, and Ardsallagh. I sampled white cheddar cheese that was tangy and tasty. The Irish Farmhouse Cheese stand carried the soft cream cheese, Brie, and blue cheeses.

The Market has strong support from the community and will continue to grow and provide a service to Belfast.

Recipes | British Isles Markets

Scalloped Oysters, Chelsea Market, London

The very first stand I saw in the Chelsea Market was Maldon Oysters. I was rather surprised to see oysters at the Market in June. It was possible to buy the oysters in the shell or shucked. The oyster stand also had several kinds of fresh fish for sale. The fish were sold whole dressed or cut into fillets.

1 pint oysters with liquor
1-1/2 cups cracker crumbs
1/4 cup butter, melted
2 cups half-and-half cream
1/2 teaspoon salt
1/8 teaspoon white pepper
1/8 teaspoon nutmeg.
3 drops hot sauce

Preheat oven to 400 degrees.

In a mixing bowl, combine all ingredients. Stir to blend. Place in a greased baking dish. Bake for 30 minutes.

Yield: 4 servings

Lemon Curd, Chelsea Market, London

Lemon curd is often served at teatime in England. The sweet, tart, velvety spread is served on freshly baked scones, muffins, crumpets and fruit breads. Lemon curd also is served on gingerbread or used as a filling for tarts and cakes. I enjoyed the most delicious lemon curd at afternoon tea in the Marriott hotel in London.

3/4 cup fresh lemon juice
1 tablespoon lemon zest
3/4 cup sugar
3 eggs, slightly beaten
1/3 cup unsalted butter

In a 2-quart saucepan, combine lemon juice, lemon zest, sugar and eggs. Cook over medium heat, stirring constantly until thickened and mixture coats the back of the spoon, about 6 minutes. Do not boil. Add butter and cook until melted. Pour into serving dish and refrigerate. The curd will keep for 2 to 3 weeks covered in the refrigerator.

Yield: 1-1/2 cups

Cranberry Almond Scones, Chelsea Market, London

The Bakery Shoppe at the Chelsea Market in London featured several types of scones with different ingredients. Most of the scones were sweetened but some were savory. They may have raisins, currants, dried fruits, nuts, or cheese as part of the ingredients. The cranberry and almond scones were the favorites at the Market. Scones are very popular in the United Kingdom and are served at breakfast and at afternoon tea.

3/4 cup all-purpose flour
2 tablespoons sugar
3/4 cup quick cooking oatmeal
1-1/2 teaspoons baking powder
1/2 teaspoon cream of tartar
1/4 cup dried cranberries
1/4 cup almonds, sliced
Zest of one orange
1 egg, slightly beaten
3 tablespoons milk
4 tablespoons butter, melted

Preheat oven to 375 degrees.

In a mixing bowl, combine flour, sugar, oatmeal, baking powder, and cream of tartar. Add cranberries, almonds and orange zest. In separate bowl, mix milk and egg. Add egg mixture to dry ingredients. Add butter. Knead dough until it holds together. Place on greased cookie sheet. Mark for 6 triangle-shaped scones. Bake for 15 to 20 minutes. Let cool for 15 minutes before serving.

Yield: 6 scones

Crumpets, Borough Market, London

English crumpets are very much like English muffins and are served with tea in the afternoon or for breakfast. They do require a crumpet ring or muffin ring in which to cook the crumpet. They are cooked on a griddle or in a frying pan.

2 cups all-purpose flour or bread flour
1 teaspoon salt
1 teaspoon baking powder
1/2 cup water
1 cup milk
1 teaspoon sugar or honey
1 tablespoon dry active yeast
Oil for frying

In a mixing bowl, combine flour, salt and baking powder. In saucepan, heat water and milk to warm. Remove from heat. Add sugar and yeast. Let set for 8 to 10 minutes for yeast to foam. Add yeast mixture to dry ingredients and stir with wooden spoon to moisten the flour mixture. Cover and let rise in a warm place for 30 to 40 minutes. Grease inside of metal crumpet rings. Heat oil in frying pan and place rings in pan. Reduce heat to medium. Pour 3 tablespoons of batter into each 3-inch ring. Cook for 6 to 8 minutes. Tiny bubbles will appear on the surface and then they burst. Remove rings with tongs. Turn crumpets, and cook for 1 minute on the other side. Serve the crumpets while they are warm.

Yield: 6 servings

Grilled Bacon-Wrapped Ostrich Steak, Borough Market, London

The meat counters at the Borough Market held almost every kind of meat and not just from the four-legged animals but even the two-legged ostrich. I had not seen ostrich meat in a butcher shop before and found the meat to look like beef. The meat was a dark red. Ostrich meat is very low in fat and cholesterol so it is sometimes enjoyed for the health benefits. Ostrich are raised domestically on farms, and the meat can be purchased on the internet or directly from the farmer.

A simple recipe is Grilled Bacon-Wrapped Ostrich Steak with a tangy marinade.

4 ostrich steaks, 5 to 6 ounces each
   (or beef steak)
4 strips smoked bacon
1/2 cup balsamic vinegar
4 tablespoons olive oil
4 tablespoons honey at room temperature
2 tablespoons chopped fresh basil
1 teaspoon dry mustard
1 teaspoon chopped garlic
1/2 teaspoon salt
1/8 teaspoon black pepper

Wrap each steak with a strip of bacon. Secure with a toothpick. In a plastic bag or glass mixing bowl, combine balsamic vinegar, olive oil, honey, basil, dry mustard and garlic. Stir or shake to blend flavors. Place steaks in marinade and place in the refrigerator for 2 to 4 hours, turning frequently.

Heat grill to 450 degrees. Remove steaks from marinade. Season with salt and pepper. Heat marinade to boiling and remove from heat. Place steaks on hot grill and close the lid. Cook for 4 to 5 minutes. Open grill and turn steaks. Brush with marinade and continue cooking for 4 to 5 minutes more until desired doneness.

Yield: 4 servings

Mushroom Barley Soup, Edinburgh Market, Edinburgh

The produce stalls in the Edinburgh Market had a variety of mushrooms. I visited with a short, stout, happy little lady who had collected many wild mushrooms. She had found shiitake mushrooms and chicken mushrooms in the woods near her home. The chicken or hen, mushrooms, as they are sometimes called, grow at the base of old oak and other hardwood trees.

Barley is a popular grain in Scotland and is used as a pottage and in soups.

1/2 cup pearl barley, uncooked
2 cups water
2 tablespoons extra virgin olive oil
1 tablespoon chopped garlic
1/4 cup chopped onion
1 large carrot, chopped
2 ribs celery, chopped
1 pound shiitake mushrooms or chicken mushrooms, sliced
1/2 teaspoon dried thyme
1 bay leaf
2 tablespoons all-purpose flour
6 cups chicken broth
2 drops hot sauce
1 teaspoon Worcestershire sauce
1 tablespoon sugar
1/2 teaspoon salt
1/8 teaspoon black pepper
3 tablespoons chopped fresh parsley
3 mushrooms, sliced for garnish on top of soup

Soak the pearl barley in 2 cups of water for 30 minutes. Drain and rinse for 1 minute. Set aside.

Place the oil in a large pot. Heat and add garlic, onions, carrots and celery. Cook, stirring until slightly softened. Increase the heat to medium high and add mushrooms, thyme and bay leaf. Cook, stirring, for 5 to 6 minutes until the liquid becomes syrupy. Add the flour to the mushroom mixture and cook for 1 minute, stirring constantly to prevent lumps. Add the barley and the remaining ingredients except the parsley. Bring to a boil, reduce heat and cook for 30 minutes until barley and vegetables are tender. Garnish with sliced mushrooms and parsley.

Yield: 6 servings

Orange Marmalade, Edinburgh Market, Edinburgh

Marmalade is an upscale jam generally made with fruit. However, *Joy of Cooking* has a recipe for "onion marmalade." The marmalade is delicious served with scones, muffins or warm toast. An attractive jar of orange marmalade also makes an impressive gift.

6 large navel or seedless oranges
2 lemons
1-1/2 quarts water
Sugar

Peel the oranges and cut the peel into very thin slices. Chop the orange pulp. Slice the lemons very thin. Combine the fruit and water in a large saucepan. Bring the mixture to a boil, reduce heat and simmer for 15 minutes. Remove from heat and cool. Refrigerate overnight. Remove from the refrigerator and heat to a boil. Reduce heat to a simmer and cook for 30 minutes until the peel is tender. Measure the fruit and liquid. For each cup of undrained fruit, add 3/4 cup sugar. Heat until the sugar is dissolved, stirring constantly. Taste for sweetness and add more sugar if needed. Bring mixture to a boil and cook for 30 to 45 minutes until the jellying point is reached. (220 degrees on a candy thermometer).

Pour into sterilized jars and seal.

Yield: 9 to 10 cups

Fillet of Sole Stuffed with Crabmeat, Billingsgate Fish Market, London

Sole is a delicate fish and requires a short cooking time. The combination of crabmeat with the sole makes a delicious dish.

3 tablespoons butter, divided
1/4 cup scallions, chopped
3/4 cup mushrooms, chopped
8 ounces fresh or canned crabmeat
3 tablespoons mayonnaise
1 teaspoon Dijon mustard
3 tablespoons lemon juice, divided
1/4 teaspoon sea salt
1/8 teaspoon white pepper
2 pounds sole fillets
Dash of paprika
Parsley for garnish

Preheat oven to 400 degrees.

In a large skillet, heat 2 tablespoons butter over medium high heat. Add scallions and sauté for 2 minutes. Add mushrooms and continue cooking for 3 more minutes until mushrooms are tender. Remove from heat. Remove all shells and cartilage from crab. Place in mixing bowl. Add mayonnaise, mustard, 1 tablespoon lemon juice, salt, pepper and sautéed scallions and mushrooms. Stir to blend. Place sole fillets on work counter. Place crabmeat mixture on half of each fillet. Cut a line along half of the sole to fold over the crab mixture. Do not cut through the fish. Fold the half sole to form a packet covering the crab. Place the fillets in a buttered baking dish. Cover with remaining butter. Pour the remaining 2 tablespoons lemon juice over the fish. Sprinkle paprika over fish. Bake for 20 minutes. Garnish with parsley.

Yield: 6 servings

Venison Stuffed Mushrooms, Borough Market, London

Venison is advertised in the Borough Market as wild game although the deer are raised for the market meat. The flavor of the venison is milder than the wild deer because of the grain and other food fed to the domestic herd of deer.

10 to 12 large button mushrooms
8 ounces lean ground venison (ground beef can be
   substituted for venison)
1 teaspoon olive oil
1/3 cup Panko Italian seasoned bread crumbs
1 large egg
1/2 teaspoon salt
1/4 teaspoon garlic powder
1/4 teaspoon ground sage
1/4 teaspoon ground thyme
1/2 teaspoon sugar
1/4 teaspoon ground black pepper
1 tablespoon Worcestershire sauce
2 tablespoons diced onion
2 tablespoons diced yellow bell pepper
2 tablespoons diced green bell pepper

Preheat oven to 375 degrees.

Clean mushrooms and remove stems. Lightly grease baking dish. Place caps in baking dish. Place venison into mixing bowl. Finely chop mushroom stems and add to venison. Add all remaining ingredients except the mushroom caps to the meat. Mix well. (I find using my hands is a good way to get ingredients incorporated.) Shape into balls to fit on the mushroom caps. Place filled mushroom caps, with meatballs facing up, in baking dish. Bake at 375 degrees for 30 minutes. If meatballs are large, bake for 40 minutes. Serve warm.

Yield: 12 to 14 servings

Pan-Fried Sirloin Steak with Sautéed Mushrooms, Borough Market, London

Much of the meat in the Borough Market was organic and quite lean. The sirloin steaks were cut about an inch thick, and that is a good thickness for pan frying. If the meat is too thin, it will dry out when fried.

4 sirloin steaks, 1 inch thick (5 to 6 ounces each)
1/2 teaspoon kosher salt
1/4 teaspoon coarse ground black pepper
1 tablespoon butter
1 tablespoon olive oil
2 tablespoons red wine
1 cup sliced button mushrooms
Rosemary sprigs for garnish

Rub steaks with salt and pepper on both sides. Heat butter and oil in a large heavy skillet to medium hot. Place steaks in hot skillet. Fry for 5 to 7 minutes. Turn steaks and fry for an additional 5 minutes for medium rare. Remove from skillet and cover with foil to keep warm. Add wine to hot skillet to deglaze. Scrape bottom to remove drippings. Add mushrooms and reduce heat to medium-low. Simmer for 5 minutes. Add mushrooms to steak. Garnish with rosemary.

Yield: 4 servings

Gypsy Toast, Borough Market, London

I found several stands selling bread and pastries in the Borough Market. The selection was phenomenal, ranging in preparation from five-day sourdough bread to half-an-hour soda bread, with a large range in between. The *Borough Market* book quotes Paul Rhodes of the Dupond's Bakery, "We use only the finest flour made from wheat grown and milled in France. Most of the bread you buy in the U.K. is made with flour from the U.S. or Canada. French wheat tastes better, and the milling process in France tends to be longer and slower." The pastries make one's mouth water. The dessert called Gypsy Toast with Roasted Plums and Clotted Cream from the *Borough Market* book includes bread and fresh purple plums.

10 plums, firm-fleshed (Victoria, Opal or Marjory)
6 tablespoons unsalted butter
2 tablespoons Marsala wine
6 tablespoons fine crystals (baking) sugar
4 eggs
1/4 cup whole milk
1 teaspoon cinnamon
2 teaspoons powdered sugar, divided
4 slices thinly cut white bread
2 tablespoons olive oil
1 small tub (4 ounces) clotted cream, or light sour cream

Preheat oven to 425 degrees.

Halve plums and remove stones. Place on a roasting pan with cut side up. Sprinkle with cinnamon and wine. Place a dab of butter in the cavity left by the stone. Dredge the tops with the baking sugar. Let plums sit for 30 minutes to marinate. Place plums in oven for 20 to 30 minutes. In a bowl, whisk eggs with milk, cinnamon, and 1 teaspoon of the powdered sugar. Soak the bread in the mixture until sodden. Melt the remaining butter with the oil in a skillet to medium hot. Fry bread slices until golden on both sides. Place on serving dishes. To serve, dust with remaining powdered sugar and spoon plum halves on top with the plum juice. Finish with a dollop of clotted cream.

Yield: 4 servings

Fried Oysters, Borough Market, London

The seafood in the Borough Market is very fresh. The sampling of fresh oysters in the Market was a delicious taste sensation. Richard Haward of Richard Haward Oysters states in the *Borough Market* book, "By law, you can only sell native 'flat' oysters between May 14 and August 4. Their flesh is more delicate than rock oysters. People think they should only eat oysters if there is an 'r' in the month. But rock oysters are perfectly safe and tasty to eat all year round."

The recipe for Fried Oysters is good at any time.

1 pint fresh oysters
1/3 cup all-purpose flour
1 teaspoon salt
1/8 teaspoon ground white pepper
1 egg, slightly beaten
1 tablespoon water
1 cup fine cracker crumbs
1/4 cup vegetable oil or butter
Lemon wedges and hot sauce

Drain oysters. In a small bowl, combine flour, salt and pepper. In a separate bowl, place egg and water. In another bowl, place the cracker crumbs. Dip the oyster first in the flour mixture, next into the egg mixture, and then dip into the cracker crumbs to coat. Heat the oil in a medium skillet. Fry the oysters until golden on each side, about 2 minutes for each side. Serve with lemon wedge or hot sauce as desired.

Yield: 4 servings

Mixed Greens with Ewe's Milk Cheese, Borough Market, London

The stand selling cheese from sheep's milk had both the soft and semi-soft cheese available. The owner was proud of the awards they had received for their cheeses. They have their own factory for producing all the cheese they sell.

6 cups mixed spring greens (arugula, frisée, mache and watercress)
1 large orange, peeled and cut into sections without white membrane
1/2 cup dried pitted cherries
1 cup semi-firm ewe's milk cheese, cut into 1/2-inch cubes

Champagne Dressing

2 tablespoons Champagne vinegar
2 teaspoons Dijon mustard
2 teaspoons honey
1/3 cup extra virgin olive oil
Ground white pepper and salt to taste

Whisk together vinegar, mustard and honey. Gradually whisk in oil. Season with salt and pepper, as desired. Place greens, orange and cherries in large bowl. Add vinaigrette and toss to coat greens. Place onto salad plates. Top with cubes of ewe's milk cheese.

Yield: 6 servings

Strawberry and Vanilla Cream Pie, Westmorland, England

Beautiful, large, bright red, fresh strawberries were for sale from the vendors at the Westmorland County Food Fest when I had the opportunity to visit the Market. The berries were freshly picked that morning and had a marvelous flowery aroma. The berries are often served with Devonshire cream, a thick sweet cream almost like melted vanilla ice cream.

Vanilla Cream Pie

1 baked (9-inch) pie shell
1-1/2 cups whole milk
1/3 cup sugar
3 tablespoons cornstarch
1/4 teaspoon salt
1 egg
1 egg yolk
1 tablespoons plain yogurt
1 teaspoon vanilla extract

In saucepan, heat milk over medium heat until steam rises from the pan. In bowl, combine sugar, cornstarch, salt, and eggs. Using whisk, blend mixture. Gradually add half of warm milk to egg mixture, whisking constantly. Pour this mixture into the remaining milk and place over medium heat. Bring to a boil and whisk constantly until mixture has thickened. Remove from heat and add yogurt and vanilla. Cover with plastic and refrigerate to cool. When cool, carefully spoon into cooked pie shell.

Strawberry Topping

3 pounds fresh strawberries, hulled and halved
1 cup sugar
2 tablespoons light corn syrup
2 tablespoons fresh lemon juice
1/4 teaspoon salt
2 teaspoons unsweetened gelatin powder
4 tablespoons water, divided
1 tablespoon cornstarch

Place 1 pound strawberries in food processor and puree until smooth. Pour into saucepan. Add sugar, corn syrup, lemon juice and salt. Simmer for 20 to 25 minutes to reduce mixture to 1-1/2 cups. Sprinkle gelatin over 3 tablespoons water. Let set for 5 minutes to dissolve. In a separate small bowl, whisk together 1 tablespoon water and cornstarch. Add cornstarch to reduced strawberry puree. Cook for 1 minute. Add gelatin mixture and heat to combine with strawberry puree. Place in large bowl, and cool to room temperature. Add remaining 2 pounds strawberries to mixture. Gently spoon the strawberry mixture over the pudding in the pie shell (above). Cover with plastic wrap and chill for several hours. Serve with whipped cream topping.

Yield: 8 servings

Scrambled Eggs with Kipper Herring, Billingsgate Fish Market, London

The term "kipper" refers to a whole herring, a small, oily fish that has been split from head to tail, gutted, salted or pickled and cold-smoked. Drying and smoking of fish has been going on for centuries as a way of preserving the fish. Records in the United Kingdom indicate this process was in use as far back as 1400. In the United Kingdom, kippers are often eaten at breakfast. The whole smoked herring is referred to as "bloater," while the hot, smoked, decapitated herring is called "birckling." These also are enjoyed at supper or high tea.

Many varieties of smoked fish were available at the Market. The restaurant in the Market listed kippers and eggs on the menu. I had to try kippers and ordered scrambled eggs and kippers for my breakfast. It was excellent.

1 tablespoon butter
2 eggs, beaten
2 tablespoons kipper herring, in chunks
Salt and pepper as desired

Heat butter in skillet to medium high. Add eggs and stir. Add salt and pepper if desired. When the eggs start to coagulate, add the kippers and continue to stir until the desired consistency is reached.

Yield: 1 serving

Braised Scallops with Wine Sauce, Billingsgate Fish Market, London

Scallops are found in all the oceans around the world. The smaller bay scallops are harvested in the water of bays. Mexico, Baja and the New England coast are home for the bay scallops. The scallops in the Market come from all around the world. Bill, my informer, told me the Billingsgate Fish Market will always have scallops because the world supply will always be there, even when one or more areas become short or have a problem.

At the Billingsgate Fish Market, the scallops are sold from ice-filled tubs in the shell or sucked and placed in plastic tubs. The scallop shell is a beautiful pink color with fluted fan pattern. It has been used as a symbol of pilgrims and in family crests. Winston Churchill's coat of arms included a scallop shell.

2 tablespoons peanut oil, divided
1-1/2 pounds fresh sea scallops
1/2 cup chicken broth
1/2 cup white wine
1 teaspoon lemon zest
2 tablespoons lemon juice
1-1/2 teaspoons cornstarch
1/4 teaspoon salt
1/2 teaspoon pepper
1 tablespoon diced shallots
Watercress for liner on plates

Dry scallops by blotting with paper towel. Place 1 tablespoon oil in skillet over medium high heat. When oil is hot but not smoking, add scallops. Cook for 3 minutes on each side and golden brown on the outside. Remove scallops to serving platter or bowl to keep warm.

Pour broth and wine into mixing bowl. Add lemon zest, lemon juice, cornstarch, salt and pepper; blend well, forming a sauce. Add remaining oil to skillet. Heat and sauté shallots until soft, not brown. Add sauce mixture to skillet. Stir until boiling. Reduce heat and boil for 1 minute, stirring constantly until mixture thickens. Remove from heat. Place scallops on bed of watercress. Top with sauce.

Yield: 4 servings or 6 appetizers

Oatmeal Raisin Muffins, Edinburgh Market, Edinburgh

When my mother served me oatmeal, she would say, "Oats makes strong horses, and your oatmeal will make you strong." The Scottish people eat oatmeal often and perhaps that is what makes them strong. At the Bakery Andante in the Market in Edinburgh, I was served a sample of a delicious oatmeal muffin. The bakery stall also had oatmeal bread for sale.

1 cup quick cooking rolled oats
1 cup buttermilk
3/4 cup all-purpose flour
1 teaspoon baking powder
1/4 teaspoon salt
3/4 teaspoon baking soda
2 eggs, lightly beaten
1/3 cup light brown sugar
1/3 cup melted butter
1/3 cup raisins

Preheat oven to 400 degrees.

Lightly grease muffin tins.

In a bowl, combine oats and buttermilk and let stand for 20 minutes. In separate bowl, sift together flour, baking powder, salt and baking soda. Stir eggs into oat mixture. Add brown sugar and butter to oat mixture. Add dry ingredients to oat mixture. Stir until combined. Batter will be lumpy. Add raisins. Spoon into muffin tins. Fill each 2/3 full. Bake for 15 to 20 minutes.

Yield: 6 muffins

Watercress Soup, Newgate Market, York

While I was at Gordon and Jane's fresh produce stand at the Newgate Market in York, I learned there are at least two varieties of watercress. One variety of greens with tiny leaves that looks like miniature watercress is called "cress." A different variety with large leaves and long stems is called "watercress." Both varieties grow in or near fresh running streams. The cress is used in salads and as a garnish to meats. Jane told me the larger watercress is often used in stews, soups and casseroles for flavor.

1/4 cup butter
1/2 cup all-purpose flour
4 cups chicken broth
1 medium onion, chopped
1 pound watercress or 1 large bunch, large stems removed
2 teaspoons sugar
1/2 teaspoon salt
1/8 teaspoon ground white pepper
2 cups half-and-half cream

In a large saucepan, melt butter and whisk in flour. Simmer for 1 minute, stirring constantly. Add chicken broth, stirring to prevent lumps. When it becomes thick, add onion, watercress, sugar, salt, and pepper. Simmer for 20 minutes. Place in batches in blender and puree to smooth. Return puree to saucepan. Add cream and heat to serve. Garnish with watercress leaves.

Yield: 6 servings

Fresh Asparagus Quiche, Newgate Market, York

The very large asparagus spears at Gordon and Jane's stall in the Newgate Market were at least 1-1/2 inches in diameter. I can't remember seeing asparagus that thick. Each bunch was wrapped with a wide paper band identifying the vegetable as "British Asparagus." I asked Jane, the attractive, middle-aged, blond owner of the stall, if she ever made an asparagus quiche. She was happy to tell me that she not only made asparagus quiche but used asparagus in soups, salads, stews and every dish except desserts.

1-1/2 pounds fresh asparagus
1 teaspoon salt
1 unbaked (10-inch) pie shell
1 egg white, beaten
2 cups shredded Swiss cheese
10 strips bacon, cooked and crumbled
4 eggs
1-1/2 cups half-and-half cream
1/4 teaspoon nutmeg
1/8 teaspoon pepper
Cherry tomatoes cut in half for garnish

Preheat oven to 400 degrees.

Cut 5 asparagus spears into 4-inch-long spears. Cut remaining asparagus into 1/2-inch pieces. In a large saucepan, boil 1 quart water. Add salt and all asparagus. Bring to a boil and reduce heat to simmer. Cover and cook for 5 minutes. Drain and set aside. Brush bottom

of pie shell with egg white. In a bowl, combine the 1/2-inch asparagus, cheese and bacon. Place mixture in pie shell. In a bowl, beat eggs, cream, nutmeg and pepper. Pour over asparagus in pie shell. Bake uncovered for 35 to 40 minutes until knife inserted in center comes out clean. Arrange asparagus spears spoke fashion on top of quiche. Place cherry tomatoes halves between the asparagus spokes.

Yield: 6 to 8 servings

Roasted New Potatoes, Westmorland, England

The small red and white new potatoes always seem like a sign of spring or early summer. At the Westmorland County Food Fair, only one produce stand had both the red and white potatoes for sale. The rather plump, middle-aged lady in a denim skirt and knit sweater, who was the owner of the stall, told me these were the first potatoes from her garden this year. She also suggested I use the following recipe in preparing the potatoes. The recipe was a hand-me-down in her family.

3/4 pound new red potatoes, 1-3/4-inches diameter
3/4 pound new white skin or Yukon gold potatoes,
   1-3/4-inches diameter
1/4 cup extra virgin olive oil
1 teaspoon dried basil
1 teaspoon crushed rosemary leaves
1/2 teaspoon dried oregano
6 garlic cloves, peeled, chopped
1/2 teaspoon salt
1/8 teaspoon fresh ground pepper

Preheat oven to 400 degrees.

Wash and clean potatoes. Cut into halves. In a bowl, combine remaining ingredients. Add potatoes and stir to coat potatoes with mixture. Place on baking sheet so potatoes are not touching. Bake for 30 minutes until tender. Serve the seasoned oil in the baking pan with potatoes.

Yield: 4 servings

Lancashire Cheese Soufflé, Westmorland, England

Lancashire cheese has been developed by the Saddleworth Cheese Company. The cultures are specially formulated to produce this cheese with its unique taste. It is a medium-soft cheese with a mild, sweet, nutty flavor. The cheese is used in baked dishes as well as snacks and in sandwiches.

6 tablespoons butter
1/2 cup all-purpose flour
1/2 teaspoon salt
1/4 teaspoon white pepper
1/4 teaspoon dry ground mustard
1-1/2 cups milk
1-1/2 cups shredded sharp cheddar cheese
6 eggs, separated

Heat oven to 350 degrees.

Grease and lightly flour a 2-quart soufflé dish or casserole or 6 ramekins. In a 2-quart saucepan, melt butter. Add flour, salt, pepper and mustard powder. Heat to bubbly, stirring to prevent lumps. Add milk and cook until mixture thickens. Add cheese, stirring until cheese melts. Remove pan from heat. Add egg yolks one at a time, beating well after each addition. In a separate bowl, beat egg whites until stiff peaks form. Fold egg whites into cheese mixture using wire whisk. Pour mixture into prepared casserole or ramekins. Bake at 350 degrees for 55 to 60 minutes. Remove from oven and serve immediately.

Yield: 6 servings

Pork, Rhubarb and Beet Pie, Chelsea Market, London

Meat pies and pasties are a common menu item throughout England. Many different foods are used in the pies, and the variety often depends on the vegetables and meats that are on hand or left over from a previous meal. The addition of rhubarb gives the dish an interesting flavor, and the beets add a bright red color to the filling. The pork, rhubarb and beet pie was one type that Timothy was selling at his stand at the Chelsea Market.

3 tablespoons vegetable oil
2 pounds lean pork, cut into 1/2-inch pieces
1 cup chopped onions
1 cup diced carrots
1 cup diced beets
1 cup fresh or frozen chopped rhubarb
2/3 cup water
1/3 cup sugar
1 tablespoon lemon juice
2 tablespoons chopped parsley
1/4 teaspoon ground thyme
1/4 teaspoon ground sage
1/4 teaspoon nutmeg
1/4 teaspoon salt
Pastry crust for 8 ramekins

Preheat oven to 425 degrees.

In large skillet, heat oil to hot. Add pork and sauté until browned. Add all remaining ingredients except the pastry. Stir to combine. Simmer to blend flavors for 10 minutes. Roll pastry to 1/8-inch thick. Cut 16 rounds to fit ramekins. Shape 8 round pastry crusts into 8 ramekins. Fill each ramekin with meat mixture. Cover with remaining crust. Pinch edges together. Pierce top with knife in several places. Place ramekins onto baking sheet and place into hot oven. Bake for 15 minutes. Reduce heat to 350 degrees and continue baking for 40 to 50 minutes. Allow pies to stand for 10 to 15 minutes before serving.

Yield: 8 servings

Portobello Burger, Chelsea Market, London

Several kinds of mushrooms were for sale at the Chelsea Market. One display that impressed me was of four portobello mushrooms nesting in a woven basket.

4 large portobello mushrooms
1/4 cup olive oil
4 Kaiser rolls or large hamburger buns
1/3 cup aioli mayonnaise
Lettuce leaves for liners
4 large slices white sweet onion
4 large sliced tomatoes

Heat grill to 450 degrees. Wipe and remove stems from mushrooms. Oil both sides of mushrooms. Place on grill. Close lid and cook for 5 minutes. Turn mushrooms and continue cooking for 4 minutes. While mushrooms are cooking, spread the sides of the buns with mayonnaise. Place lettuce leaves on buns. Top with onions and then with tomatoes. Place grilled mushrooms on top of tomatoes.

Yield: 4 servings

Roast Beef and Yorkshire Pudding, Westmorland, England

When wheat flour came into common use for making cakes and puddings, cooks in the north of England devised a means of making use of the fat that dripped into the roasting pan to cook a batter pudding while the meat roasted. In 1737, the following recipe for A Dripping Pudding was published in *The Whole Duty of a Woman*.

Make a good batter as for pancakes; put in a hot toss-pan over the fire with a bit of butter to fry the bottom a little, then put the pan and butter under a shoulder of mutton, instead of a dripping pan, keeping frequently shaking it by the handle, and it will be light and savory and fit to take up when your mutton is enough; then turn it in a dish and serve it.

The name "Yorkshire" pudding was established by Hannah Glasse in her book, *The Art of Cooking Made Plain and Simple*, published in 1747. It is often claimed that the purpose of the dish was to provide a cheap way to fill the diners because the Yorkshire pudding was much cheaper than the other items served at the dinner. It was often served first at the meal.

In some parts of England, the pudding is served as a snack with jam or at teatime as a pudding.

3-1/2 to 4 pounds boneless beef roast, top round, rib or sirloin
2 tablespoons vegetable oil
2 teaspoons salt

Preheat oven to 425 degrees.

Place roast, fat side up, into roasting pan. Coat with oil. Sprinkle with salt. Cook until meat thermometer reads 140 degrees for medium done or 150 degrees for well done. Remove from oven. Place on a platter and cover with foil while meat rests.

Yorkshire Pudding

3 eggs, slightly beaten
1 cup all-purpose flour
1/2 teaspoon salt
1 cup milk
2 tablespoons vegetable oil

While meat is roasting, beat eggs. Place flour and salt into blender. Add milk, oil and eggs. Blend until smooth, about 10 seconds. Refrigerate until meat is at desired temperature of doneness. Remove meat from roasting pan. Stir the hot drippings in the pan to loosen meat scraps and to blend. Stir the pudding batter and pour into hot drippings. Bake for 20 minutes at 425 degrees. Reduce temperature to 350 degrees and continue baking for 15 to 20 minutes until the pudding is a golden brown. Serve immediately.

Yield: 6 servings

Finnan Haddie, Edinburgh Market, Edinburgh

There are references to smoked fish in Scotland going back to the sixteenth century. James Boxwell wrote about them in the eighteenth century, mentioning that Scottish smoked fish could be obtained in London. But these were heavily smoked (as a preservative) and a bit tough. In the late nineteenth century, as fast transportation by train became available, the Aberdeen fishing village of Findon (pronounced locally as "Finnan") began producing lightly smoked and delicately flavored haddock (haddies) that were of a much finer texture. They were an immediate success, and variations on these tasty fish have become very popular. As a child, we often had Creamed Finnan Haddie in the wintertime. The smoked

haddock was kept in a wooden box that stayed frozen on the porch during the South Dakota winters. I was surprised and delighted to see the smoked haddock in Scotland and England. Following is the recipe that my mother used in making Creamed Finnan Haddie. It is a recipe with milk and onions for a delicately, smoky-flavored fish stew.

1 large onion, sliced thin
1 pound smoked haddock
1-2/3 cups milk
1/2 teaspoon ground white pepper
1 teaspoon dry mustard
2 tablespoons melted butter
1 tablespoon all-purpose flour
1 tablespoon chopped green onion
1 tablespoon finely chopped parsley

Place the onion slices in a large pan. Cut the haddock into pieces about 1-inch wide. Place fish on top of onions. In separate bowl, mix milk, pepper and mustard powder and pour over fish. Heat to boiling and reduce heat to a simmer. Cover and cook for 5 minutes. Uncover and simmer for another 5 minutes. Remove fish from pan using a slotted spoon allowing the liquid to run off the fish. Place fish on platter and keep warm. Continue to simmer the milk mixture for additional 5 minutes, stirring frequently. Mix the warm butter with the flour and add to the milk. Stir over low heat until mixture comes to a slow boil and thickens. Add green onions and stir. Gently place fish into milk mixture. Serve hot with garnish of chopped parsley.

Yield: 6 servings

Rosemary Braised Lamb Shanks, Edinburgh Market, Edinburgh

Lambs raised in Scotland are of the Highland breed that provides a high quality meat and a good yield. Many of the farmers have small herds of sheep and raise some lambs to sell at the market.

4 lamb shanks (2 to 3 pounds)
1 tablespoon kosher salt
1 teaspoon fresh ground black pepper
2 tablespoons olive oil
2 sweet onions, chopped
2 leeks, chopped, white only
3 carrots, peeled and cut into 1/2-inch rounds
4 cloves garlic, minced
3 cups red wine
1/4 cup balsamic vinegar
1 can (28 ounces) whole peeled tomatoes with juice
1 can (10.5 ounces) condensed beef broth
2 tablespoons fresh chopped rosemary
1 teaspoon dried thyme

Rub shanks with salt and pepper. Place oil in heavy large pot over medium high heat. Sauté lamb shanks until golden brown on all sides, approximately 8 minutes. Remove shanks from pot and cover with foil to keep warm. Add onions, leeks, carrots and garlic to hot pot and sauté for 10 minutes. Add wine, vinegar, tomatoes, beef broth, rosemary and thyme. Return lamb shanks to pot. Cover and simmer for 2 hours until the meat is very tender and tends to fall off the bone. Remove shanks from pot. Simmer vegetables in pot to thicken for about 15 minutes. Serve the sauce with the lamb shanks.

Yield: 4 to 6 servings

Smoked Salmon Pâté, St. George's Market, Belfast

Some of the best salmon in the world is caught off the coast of Ireland in the ice cold waters of the North Sea and the Atlantic Ocean. The markets in Belfast, Dublin and Cork all sell a variety of salmon. In Ireland, there is a story of a monk who fell asleep and a salmon came to him in a dream. The salmon fell into his fire and burned. When the monk pulled the salmon out of the fire, some of the cooked flesh clung to his fingers. He immediately put his fingers in his mouth and was amazed at the wonderful taste of the salmon. He became very wise, and the story tells anyone who eats salmon will be wise.

4 ounces cream cheese, softened
1/2 cup mayonnaise
4 ounces smoked salmon
1/3 cup chopped green onions
1 tablespoon capers, drained

In a bowl, mix cream cheese and mayonnaise until smooth. Remove skin and dark meat from smoked salmon. Crumble salmon into cheese mixture. Add green onions and capers and stir to blend.

Refrigerate before serving. Serve with crackers.

Yield: Approximately 1 cup

Irish Soda Bread, St. George's Market, Belfast

Irish soda bread was first prepared in the nineteenth century in Ireland. The wheat flour used was a soft, less expensive product. Soda is used as the leavening agent and when mixed with the sour milk or buttermilk gives the bread some degree of leavening. The ingredients for soda bread were and are readily available throughout Ireland.

3 cups all-purpose flour
1 teaspoon baking soda
1/4 cup sugar
1 teaspoon salt
1/4 cup butter, cut into tiny pieces
1/2 cup raisins or currants
1-1/4 cups buttermilk

Preheat oven to 350 degrees. Lightly coat baking sheet with non-stick vegetable spray.

In large bowl, combine flour, baking soda, sugar and salt. Cut butter into flour mixture using pastry cutter. Add remaining ingredients. Mix in bowl. Turn onto floured surface and knead 9 times. Shape into a loaf 6 inches round and 2 inches thick. Place on baking sheet. Cut a 1-inch deep and 4-inch long cross on top of loaf. Bake for 50 minutes until golden brown. Cool on rack before slicing.

Yield: 12 to 16 servings

Colcannon (Cabbage Potato), St. George's Market, Belfast

Cabbage and potatoes are two of the traditional foods used by the Irish population. During the famine, the potatoes were not edible, and the people suffered. At the St. George's Market in Belfast, the counters were well supplied with fresh green cabbage and bright green bunches of kale. Often kale is used in place of or with the cabbage in this dish. Colcannon is a tasty, easy and inexpensive dish to prepare.

4 medium potatoes, peeled and quartered
1/3 cup whole milk or half-and-half cream
2 tablespoons butter
1/4 cup chopped onion
1-1/2 cups shredded green cabbage
1/2 teaspoon salt
1/8 teaspoon white pepper

In a large saucepan, cook potatoes until tender. Remove from water. Mash potatoes. Add milk and butter. Place onion and cabbage in saucepan with 3/4 cup water. Cover and cook for 12 minutes until tender. Drain and add cabbage and onion to mashed potatoes. Season with salt and pepper. If the mixture is too thick, add more milk.

Yield: 6 servings

Bread Pudding with Irish Whiskey Sauce, St. George's Market, Belfast

Bread Pudding is a common dessert generally made with stale bread, eggs and milk. It is inexpensive, tasty and easy to prepare. The Irish have been distilling whiskey for centuries. The Bushmills Distillery in northern Ireland claims to be the oldest licensed distillery in the world. It is not surprising the Irish used whiskey in cooking. The sweet Irish Whiskey Sauce with its unique flavor makes the common bread pudding a festive dish.

1/2 cup golden raisins or currants
1/2 cup Irish whiskey
4 large eggs
2 cups milk
3/4 cup sugar
1/2 teaspoon vanilla
1/4 teaspoon nutmeg
12 slices white bread

Preheat oven to 375 degrees.

Soak raisins in whiskey for 1 hour. Butter or spray with non-stick cooking spray a 2-quart baking dish. In bowl, combine eggs, milk, sugar, vanilla and nutmeg. Whip to blend. Tear bread into pieces and place in prepared baking dish. Drain raisins and save whiskey. Put raisins into baking dish with the bread. Pour egg-milk mixture over bread in baking dish. Stir briefly to blend raisins. Place baking dish in pan and add water to the pan about 1 inch deep. Bake for 40 minutes until toothpick inserted in the center of the pudding comes out clean.

Yield: 8 servings

Irish Whiskey Sauce

1/3 cup cream
1/2 cup butter
3/4 cup sugar
1/4 to 1/2 cup whiskey (left from soaking raisins)

In saucepan on medium heat, place cream, butter and sugar. Simmer on low until sauce thickens. Add whiskey that was left from soaking raisins. Serve hot over bread pudding.

Yield: 8 servings

Fish and Chips, Billingsgate Fish Market, London

Most of the fish that is sold in London as Fish and Chips comes from the Billingsgate Fish Market. When Fish and Chips were first introduced in England and Ireland in 1858, cod and haddock were the fish used. Today, the Market sells whitefish, cod, haddock, pollock, coley, plaice, skate, rock salmon and tilapia to be used in preparing Fish and Chips. I learned that some of the fish shops in England have a standing order at the Market for a particular type of fish they use in their restaurant so they are assured of the availability of the fish when the supply gets short.

Fish and Chips are often used as a snack food and are sold as a "take away." However, deep fried fish has been on the supper menu of the working class for a century.

2 pounds whitefish fillets, skinless, boneless
2 to 2-1/2 cups peanut oil for deep frying.

Batter

1 cup all-purpose flour
3 tablespoons cornstarch
1 teaspoon kosher salt
1/4 teaspoon ground black pepper
1/2 teaspoon ground marjoram
1 cup beer (if batter is stiff, add more beer)
1 tablespoon vegetable oil

Cut fish fillets into 6 pieces. Pat dry. Heat oil in deep fat fryer or large saucepan to 375 degrees. Oil should be about 2 inches deep in fryer. Combine all ingredients for batter. Dip each fillet into batter. Allow the excess batter to drip off fillet. Fry in hot oil until golden brown for 4 to 5 minutes, turning the fish once during cooking. Cook in batches so as not to crowd the fillets in the oil. Drain on paper towel. Serve with malt vinegar and sea salt.

Yield: 6 servings

Grilled Prawns, Billingsgate Fish Market, London

Prawns and shrimp are often used interchangeably. However, in the United Kingdom the term prawns is almost universally used when referring to shrimp of any type. At the Billingsgate Fish Market in London, prawns are the large shrimp—only ten to fifteen per pound. The Market also carries small crustaceans with a brownish shell that are called shrimp and are used to make potted shrimp. Bill, who has worked n the Market for forty years, was a great source of information. He told me much of the shrimp and seafood comes from shrimp farms in Asia. There are dozens and dozens of varieties of shrimp, and the Billingsgate Market carries many types. Bill also said there is a difference in taste and texture of the shrimp depending on the variety. A shrimp-like crustacean called Norway lobster is ideal for making scampi. Some of the chefs who shop at the Market purchase the type of prawns best for the dish they plan to prepare and serve in their restaurants.

2 pounds jumbo shrimp or large prawns
1/2 cup olive oil
2 cloves garlic, crushed
1/4 cup fresh lime juice
Pinch red pepper flakes
1/4 teaspoon salt

Remove shells and heads from shrimp. Devein shrimp. Place oil, garlic, lime juice, pepper flakes and salt in large plastic bag. Add shrimp to the bag and coat the shrimp with the marinade. Refrigerate for 2 hours, turning occasionally. Thread shrimp onto skewers. (If using wooden skewers, soak them in water for several minutes before using.) Place shrimp onto hot grill 5 to 6 inches from heat. Cook for 3 to 4 minutes on each side until shrimp are pink and firm.

Yield: 6 servings

Shepherd's Pie, St. George's Market, Belfast

England, Ireland and Scotland all claim to be the birthplace of Shepherd's Pie. Meat pies have been part of the diet in these countries for centuries. They were generally made with the leftover bits of meat and vegetables. However, in the Elizabethan time, mince pies made with shreds of beef or mutton and suet seasoned with cloves, mace, pepper and some saffron plus raisins and prunes were popular. This is similar to the recipe for the Christmas mince pies of today. Shepherd's Pie is a lamb or mutton stew with bits of meat and vegetables, such as carrots, peas, onions in gravy, with the top of the dish covered with mashed potatoes. Originally, the potatoes were sliced on top of the stew. If beef is used in the pie, it is called a "cottage pie."

2 tablespoons olive oil
1 large onion, chopped
1 cup diced carrots
1 cup diced celery
1 pound cooked lamb, cut into bite-sized pieces (leftover roast lamb is good)
1 cup fresh or frozen peas
2 tablespoons cornstarch
2 cups broth
3 medium potatoes, peeled and cubed
1 tablespoon butter
1/4 to 1/3 cup milk
Salt and pepper for seasoning

Preheat oven to 375 degrees.

Heat oil in large skillet. Add onions, carrots and celery. Cook for 6 to 8 minutes. Add cooked lamb. Simmer for 5 minutes. Place in casserole or baking dish. Combine cornstarch with broth and stir to blend. Cook over medium heat, stirring until thickened. Add to meat and vegetables in casserole. Add peas and stir to blend. In a separate pot, cook potatoes until tender. Drain. Return to heat and mash. Add butter, milk, salt and pepper to make firm mashed potatoes. Cover the stew in the casserole with mashed potatoes. Bake casserole 40 minutes until potatoes are golden.

Yield: 8 servings

Roast Leg of Pork, Newgate Market, York

The whole leg of fresh, not smoked, pork was a specialty of the Swain Family Butcher Shop at the Newgate Market. It was available with bone in or boneless. Fredrick, the butcher, told me that most of the customers want the bone in so they can use the bone for soup. The whole leg of pork weighs fifteen to twenty pounds. The butcher shop also had pork fillet, sliced pork belly, pork ribs and pork chops. Several kinds of homemade sausages were available. Each variety of the homemade sausage was prepared with different ingredients. Some that I saw in the case were pork and chives, pork and leeks, pork, tomatoes and basil and the traditional sausage mixture of pork and spices.

1 fresh leg of pork, 15 to 20 pounds
1 tablespoon salt
1/2 teaspoon black pepper

Preheat oven to 350 degrees.

Place pork leg on a rack in a large shallow roasting pan. Roast for 4 to 5 hours or until meat thermometer inserted in the thickest part of the meat registers 150 degrees. Remove from oven. Cover with foil and let meat rest for 20 minutes before slicing. An orange marmalade glaze can be used to coat the meat one hour before it is fully cooked.

Serve with chutney if desired.

Yield: 10 to 14 servings

Beet Root and Carrot Slaw, Newgate Market, York

The produce at the Newgate Market was very fresh, having been harvested the morning of the Market. Several trays of root vegetables were displayed. Two varieties of beets, carrots, turnips, new potatoes, onions and scallions were for sale. The sign for the beets listed them as "beetroot," which was accurate because the beet leaves were removed. However, it was a term I had not seen before. Chioggia beets do not bleed and work well in this slaw.

1/4 cup Greek style yogurt
1 teaspoon orange zest
3 tablespoons fresh orange juice
1 tablespoon fresh lemon juice
1 tablespoon chopped fresh dill
3 medium-sized Chioggia beets, peeled and
   julienned
3 medium carrots, peeled and julienned
Kosher salt and ground black pepper

In a medium bowl, combine yogurt, orange zest, orange juice, lemon juice and dill. Stir to blend. Add beets and carrots. Stir only to coat with dressing. Season with salt and pepper.

Yield: 6 servings

Markets of Scandinavian Countries

As early as the ninth century, the Vikings from Norway, Sweden and Finland were establishing trading routes. They are credited with establishing trading posts along the ports of England, Ireland, Scotland, France, Spain, and Denmark and even along the Russian rivers. In their long boats, they brought grains, cattle, corn, tropical fruits and wine back to the Scandinavian countries. More than one thousand years ago, the descendants of the Vikings, fishermen and farmers settled in the majestically beautiful land. The settlers raised sheep

and goats and fished for their survival in this harsh environment. The fishermen also moved to the natural harbors along the shore of the North Sea. Boats were their only means of transportation and made communication with other areas possible. Over time, marketplaces were set up in the villages in the squares, and those wishing to sell their wares were charged a toll or a stallage fee by the landlords or the authorities who owned the marketplace.

To avoid the charges, the farmer or his wife would sell the items directly to the consumer. Some would set off once a year during a slack farming season to peddle their surplus door to door. It was more common for the farmer to sell his products at the local fair. This was a time of socializing and entertainment as well as conducting business. After a year of a bountiful harvest, the farmer might attend several of the fairs held in his area.

Sweden occupied Finland and Norway, and it became part of the Swedish kingdom for five hundred years. Trade of food and labor moved freely from one area to another in this domain. Helsinki was founded by King Gustav I of Sweden in 1550.

By the eighteenth century, there was an increase in markets for agricultural products as towns grew and specialized secondary production increased. The fishermen contributed to this expansion with their freshly caught fish from the cold waters surrounding the countries.

Today, the markets are well-organized. The farmers, producers, processors and the distributors are recognizing the consumer's interest in and desire for healthful foods. The demand for organic and natural food and those products with a small carbon footprint has greatly increased. Certified organic production has been practiced by a few farmers since 1931. However, the great increase in organic production has been a result of farmers', consumers' and the intellectuals' strong interest in organic food. The government of these countries has made economic subsidies to farmers producing certified organic products.

The requirements for those who are selling their wares at the organic farmers' market are: They must have bred, caught, raised, won, baked, smoked, pickled or otherwise processed the food. The person selling the food must be able to tell the consumer how and where the product was raised and how it was processed for the market.

The law of the land, particularly in Norway, grants the oldest son ownership of the farm when his parents die. The other siblings often purchase parts of the family farm. Land division results in farms becoming small with only a few acres. The farmer with a small acreage was the ideal subject for organic farming. The goal is to have 20 percent of the agriculture production in Norway organic by 2020, and the Swedish government has set a goal of 30 percent of the farmland in organic production by 2020.

Bondens Market | Oslo, Norway

At the the Environmental Festival 2010, held on June 5, the organic Market was the main feature, along with environmental lectures and entertainment. The twenty vendors set up their tents and stalls early in the morning along Karl Johans gate. The products for sale were honey, jellies and jams, cheese, smoked fish, meat, healthful fruit juices, beverages, flatbrod, sausages, bread and muffins, tomatoes, lettuce and basil.

Christian Dante Ferguson, an organizer for the Environmental Market, was a great source of information. Chris represents an organic fruit and vegetable delivery company. She is working with farmers to incorporate their products into the restaurant menus. She also oversees delivery of the organic products to markets and individual clients.

Eleanor, an attractive blond, blue-eyed young lady, owned a smoked and dried fish stall. She told me she caught, cleaned, dressed and smoked the fish herself. Her packages of fish were very attractive. I was impressed. Two stalls were selling fresh fish fillets that were on crushed ice. The salmon, halibut, cod, and silver skin sole glistened in the display.

Two stands were selling all-natural, concentrated fruit juice, mostly berry juice. A gentleman named Rune Fatleh was the owner of the Vikja Company. He raised livestock on his all-organic farm and sold the meat at farmers' markets and to some supermarkets. He also had elderberry bushes by a creek on his land and was selling the concentrated juice

of the elderberries at the Market. After I tasted a sample of the juice, he insisted that I accept a small bottle of the juice as a gift. The juice had a tart, tangy taste rather like cranberry juice. Rune told me I would need only a little bit each day for good health.

A truly Norwegian stand was the Kal Skrippe Shop making tissue-paper thin *flatbrod*. The fifteen-hundred-year-old recipe called for ground wheat flour, salt and water. I learned there is no yeast in

flatbrod. The two friendly ladies manning the stand were making a type of pancake on a large round griddle. This type of griddle would also be used in making lefse. The pancakes are eaten with sour cream and butter.

Organic cheese was being sold from several stands. Samples were available for all the visitors to the Market. One stand had a round block of gjetost—a brown goat's milk cheese that was unusually soft and slightly sweet.

I enjoyed talking with Carol, who was selling her organic jams and jellies. She told me that she raised most of the fruit and berries she uses in her products. The other fruits she buys from farmers who raise organic fruits.

As part of the program on education regarding organic production, the Market had a stand providing information on organic products. It was manned by an attractive young blond lady with a wonderful warm smile. She, like everyone else at the Market, spoke excellent English. The vendors were happy to talk with me about their products and the growth and interest in organic products.

In 2009, there were twenty sites of farmers' markets in Norway meeting all the criteria. This seems to be a very low number considering the interest in organic food. From the literature I picked up at the Market, I counted eight different sites for organic markets in Oslo. There seemed to be an organic market held every week from June 5 through the middle of December.

Fisketorgel, Bergen Fish Market
Bergen, Norway

I was surprised to see large chunks of fresh whale meat and slabs of dark burgundy, smoked whale meat for sale at the Bergen Fish Market, Fisketorgel. I suppose I should not have been shocked for the recorded history shows that whales have been hunted in the waters around the Scandinavian countries since the ninth century. The fishermen brought their catch to the village called Bryggen for trade. They brought stockfish, cod and whitefish that they had dried without salt during the long winter.

In spite of hardships and fire, the Bergen Fish Market has survived. Today, fresh, smoked, cured, dried and canned fish are sold to local customers and curious tourists from the stalls of the Market. Of

the twenty-six or more shops, most were selling fish and seafood. There are no fishermen present in the Market today. All the products are purchased from seafood wholesalers and processors who buy from the fishermen and large fishing companies. The products come from around the world.

The fish stalls had large quantities of fresh fish for sale. Cod and salmon were the best sellers. Other fresh fish available were red fish, monkfish, tusk, mackerel, black haddock, whale, capelin, halibut, pollack and herring. The fjord salmon that is found only in the cold waters of the rivers entering the North Sea was promoted as the VERY best. About 90

percent of the salmon and 40 percent of the trout sold in Norway are farm-raised, according to Thormod Johansen, director of the Norwegian Fisheries Museum in Bergen. In the late 1980s, Norway copied Denmark in establishing fish farms. In less than twenty years, 50 percent of the money from the fishing industry was coming from farmed fish.

At the Bergen Fish Market, the orange-red salmon fillets were sold marinated, cured and smoked, as well as fresh. I learned there are two methods for smoking salmon. The fast smoked is done in two hours at a fairly high temperature, and the slow smoked is held in the smoker for two days at a lower temperature.

The vendors at the salmon-laden stands were encouraging the observers and potential customers to taste their product. They would slice a small morsel of salmon with a wide-blade long knife and hand the bit of salmon on the blade to the recipient. I found the fast-smoked salmon to be soft and to crumble when sliced. The slow-smoked salmon was more firm and could be thin sliced. One young, enthusiastic salesman told me he would put the salmon in a foil bag, and I could carry it for two weeks without refrigeration. At one time, the fish sold at the Market was smoked along the Bergen wharf and the smell of the wood smoke penetrated the area. Today, the smoking is done in large processing plants along the coast south of Bergen.

The whole dressed herring, with heads and tails intact, were smoked and called klippfisk. Dry strips of smoked herring were also available. The vendor told me, "It would keep forever."

Cod and haddock are also smoked. For years, cod was dried and packed in salt for use throughout the long winter when fishing on the wild, icy waters was impossible.

Only one stand had dried cod hanging from hooks around the top railing of the stand. I was told that this cod is the real lutefisk. Lutefisk is a popular dish for some Norwegians in the United States and is eaten mainly at Christmastime. It has a reputation of having a very strong fishy smell when being cooked. The reconstituted lutefisk was for sale in vacuum-sealed packages.

Almost every stall had cooked crab on display. The large, red king crab legs were on crushed ice. Some of the legs were as large around as my wrist. The cooked stone crab claws were piled high on the counters. The Norwegian commercial catch of the red king crab did not start until 2002. It is now a valuable resource, but, as a non-native species, great care is taken in Norway to prevent it from dispersing to new areas.

Two of the vendors had large cement tanks, approximately 6-by-6-feet and 3-feet deep, in back of their stands adjacent to the harbor. Two of the tanks held live brown crab, also known as common crab. They are caught along the Norwegian coast in a depth up to fifty meters. In another tank, I saw the large pale prawns. The deep water prawns are found in the fjords, offshore banks and in the Arctic regions. The pink, deep-water prawn is the most common caught. The cooked prawns were piled high on the stands, and dishes of cooked prawns could be purchased for a snack or lunch.

Another tank held live lobsters, called clayfish, not crayfish. The lobster is one of the largest crustaceans found in Norwegian waters. They only thrive in shallow waters, in depths of forty meters or less with rocky or stony beds where they can find plenty of hiding places. There has been a dramatic drop in the stock of lobster in Norwegian waters during the last fifty years, and that is why they are now protected by conservation orders. Minimum-sized lobsters may only be caught using lobster pots. Attempts are being made to develop lobster farming, sea ranching and/or stocking with young lobsters raised in captivity to bolster local stocks.

Several fish stands had canned herring, sardines and mackerel for sale. In 1875, there were seventy fish canning factories around Bergen. The last canning plant closed in 2008, and now all the canned fish sold at the Market comes from Poland and other countries.

One does not think of Norway as a source of caviar, but several stands had a surprisingly large display of small jars of caviar. There were several kinds of caviar for sale. The Arctic caviar is from the capelin, the Norwegian caviar is from the seahaug, the red caviar is from the salmon, both wild and farm-raised, and the yellow is from the herring. Smoked salmon roe also is used for caviar.

Kaviar is a special processed cod roe sold in a tube similar to a large toothpaste tube. I was served a small dab on the end of my finger. It had a sweet, salty taste and a slightly grainy texture. I thought it tasted very good. Swen, the middle-aged vendor who looked like I imagined a Viking would look, said, "As a boy, I ate Kaviar on bread, and my mother told me if I ate it every day, I would be clever."

Fish is certainly the major part of the Bergen Fish Market, but there are two or three produce stands at the Market. When I visited the Market in early June, there were no vegetables for sale at the stands. The two stalls that were open had large bing cherries from Turkey, blueberries from Spain, strawberries from Belgium, oranges, lemons and grapefruit from Spain, apples from France and locally grown rhubarb. Johan, the owner of a stand, informed me the rhubarb was used for making fruit soup.

The only meat stand was run by a white-haired, mature gentleman. He sold "polse," meaning sausages. His sausages were made with local products with different spices. Reindeer and moose sausage were the most popular. He also had smoked sausage made with whale meat. Chorizo, a Mexican type of sausage, was made with a mixture of pork and different meats and spices. Lamb sausage was available, as was the salt-cured and dried whole leg of lamb. This delectable treat is sliced thin and served as a cold cut of meat. This stand also had small half-pound to one-pound pieces of salt-dried pork for sale.

The Fisketorgel has changed over time, as to be expected. It is still a popular fish Market for the local residents and certainly a tourist attraction for all the foreign visitors.

Hotorget Farmers' Markets
Stockholm, Sweden

The Hotorget Hay Market in Central Stockholm was appropriately named back in the 1600s. In the summer, the farmers from Roslagen, north of Stockholm, would pack their carts or wagons early in the morning to go to the market in Stockholm. This would be done at 2 or 3 o'clock in the morning because the sixtieth latitude in north Sweden is the land of the midnight sun. In June, there are about nineteenth hours of light. The horse-drawn wagons would bring hay, grain, eggs, potatoes, farm produce, chickens, and animals for sale to the crowds in the fast-growning town.

After a day at the market, the farmers often would gather at a local tavern. Sometimes the camaraderie and the party would go on long into the night. In the morning, the farmers would return home with less money because they helped the economy of the tavern.

The farmers were allowed to bring their horse-drawn wagons to the market until 1920 when congestion became too great. The farmers then took and sold their products at other markets. There were several markets around Lake Malaren at that time.

The new Hotorget Market, built in 1965, is located in the square in front of the large Concert Hall. The landmark is known by the larger-than-life bronze statue named Oreus Group by Carl Miller. The work of art overlooks the Market from the steps of the Concert Hall.

During the summer and during mild weather, the fruit, vegetable and flower stands are out of doors in the square.

I arrived at the Market early in the morning when the stands were just being set up by the merchants. The trucks and vans filled with the produce from the wholesale houses were backing into the square to unload their wares. No longer are there farmers at the Hotorget Market. The vendors and workers at the fruit, vegetable and flower stands were all young men with dark complexions, dark brown eyes and dark hair. I was told the men came from Southern Europe, Turkey and Asia.

When the Market is open, it is a noisy place. The vendors shout to the customer the availability of their products. My Swedish guide translated the shouting as "Buy my berries!" and "Best berries in the market!" The vendors haggle with the customers who want a lower price. A large man selling the berries would

hold his hand over his heart and say, "Lady, I can't sell it for less, my children will starve." Late in the day, before the Market closes, the vendors do lower their prices and holler even louder about the good price they will give the one who buys their products. I found all the vendors at the markets I visited spoke Swedish, Norwegian and English, and they conversed with me in English.

At the time I was at the Market, in the middle of June, the only produce from Sweden in the Market was raised in greenhouses close to Stockholm. The selection of vegetables included several types of lettuce and greens, red, green, white and yellow onions, potatoes, tomatoes, leeks, celery and most other vegetables. What impressed me the most were the piles of neatly arranged white asparagus. The fat stalks were 8 to 10 inches long and 1 to 1-1/2 inches thick. Aaron, a very pleasant talkative man, told me the white asparagus came from Germany. The thick stalks needed to be peeled before cooking. The taste of the white asparagus in much milder than the green asparagus.

At this time of year, fresh berries were displayed at every stand. There were fresh, plump blueberries, red raspberries and large, fat blackberries. The fresh strawberries had a wonderful aroma, and I could smell them before I saw them at the stall. My new talkative friend told me the berries came from Spain, the shiny, dark red cherries from Turkey, melons from southern France and the oranges from Portugal.

In the lower level of the large building facing the square are the meat, fish, cheese, bread and prepared food shops.

The area reminded me of a large supermarket except there were several meat shops and fish counters throughout the open area. The fish vendors had a large selection of fresh, marinaded, and smoked fish. One stand was preparing kabobs of square, thick cuts of salmon, halibut and monkfish topped with a fat tiger prawn. They looked beautiful. One busy counter was making and selling sushi made with fresh salmon and tuna. I visited with the customer who told me sushi was very popular in Sweden.

Several types of shellfish, shrimp, lobster, crayfish, and mussels were for sale. These are caught along the west coast of Sweden. The salmon and other fish are fished from the Baltic Sea.

The four meat counters at the Market held beef, lamb and pork of various cuts. One stand even had pig's ears for sale. The roast looked well-trimmed and neatly rolled. The butterfly lamb chops were cut across the full loin so they appeared as two chops connected in the center. Organ meats were available at two of the meat stands.

I found only one bakery stand. Most of the loaves of bread were a type of rye bread. There was light rye, dark rye and pumpernickel rye and a sourdough rye on display. Everyone has heard of Swedish limpa and, to my embarrassment, I found that limpa means loaf and not a type of bread.

In the center part of the large open area were two well-stocked cheese markets. I asked where the different cheeses came from. Eric, the young Swedish salesman, told me France, Italy, Germany, Poland, Spain and Finland. I thought Sweden would be the major producer of cheese for the Market. He showed me the large round wheels of cheese on the counter and said these are the cheese of Sweden. I tasted the samples he gave me, and the cheese tasted like sharp cheddar and a Swiss mixture. It was very good.

Ostermalmshallen Market
Stockholm, Sweden

The beautiful red brick structure with an impressive tower was built by the city of Stockholm in 1888 for the sole purpose of an enclosed marketplace called Ostermalmshallen to replace an outdoor market in the square that was crowded, dirty and unsanitary. It has operated as a marketplace ever since that time. The building is large, at least two hundred feet long and one hundred feet wide. The aisles are fairly narrow, but they may have just seemed narrow because of the crowd of people in the Market. In spite of the congestion, the Market was not unusually noisy, and the vendors were not shouting about their products like those in the outdoor Hotorget Market.

The first stall I saw as I entered the Market was a large, rectangular, four-sided meat market. This large shop had an extensive variety of meats. The beef was available in steaks, roasts and sections of the animal as the whole leg or entire loin. The T-bone and porterhouse steaks and the rib roasts had a thick 1-1/2-inch covering of creamy white tallow. The centerpiece of the shop was a tall-glass enclosed case holding a whole beef loin with temperature and humidity control for aging the meat.

I was surprised to see horse meat steaks for sale. A clerk named Mike told me the horse meat is prepared the same way as beef. The horse meat sold by this Market comes from a slaughterhouse in the south of Sweden.

The shop had many special products. The large, bright red, eight-ounce beef patties were interesting because of the ingredients that were added to the meat. Mike explained the different patties. The first was beef tartare and was to be eaten raw. Another tray of patties was made with a mixture of ground beef and pork and, of course, did require cooking. Other patties had different ingredients added; one contained chopped fresh garlic, another green capers, one set had blue cheese mixed with the beef and another contained chopped green onions. Mike said they added salt, pepper and egg to all the meat mixtures.

Next to the display of beef steaks in the counter were small, square, one-fourth-cup sized containers of flavored butter. Some of the butter had cheese added; others had roasted garlic mixed with the butter. The flavored butter was to be placed on the hot steaks just as they came off the grill as the steak was being served.

I was interested in a large, baseball-sized, round dough filled with a pork and beef mixture. A friendly young clerk at the shop wrote the name of the product, "kroppkakor," on a slip of paper for me because I could not even pronounce the word, let alone spell it. He told me the ball is cooked in boiling water before eating. It really is a large dumpling. The dough looked like potato dough.

The glass-enclosed, refrigerated case held an orderly display of dressed chickens. The whole dressed birds were in perfectly straight rows as if they were a marching band. Even the cut pieces of chicken were arranged in an orderly, neat fashion. Each piece was carefully trimmed, and there were no ragged cuts or hanging fragments.

The cheese stalls were packed with a wide variety of cheeses. The wedges cut from large wheels were cheeses from Sweden. It is mild cheddar. Several other pieces of cheese were from Europe.

There were several well-stocked fish counters in the Market. Salmon was available at every stand. Much of the salmon comes from Norway. Also fish farms that raise salmon and trout are nearby in the Baltic Sea and supply the Market. Eel that is for sale in the Market is also caught in the Baltic Sea. The lobster comes from Scotland and the East Coast of the United States. The large shell-on-shrimp also comes from Scotland. The fresh waters in and around Sweden supply the Market with perch, pike, fresh water trout, whitefish and sturgeon. The most frequently seen salt water fish were cod, tomfish, turbot, flounder, sole, torsk, stromming, and herring. I am sure I am forgetting some of those for sale at the Market.

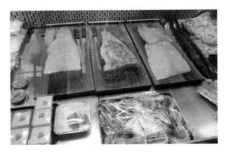

At one stall, I found small, round appetizers made with minced fresh salmon placed on a little round of toast and another of smoked chopped fish on a similar round. These were very attractive.

The bakery shops at the Ostermalmashallen Market displayed large loaves of bread in various shapes. The round, the elongated oval, the square and the diamond-shaped bread were stacked on wooden shelves and displayed on the counters. "Rolland," the long baguettes, were in a basket near the aisle next to the customer traffic. The Swedish people like rye bread, and rye flour is used in most of the loaves at the bakeries. The recipe for breads varies in the different regions of the country. The round waffle-like bread "kagkaka" is popular in the north of Sweden. According to Ingrid, the shop owner, the light rye bread contains some white wheat flour. Pumpernickel bread is quite dark, as is the molasses bread sold at the stand. She said the large, round, flat loaf is generally walnut bread, although other nuts are also used in the round loaves. The spice anise seed is used in some rye bread as well as raisins, fruit or dried orange peel. Of course, multigrain breads are gaining in popularity because of the desire for more healthful food.

The flat bread was so thin it looked like perforated tissue paper. Rye krisp is served at every meal and is sold by the sheet.

One stall was selling fresh pasta in different shapes. Some were stuffed with fillings of meat, cheese or vegetables.

The flowers at all the markets in Stockholm were fantastic. In the morning, the vendors arrived at the markets with large pallets of potted and cut orchids, the entire pallet wrapped in clear plastic. Another abundant flower at the markets in June was the Oriental lily. Some stalls had dozens of buckets holding large bouquets of lilies. The aroma was almost overwhelming from these flowers. The blossoms were of many different colors, making it difficult to choose. White lilies seemed to be the most popular.

Plants of garden vegetables also were being sold at the outdoor markets.

Sodermalmshallana Market
Stockholm, Sweden

The island of Sodermalm is the largest borough of Stockholm and can be reached by ferry boat across Lake Malaren or by the train/subway from Old Town (Gamla Stan). It has about one hundred thousand residents and an active, busy commercial life.

The Sodermalmshallana is the Market Hall in Sodermalm next to a square with booths of flowers and some fruit stands. The main Market is in the Hall by Medborgargtalsen on Sodermuim. This is the newest of the three main markets in Stockholm and was opened in 1992.

Down a few steps from the square is the large open market area in the building. It is bright, neat, sparkling clean and looks inviting. It is not as large a space as the other markets. The counters of meat, fish, cheese, bread and deli foods are randomly placed so the same type of products are not necessarily next to each other. The selection of the different foods was more than adequate. All the markets sold some organic foods. The Sodermalmshallana seemed to have a larger selection of organic products, and they were available from more merchants.

The large Sandstrom's meat market dominated the fresh and smoked meat section of the Market. The meat looked to be the very best quality, bright red with very little fat. I met Daniel, a studious, attractive, young man in a perfectly white butcher coat, who told me that all their meat is organically raised on farms on the Gotland Island south of Stockholm. He said, "The cattle eat the best grass in Sweden that also has herbs growing in

it to make the meat taste better. There are no chemicals used on the land, and the Charolais cattle do not get medicine." Some of the beef, particularly the meat for steaks, is aged for three weeks. Another attendant in the meat market took great pride in telling me of the care he takes in smoking the sausages. He personally smokes and cures the bacon, ham and sausages. He had five different sausages made with recipes from different countries, Germany, Poland, Spain, Italy and Sweden. He uses different spices, as well as different kinds of meat and cheeses, in the sausage recipes. He told me the length of the time to smoke the products varied. The array of sausages went on and on.

The pigs raised on the farm in Gotland also are certified organic. The pork roasts did have a stamp, and I was told the stamp was for sanitation and pure food inspection, not organic.

The two cheese shops had most of the same kind of cheese. I saw cheese from several European countries. The large, cream-colored wheels of cheese from sheep and cow's milk displayed on the top of the glass case was from Sweden. I asked, "From what part of Sweden does the cheese come from?" The vendor found a long cylinder by the counter and pointed on it to demonstrate the parts of Sweden producing cheese. According to the improvised map, the Swedish cheese is produced in the far south and all along the way up north to cover three-fourths of the country. Much of the cheese at both stands was organic.

I saw only one long fresh fish stand with a variety of whole and sectioned fish on crushed ice. The selection was extensive. The only seafood I saw at the Market was shrimp. A section of the counter had a display of smoked fish. The vendor said that they sell a lot of smoked fish because the Swedish people really like smoked fish.

The large, two-sided fresh produce stand was colorful and the different shapes and sizes of the fruits and vegetables made a fantastic picture. The extensive selection contained fruits from Europe, Asia and home-grown Swedish strawberries and rhubarb. In the square outside the Market, I found a small fruit stand. The young lady selling the fruit told me the large yellow pears with brown freckles came from Argentina, South America.

The square was also home for several flower stands filled with peony blossoms and fragrant lilies.

Kauppatori Market | Helsinki, Finland

beautiful fresh cherries from Spain filled one stall. Two stands had large, fresh stalks of red rhubarb for sale. These were obtained from a nearby gardener, the young, tall, blond salesman told me.

At a well-stocked vegetable stall, I saw a basket of root vegetables arranged for a stew. It contained parsnips, celery root, red onions, scallions, potatoes and a root of fresh horseradish. This was the first fresh horseradish I had seen at a market.

Several stands had tiny, round potatoes. Some of the white potatoes were the size of a marble. The darker potatoes were the size of Ping-Pong balls. The lady selling the potatoes said, "The potatoes are from Poland, but Finland raises lots of potatoes." I saw small cauliflower the size of a sauce dish and long, thick spears of white and green asparagus. These came from France, as well as the large, white garlic bulbs and the scallions that were four to five inches long.

I met Maraki, a slender lady in her 30s who was wearing a colorful jacket and

The early settlers in Finland were called "wanderers and gatherers." To be more accurate, they should be called "fishermen and gatherers" because their subsistence came from the Baltic Sea, the White Sea, the Gulf of Finland and the thousands of inland lakes. Many of the settlers were from the neighboring land of Sweden.

The Market Hall was built in 1889, but the market had been in existence for years before the government decided to build an enclosure to provide shelter for the vendors during the long winter.

The Kauppatori Market and the Market Hall, or Old Store Hall, is located at the South Harbor where small boats, yachts and cruise ships dock. On the eastern end

of the harbor is the beautiful orthodox Uspenski Cathedral overlooking the Market from its location on a small hill. Looking down on the Market from this vantage point, I could see rows of orange-topped tents and clusters of small tables.

In the middle of June, when I visited the Market, many of the fresh vegetables and berries were just coming to market. Almost every stall had a beautiful display of large blueberries, raspberries and strawberries. I learned from a saleslady that most of these were imported, and the strawberries were the only locally grown fruit. Later in the season, the stalls will have loganberries, blackberries, and cloudberries found in the woods. Cranberries are raised in the bogs and sold at the Market. The berries that grow wild are smaller but have fantastic taste compared to the farm-raised. Boxes of

hat. She gave me a lesson on Finnish mushrooms. Most of the mushrooms sold at the Market are found in the woods. They grow wild and can be picked all summer long. The large tray of small, golden mushrooms and the large black ones that looked like truffles are used in cooking and not eaten fresh.

Emma's stand had tomatoes, fresh peas in the pod, green onions, leaf lettuce, parsley, dill, carrots, beets, cauliflower, cucumbers and green beans.

I saw only two bakery shops selling bread: one in the square and the other in the Old Market Hall. The Finnish people enjoy rye bread so the bakery stocked several types of rye breads of different shapes and different-sized loaves. Some were made with molasses, some with potato flour and others had caraway seed, anise seed or sesame seed on the loaves. The flat round bread was a nut bread. Many of

the breads were made with whole grains grown in Finland.

The Market Hall is the home for fresh meats, processed meats, fish, both fresh and smoked, cheeses, breads, jellies, jams and syrups, as well as prepared foods. The two long parallel aisles run the full length of the very long building. In the center of the structure is a lobby or foyer where

one can sit. On one side is a tall, arched, clear glass window.

The section of fish stalls was very interesting. There were at least ten stalls each about ten feet long. Both wild and farm-raised salmon fillets from the cold waters of the Baltic Sea were sold fresh, marinated and smoked. Various marinades and rubs were used. Some of the slabs of trout and salmon were dressed with dill, parsley or crushed peppercorns. Other species of fish were for sale, whole or cut into pieces. Small, whole, cleaned silvery fish, about four to five inches long like sardines or smelts, were sold fresh, smoked or deep fried.

Finland is a country of thousands (187,888) of lakes. Its largest lake, Saimaa, is the fourth largest in Europe. Fresh water fish, such as perch and northern pike from the lakes, are sold at the Market. Smoked herring, salmon and whitefish were arranged in an attractive display in the refrigerated cases. Shrimp from tiny to large prawns were piled in metal bins. Marinated shrimp and several different recipes of shrimp salad were in tubs or oval-shaped ceramic dishes. Some were arranged as appetizers or snacks in round, serving-sized bits. Snails in the shell were steamed and stuffed with a soft cream cheese mixture. All the appetizers looked very delicious.

The fresh meat cases had beef, pork and lamb cut for roasts, steaks or chops. The

dark red reindeer meat was for sale in several refrigerated cases already cut for roasting or broiling. Reindeer meat and moose meat also are made into sausages. The reindeer are raised in Lapland for sale to the markets.

The Market had several stalls selling sausages of all sizes and meat mixtures. In talking with John, a sausage purveyor, I learned the Finnish people eat a lot of sausage. He said, "The best of life is to get out of the sauna and have a cold beer and a grilled sausage." The Finnish people take a lot of saunas, at least three or four times a week, so that would mount up to a goodly amount of sausage every year.

I was impressed with the several long, glass-enclosed counters with a variety of appetizers and salads. There were large bowls of marinated fillets and smaller cutlets of herring in wine or other marinades. Several different cabbage salads were favorites of the shoppers.

Some of the counters held trays of olives from bright green to gray green to jet black. Several of the trays held a combination of olives and seasonings. A seafood salad had squid, shrimp and crab as its ingredients. The bite-sized canapés were topped with mixtures of seafood or of ham.

In the Market Hall, it is possible to select a delicious lunch from the prepared food vendors. The menus list fish soup, potato soup, cabbage soup, reindeer burgers, sausages on a bread wrap, smoked salmon, pickled herring, shrimp salad or cooked, peeled shrimp and many other choices. Seating is limited because the aisles are not wide. In one area, a narrow table is attached to the wall with stools along the one side for the diners. The prepared food stands are just across the aisle.

Recipes | Scandinavian Markets

Potato Fennel Soup, Bondens Market, Oslo

Potatoes are the most common starch in the Norwegian diet. They are used in stews, soups, eaten boiled with butter or cream sauce with lutefisk and as the base for the thin Norwegian bread, lefse.

1/2 tablespoon olive oil
1 fennel bulb, chopped
1 cup chopped leeks (about 1 large leek)
1 large baking potato, quartered
2 cups vegetable broth (enough to cover potatoes)
1/2 cup half-and-half cream
Nutmeg, salt and white pepper
1/2 cup sour cream
Fennel fronds for garnish

In large soup pot, heat olive oil over medium heat. Add fennel and leeks. Sauté until vegetables are soft, about 6 minutes. Stir in potatoes, vegetable broth and cream. Cover and reduce heat to simmer for 20 minutes until vegetables are soft. Add nutmeg, salt and pepper to taste. In a blender or food processor, puree the soup until smooth. You will need to do the blending in batches. Return to the soup pot. If the soup is too thick, add more cream. Heat before serving. Ladle into bowls. Garnish with a dab of sour cream and fennel frond.

Yield: 4 to 6 servings

Norwegian Pancakes, Bondens Market, Oslo

The Norwegian pancake is a buttermilk pancake that's eaten with butter and sugar or "brun ost" and sour cream. It is cooked on a large round griddle that is also used for cooking lefse.

5 large eggs
2 cups sugar
1 quart buttermilk
1/4 cup butter, melted
2-1/2 cups all-purpose flour
1 teaspoon baking powder
1 teaspoon baking soda
Oil for frying

In a mixing bowl, combine eggs, sugar, buttermilk and butter. Beat well to combine Add flour and mix only to combine. Add baking powder and baking soda. Place 1/2 cup to 1 cup batter on hot greased griddle, depending on the desired size of pancake. (The large ones are difficult to turn unless you have a large, flat turner.) Fry until golden on griddle side, turn and cook for 1 minute on the second side until golden. Serve with butter, sour cream or fruit sauce.

Yield: 10 to 14 pancakes

Smoked Trout Salad, Bondens Market, Oslo

The sea trout are caught in the North Sea and the Baltic Sea by Eleanor, a vendor at the Bondens Market in Oslo. She not only caught the trout, she cleaned, smoked, and packaged the fish. Smoked fish will keep all winter if held in a cold place.

1/2 cup crème fraiche or sour cream
2 tablespoons lemon juice
2 tablespoons fresh dill, chopped
Kosher salt, as desired
In medium bowl, combine crème fraiche, lemon juice and
    dill. Set aside.

6 tablespoons extra virgin olive oil
2 tablespoons lemon juice
Ground black pepper, as desired
1 pound smoked trout, skinless and deboned
1 medium-sized seedless cucumber, peeled, sliced thin
1/2 cup thinly sliced scallions
Lettuce leaves for plate-liners

In a large bowl, whisk oil, lemon juice, and black pepper.
Break trout into bite-sized pieces. Add cucumbers, scallions
and trout to oil mixture. Marinate for 15 minutes. Arrange
lettuce leaves on salad plates. Arrange sliced cucumber
mixture on lettuce leaves. Top with trout and bits of scallion.
Garnish with a fresh dill sprig.

Yield: 6 servings

Fruit Soup, Fruktsoppa, Bondens Market, Oslo

Fruit soup is a traditional Scandinavian dish that can be served cold or hot. The recipe can vary according to the fruit and fruit juice available in the pantry of the home. Some recipes do not use sugar or honey for sweetening and have only the sweetness of the fruit. Fruit soup is served as a dessert, a snack or as a fruit at breakfast.

1/2 cup chopped dried apricots
1/2 cup chopped dried prunes
1/2 cup dried cherries
1 cup water
1/2 cup golden raisins
1 fresh apple peeled, sliced
1 lemon, sliced
1 cinnamon stick
1/2 cup sugar
2 tablespoons quick cooking tapioca
1-1/2 cups fruit juice (cranberry or lingonberry
    or elderberry)

Place the dried apricots, prunes and cherries in a large saucepan. Add 1 cup cold water and let stand for 30 minutes. Add remaining ingredients and heat to a boil. Cover the pan and reduce heat to a simmer for 15 minutes. Stir occasionally to prevent sticking. Remove cinnamon stick and lemon slices. Cover and refrigerate for 4 hours. Garnish with dollop of sour cream or plain yogurt.

Yield: 4 to 6 servings

Rommegrot, Bondens Market, Oslo

Rommegrot is a traditional Norwegian cream dessert. It is made with cream, milk and flour. That sounds like a recipe for paste. However, the addition of sugar and cinnamon makes it a more appealing dish. In cooking the cream mixture, it gradually becomes thick and smooth. The butterfat will melt and float to the top of the cooking dessert. It can be scooped up and removed although some enjoy having their dish of Rommegrot topped with the butter along with cinnamon and sugar.

1 quart heavy cream
1 quart whole milk, scalded
1 cup all-purpose flour
1/2 teaspoon salt
3 tablespoons sugar
Cinnamon and sugar for topping

Place cream* in a heavy kettle and bring to a boil. (I use a slow cooker.) Reduce heat and simmer for 15 to 20 minutes stirring constantly. A wooden spoon works well. Sift flour into cream and continue to stir. Cook until butter forms on top. Skim off butter and save. Gradually add scalded milk. If the product is too thin, sift more flour into the cream mixture and continue to cook. Add sugar and salt. Serve warm in a bowl with a little melted butter, cinnamon and sugar.

Yield: 8 servings or more

*If you use homogenized milk or cream, the butter does not separate.

Greens Salad with Lemon Pepper Dressing, Kauppatori Market, Helsinki

2 cups red leaf lettuce, bite-sized pieces
2 cups green leaf lettuce, bite-sized pieces
2 cups endive, bite-sized pieces
1 cup fresh basil, bite-sized pieces
3 garlic cloves, minced

Wash greens and tear into bite-sized pieces. Measure by packing them into a measuring cup. Place greens in a large bowl. Add garlic and toss. Drizzle with dressing.

Yield: 4 to 6 servings

Lemon Pepper Dressing

2 tablespoons lemon juice
1/4 cup extra virgin olive oil
1/2 teaspoon prepared Dijon mustard
2 tablespoons diced roasted red pepper
2 tablespoons diced shallots
1/4 teaspoon sea salt
1/8 teaspoon freshly ground black pepper

Using a wire whip, blend lemon juice, olive oil and mustard. Just before serving, add pepper, shallots, salt and pepper. Whip to blend.

Yield: 3/4 cup

Crab and Shrimp Cakes, Bergen Fish Market, Bergen

The assortment of shrimp at the Market was extensive. This included the large white shrimp from the deep water to the small pink shrimp caught in the bay or farm-raised. There also were several kinds of crab, both raw and cooked, for sale. The cooked crab meat was sold by the kilo.

2 cups cooked crab meat
2 cups chopped bay shrimp
1/4 cup chopped green onion
1/2 tablespoon chopped fresh parsley
1/4 teaspoon chopped fresh thyme
2 tablespoons mayonnaise
1 tablespoon Dijon mustard
1 tablespoon lemon juice
1 tablespoon dry white wine
Dash celery salt
Dash white pepper
Dash hot sauce
1/4 cup bread crumbs
2 eggs, beaten
Olive oil for frying cakes

In a mixing bowl, combine all ingredients and mix well. Refrigerate for 1 hour. Form mixture into cakes, approximately 3-1/2 inches in diameter. Pan-fry cakes until golden brown on each side.

Yield: 6 cakes

Broiled Salmon Fillet with Pepper Jelly Glaze, Bergen Fish Market, Bergen

The pepper jelly used as a glaze for the salmon adds a slightly hot-sweet taste and gives the fish a glossy appearance.

2 pounds salmon fillet
2 tablespoons jalapeño pepper jelly
1/4 teaspoon kosher salt

Heat broiler to 450 degrees.

Spray broiler pan with non-stick spray. Place 1/2 to 1 cup water in lower part of broiler pan. Place salmon, skin side down, onto broiler pan. Spread jelly over fish. If the jelly is stiff, heat it in the microwave oven for a few seconds. Sprinkle with salt. Broil for 10 to 12 minutes until salmon flakes.

Yield: 6 servings

Tipsy Cherries, Bergen Fish Market, Bergen

The produce stands at the Bergen Fish Market all had their counters full of beautiful, large, sweet red cherries. They are a tasty snack or delicious dessert. I had made brandy cherries and thought it would be a great combination of the market cherries and the Norwegian liquor Aquavit. After marinating in the Aquavit for a couple weeks, the cherries and sauce can be used as a topping on ice cream, angel food cake, custard, plain yogurt or waffles. Enjoy!

1 quart fresh sweet cherries, stems and stones removed
1/2 cup sugar
1/2 cup Aquavit (Norwegian liquor), more if needed

Wash, stem, pit and cut cherries in half. Pack cherries tightly into quart canning jar. Pour sugar over cherries. Add Aquavit to fill the jar. Cover tightly. The jar of cherries does not need to be refrigerated. Shake the jar occasionally to distribute the sugar and Aquavit. Cherries are ready to serve after two weeks but will keep for a year in the refrigerator.

Yield: 1 quart

Braised Whale Steak with Lingonberry Salsa, Bergen Fish Market, Bergen

I was surprised to see whale meat at the Bergen Fish Market. However, I learned that the Norwegian fishermen apply for licenses to hunt a limited number of whale each year. The meat is dark red, almost burgundy in color. The elderly, gray-haired man selling the fish told me that whale is cooked the same as tuna. I always thought whale was fatty, but this meat seemed very lean.

2 tablespoons butter, melted
4 whale steaks, each 5 to 6 ounces and 1 inch
   thick (or tuna)
1 teaspoon salt
1 teaspoon lemon pepper
Parsley for garnish

Heat the butter in a large skillet to brown the butter. Season steaks with salt and pepper and place in hot butter. Cook for 4 to 5 minutes. Turn steaks and continue cooking for additional 4 minutes. Remove from skillet and place on serving dish. Garnish with parsley. Serve with lingonberry salsa.

Yield: 4 servings

Lingonberry Salsa

1 bag (12 ounces) fresh or frozen lingonberries
1 quart water
2 cloves garlic, minced
1/2 jalapeño chili, seeded and diced
1/2 cup diced green pepper
1/4 cup diced onion
Juice of 3 limes
Salt to taste

Boil lingonberries for 1 minute in quart of water. Drain well. Place in a bowl and add remaining ingredients. Stir and mash some of the whole lingonberries. Refrigerate until serving.

Yield: Approximately 2 cups

Fresh Berry Parfait, Hotorget Market, Stockholm

The vendors at the Hotorget Market in Stockholm had their counters filled with fresh fragrant strawberries. They also were selling blueberries, raspberries and some blackberries. The stalls were beautiful because of the array of colors, and the air was filled with the fragrance of the berries.

1 cup fresh strawberries, sliced
1 cup fresh blueberries
1 cup fresh raspberries
1 pint vanilla yogurt

Using 4 parfait glasses, place 2 tablespoons yogurt into each glass; divide blueberries among the parfait glasses. Top each with 2 tablespoons yogurt. Divide strawberries among parfait glasses. Top with 2 tablespoons yogurt. Add the raspberries, divided among the 4 glasses. Top with yogurt. Garnish the top with a berry.

Yield: 4 servings

Kropp Kakor, Hotorget Market, Stockholm

Kropp Kakor is a traditional Swedish potato dumpling that is popular in both Norway and Sweden. In Norway, the dish is called Potato Klubb. The recipe varies in the different regions of the country. In the northern part of Sweden, raw potatoes are used in the dough, and in the southern part, the dough is made with cooked potatoes. It is served as a main dish most often in the fall and winter. (The spring potatoes have too much moisture.) The filling is generally cooked pork, ham or bacon. Some recipes call for a small meatball to be inserted into the ball. The use of allspice also varies with the cook's taste.

Kropp Kakor is served with lingonberries or whortleberries jam and melted butter. They are often served the second day sliced and fried in butter.

3/4 pound ground beef
3/4 pound ground pork
1 tablespoon oil or bacon drippings
1/2 cup onion, finely chopped
1-1/2 to 2 pounds potatoes, quartered (about 6 medium-sized potatoes)
1 egg yolk, slightly beaten (a second egg can be used if the dough is too stiff)
1/2 teaspoon allspice
1-1/2 teaspoons salt
1/8 teaspoon black pepper
2 to 3 cups flour

Combine pork and beef. Heat oil in skillet. Add onion and sauté for 3 minutes. Add pork and beef and sauté until cooked, about 5 minutes. Set aside. Boil potatoes for 20 minutes, drain and cool to room temperature. Mash or rice potatoes. Add egg yolk, allspice, salt and pepper to potatoes. Add flour 1 cup at a time to mixture so dough can be handled and shaped into balls. Turn dough onto floured surface and knead 5 or 6 times. Use your hands to shape the dough into balls about the size of a baseball. Punch a hole in each ball. Fill the hole with 1 tablespoon meat mixture. Close the hole and drop the balls one at a time into 2 quarts boiling, salted water. Cook only as many dumplings at one time that will float uncrowded in the pan. Cook for 15 to 20 minutes. Remove with a slotted spoon. Serve warm with melted butter and jam.

Yield: 6 sevings

White Asparagus with Brown Butter Sauce, Hotorget Market, Stockholm

The white asparagus for sale at the Hotorget Market were unusually long and thick. The huge asparagus spears must be peeled before cooking. The white asparagus has a milder flavor then the green asparagus. The Brown Butter Sauce will enhance the flavor of the asparagus.

12 large stalks fresh white asparagus spears, trimmed (if large, they may need to be peeled)
4 tablespoons butter
1 cup fresh bread crumbs
1 teaspoon chopped fresh parsley

Cook asparagus in saucepan for 10 minutes until crisp tender. Drain and set aside. In large skillet, heat butter to hot and turning golden. Add bread crumbs, stirring until well coated and golden brown. Add asparagus and sauté until well-coated with brown butter bread crumbs. Garnish with chopped parsley.

Yield: 4 servings

Broiled Seafood Kabobs, Hotorget Market, Stockholm

The seafood kabobs that were being prepared at the Market were a beautiful assortment of colors from the different fish and shellfish. The kabobs were selling fast, and the young men were busy keeping up with the orders from the customers.

1 pound salmon fillet, cut into 8 pieces
1/2 pound halibut fillet, cut into 4-inch pieces
1/2 pound ahi, cut into 4 pieces
4 large jumbo raw shrimp, peeled and deveined
4 sea scallops
1 zucchini, cut into 8 slices of 1/2 inch each
1 yellow summer squash, cut into 4 slices of 1/2-inch each
1/2 small red onion, cut into 8 slices
2 tablespoons olive oil
2 tablespoons lemon juice
1/2 teaspoon salt
1/4 teaspoon fresh ground black pepper
4 skewers, oiled

Heat broiler to 500 degrees.

On each skewer, place: onion slice, ahi, yellow summer squash, scallop, zucchini, salmon, shrimp, zucchini, halibut, salmon and onion slice. Brush fish with olive oil and 1 tablespoon lemon juice. Sprinkle with salt and pepper. Place onto broiling pan that has been coated with non-stick cooking spray. Broil 5 inches from heat for 4 minutes. Turn and continue broiling for 4 to 5 minutes. Remove from broiler and brush with remaining lemon juice.

Yield: 4 servings

Fresh Poached Pear with Red Wine Sauce, Hotorget Market, Stockholm

4 firm ripe pears, peeled
2 tablespoons lemon juice
1/2 cup sugar, divided
2 cups red wine
3 cloves, whole
3 cardamom pods, whole
3 anise seeds, whole
1 stick cinnamon, whole

Peel pears and cut a slice off the bottom so pears stand straight. Leave on stems. Place in saucepan and add water and lemon juice to cover pears. Add 1/4 cup sugar. Place on medium heat. Cover and simmer for 15 minutes. Remove from heat and let cool.

To make the wine sauce, place wine, cloves, cardamom, anise, cinnamon and 1/4 cup sugar in saucepan. Place on medium high heat and bring to a boil. Reduce heat and simmer for 20 minutes to reduce sauce.

Refrigerate to cool completely. Divide sauce into 4 serving dishes. Remove pear from liquid with slotted spoon and gently set in the center of the wine sauce.

Yield: 4 Servings

Strawberry Rhubarb Pie, Sodermalmshallana Market, Stockholm

Locally grown rhubarb can be found in the markets in Stockholm in May and June. The home-grown strawberries, however, do not come to the markets until later. The strawberries in the Market when I visited had been imported from Spain.

2 unbaked (9-inch) pie crusts
1/2 cup plus 1 tablespoon all-purpose flour
1 cup sugar
1/2 teaspoon salt
2 pints fresh strawberries, sliced
1 pound fresh or frozen rhubarb, cut into 1 inch pieces
1 tablespoon butter
1 egg
1 tablespoon sugar

Preheat oven to 425 degrees.

In a large bowl, combine flour, sugar and salt. Add strawberries and rhubarb. Stir to coat fruit with sugar and flour mixture. Let stand for 5 to 8 minutes. Prepare pie crust in 9-inch pie pan. Pour fruit into pie shell. Place dabs of butter on top of fruit mixture. Cover top with second crust (or do a lattice weave with the crust over the top). Seal edges of crust. Beat egg in small bowl. Add 1 teaspoon water. Brush crust with egg. Sprinkle with 1 tablespoon sugar. Bake pie at 425 degrees for 15 minutes. Reduce heat to 375 degrees and bake for 50 minutes until the juice bubbles and crust is golden. Cool on rack.

Yield: 8 servings

Pickled Beets, Sodermalmshallana Market, Stockholm

The beets for sale in the markets were small, round bulbs with long green stems. The stems could be used as cooked greens. The Ping-Pong ball size of the beets was ideal for pickling. The pickled beets are often served as a salad or with a sandwich. All the Swedish recipe books that I checked had a recipe for pickled beets.

1 pound small, fresh beets
1/2 cup beet cooking liquid
1/3 cup sugar
1/3 cup cider vinegar
1/2 teaspoon salt
3 whole cloves
2 whole allspice
1/2 stick cinnamon

Scrub beets well to remove all dirt. Leave the root ends and about 2 inches of stem on the beets. Place in a pot of water and bring to a boil. Cover and simmer until tender, about 25 minutes. Drain, reserving 1/2 cup of liquid. Cool beets and slip off the skins, remove stem and tail. In a medium-sized saucepan, place beets, 1/2 cup cooking liquid, sugar, salt and vinegar. Tie the spices in a cheesecloth and put into pan with beets. Cook until mixture comes to a boil, stirring occasionally. Reduce heat and simmer for 5 minutes. Remove spices from liquid. Beets will keep for several weeks if placed in a sterile jar and tightly closed.

Yield: 2 cups

Rich Cheese Sauce, Sodermalmshallanan Market, Stockholm

The cheese cases in the markets had a large variety of cheese not only from Sweden but from Europe and around the world. In reading the cheese signs, I saw Adelost, Graddost, Greve, Sveciaost, Vasterbottenost, Herrgaardsost, Prastost and Hushallsost. "Ost" must refer to cheese. When I asked what part of Sweden the cheese comes from, I was told from one end of the country to the other. The merchants were very generous in giving me samples of the wonderful, flavorful cheeses.

1/2 cup butter
1/4 cup all-purpose flour
2 cups milk
1/8 teaspoon cayenne pepper
1 tablespoon Worcestershire sauce
1 cup shredded sharp cheddar cheese
1 cup shredded Swiss cheese
1 cup shredded Parmesan cheese
12 ounces beer
Dash of nutmeg

In a large saucepan, melt butter. Add flour and cook over medium heat, stirring constantly. Add milk and stir while cooking until thickened. Add pepper and Worcestershire sauce. Gradually add cheeses. Cook over medium heat, stirring until cheese is melted. Add beer and stir to blend. Add nutmeg and serve.

Yield: 8 servings

Broiled Gourmet Beef Patties, Ostermalmshallen Market, Stockholm

The large butcher shop near the front of the Market had several trays of beef patties in their refrigerated counter. The patties were large, perfectly shaped and mixed with different, interesting ingredients. One tray of fresh beef patties was beef tartar to be eaten raw. One tray held patties containing green capers, another mixture of beef and pork also contained chopped green onions. One that sounded tasty and different to me was the beef patty mixed with blue cheese.

1 pound lean ground beef
2 eggs, slightly beaten
1/2 teaspoon salt
1/8 teaspoon fresh ground black pepper
In a large mixing bowl, combine all ingredients and mix, do not over mix

Various additions

1/2 cup crumbled blue cheese
Or
1/2 cup green onions, chopped
Or
2 tablespoons cloves garlic, minced
Or
1/4 cup green capers

Heat broiler or grill to hot. Oil grill or broiler pan. Shape meat mixture into patties of desired size. Broil 3 inches from heat for 7 minutes on each side for medium done. It is recommended that ground meat be cooked well done.

Yield: 2 to 4 servings

Swedish Rye Bread, Ostermalmshallen Market, Stockholm

Rye grain was introduced to Sweden around 500 A.D. and proved to be a productive crop. Rye bread is the most popular bread in Sweden and is eaten at every meal. Several types of rye bread are sold at the markets. Not only are the loaves of different shapes but the ingredients also vary. Some of the rye bread might have caraway seeds, aniseed, citrus peel, dill seeds or nuts added. The bread may be a light rye or the dark pumpernickel.

2 packages active dry yeast
1 teaspoon sugar
1/4 cup warm water
1 cup warm milk
1/2 cup warm water
1/2 cup orange juice
1/4 cup dark corn syrup
1/4 cup vegetable oil

2 teaspoons salt
1 teaspoon aniseed
1/2 teaspoon ground cardamom
1 to 2 teaspoons orange zest
2 cups rye flour
5 cups all-purpose flour
Melted butter for brushing

Combine yeast sugar and 1/4 cup warm water in a bowl. Stir to dissolve. Let rest for 5 minutes. Combine rye flour and white flour in a large bowl. Place 1 cup warm milk, 1/2 cup warm water and 1/2 cup orange juice in mixing bowl. Add yeast mixture to liquid. Add three cups of flour mixture to liquids. Stir to combine flour into liquid. Cover bowl and let sponge rise for 1 hour until double in volume. Add brown sugar, syrup, oil, salt, aniseed, cardamom and orange zest to mixture. Gradually add remaining flour to form stiff dough that may be sticky. Place on floured surface and knead dough until smooth and elastic. Place into well greased bowl and turn dough to coat with oil. Cover and let dough rise to double in size, about 1 hour. Punch dough down Turn out dough onto lightly floured surface, kneed and form into two round balls or loaves. Place balls on greased baking sheet. Cover and let rise in a warm draft free place for 45 to 50 minutes. Bake at 375 degrees for 1 hour until bread sounds hollow when tapped and is golden brown. Brush the hot loves with melted butter. Cool before slicing.

Yield: 2 loaves

Finnish Appetizers. Kauppatori Market, Helsinki

Small tidbits or snacks with various food combinations are popular in Finland. The selection of prepared appetizers, spreads and toppings available in the markets was endless. They were arranged in an attractive pattern in the refrigerated cases.

Shrimp Spread

1 tablespoon chili sauce
1 tablespoon lime juice
1/3 cup mayonnaise
1/4 cup chopped green onion
1/4 cup chopped water chestnuts
1 cup chopped cooked shrimp

In mixing bowl, combine chili sauce, lime juice and mayonnaise. Mix to blend. Add onions and water chestnuts. Gently stir in chopped shrimp.

Yield: 1-1/2 cups

Smoked Salmon

3 ounces soft cream cheese
4 ounces smoked salmon, skin removed and crumbled
1/4 cup chopped fresh tomato
1/4 cup chopped green onions
1 tablespoon capers
12 baguette rounds, toasted or 12 large round crackers

For each appetizer, spread the baguette or cracker with cream cheese. Place salmon, tomato, onion, and capers on top of cream cheese.

Yield: 10 to 12 servings

Avocado Crab Crostini

24 baguette rounds or crackers
3 ounces soft cream cheese
6 ounces crab meat, shell and fins removed
1/4 cup mayonnaise
1/4 cup sour cream
2 tablespoons finely chopped green pepper
2 tablespoons finely chopped red pepper
2 tablespoons grated Parmesan cheese
1 teaspoon lemon zest
1 tablespoon lemon juice
1/4 teaspoon salt
2 ripe avocados, peeled, seeded and cut into 24 slices

Toast baguettes slices to golden brown. In mixing bowl, combine cream cheese, crab, mayonnaise, sour cream, green pepper, red pepper, cheese, lemon zest, lemon juice and salt. Top each baguette with 1 tablespoon crab mixture. Top with slice of avocado.

Yield: 24 servings

Reindeer Mushroom Soup, Kauppatori Market, Helsinki

Reindeer are raised in Lapland for the markets in Helsinki. The meat is sold fresh and cut for roasts, steaks, cubed and ground. A large amount of the meat is used for making sausages.

2 tablespoons olive oil
1/2 cup chopped onion
1 clove garlic, minced
1 pound venison steak, cut into 1/2-inch long strips by
    1-1/4-inch thick
4 cups sliced mushrooms
2-1/2 cups chicken broth
1/8 teaspoon dried thyme
3 tablespoons butter
1-1/2 tablespoons cornstarch
1-1/2 tablespoons flour
1-1/2 cups half-and-half cream
1 teaspoon salt
1 teaspoon sugar
1/4 teaspoon white pepper
2 tablespoons sherry wine (optional)

In a large, heavy saucepan, heat 1 tablespoon oil to medium high. Sauté onions in oil. Remove onions from pan and set aside. Add remaining oil and heat to medium high. Add meat and cook for 15 minutes. Remove from pan and set aside. Place mushrooms into pan and add chicken broth and thyme. Cook covered for 20 minutes. In a blender or food processor, puree mushrooms, keeping some chunks whole. In saucepan, melt butter. Stir in cornstarch and flour and cook for 2 minutes. Gradually add cream, stirring constantly as it thickens. Add mushrooms and broth, salt, sugar and pepper, stirring to blend. Add cooked reindeer meat. Cook for 5 minute. Remove from heat. Add sherry wine.

Yield: 6 to 8 servings

Finnish Flat Bread, Kauppatori Market, Helsinki

Bread is a staple in the Finnish diet. During periods of scarcity, the bread was the difference between life or starvation. Crisp breads are traditional thin, cracker-like breads usually made with some rye flour. In Finland, the leavened rye breads are dried into thin crisps. They are sometimes made using sourdough and also based on combinations of flours, including wheat, barley or potato. The various flat breads are usually made from unleavened dough and baked in flat, round loaves. Flat breads are most often served with soups, salad or cheese. Crisp breads are common throughout Finland.

1-1/2 cups all-purpose flour
3/4 cup rye flour
1 tablespoon sugar
1-1/2 tablespoons baking powder
1/2 teaspoon baking soda
1 teaspoon salt
1/2 cup cold butter
1 cup buttermilk

Preheat oven to 350 degrees.

In a large bowl, combine flours, sugar, baking powder, soda and salt. Cut butter into flour mixture until mixture resembles coarse crumbs. Add buttermilk and mix to blend. Grease and flour large baking sheet. Place dough on pan and spread to 1/4-inch thick. Pierce dough with a fork. Bake for 20 to 30 minutes until lightly brown.

Yield: 1 large pan, approximately 24 servings

Markets in the Eastern European Countries

Throughout the centuries of war, invasions, occupations and waves of migration, the societies of the Eastern European countries have amalgamated and blended. In the tenth century, the German Babenberg dynasty acquired the lands of Austria, Hungary and neighboring states and, during their reign of three hundred years, became a major trading center. During the Habsburg reign of six hundred years, the empire included Austria, Bohemia, Hungary, Czechoslovakia, Germany and parts of the Balkans. World War I and World War II—with the occupation of Russia in Poland, Hungary, and Czechoslovakia and Germany's influence in Austria—again resulted in a significant change in the culture and the availability of food and markets.

Over the centuries, the ups and downs of trade and existence of markets varied with the policies of the different rulers and the impact of war. The rivers in Eastern Europe played an important role in transportation, immigration and trade to the land-bound countries. The rivers—Danube, Rhine, Elba, Odra, and Seine—all had trading posts established along their banks. As early as the twelfth century, markets were thriving in the towns. The town square for holding the market was adjacent to the church or castle, and permission for the market was granted by the church bishop, the nobility, such as king, lord and land owner, or the city council.

The markets were the place where the farmers and craftsman would bring their products to sell directly to consumers. Market Day was a time of socializing, of political events, entertainment and even an occasional public execution.

Today, the Market is still a center for gathering and purchasing the freshest foods available. Organic and bio-foods have arrived in the Eastern European Markets. During the Communist occupation, the farmers were unable to pay the price for chemical fertilizers and pesticides. Their small farms were worked in the same traditional farming methods as previous generations. These methods made conversion to organic farming less difficult. The European Union also has helped the farmers in growing and producing organic products.

The Markets in the Eastern European countries tend to have similar foods for sale, and some of the traditional recipes of one country are popular in adjacent countries.

The Great Market Hall did not have many organic products for sale. The lack of demand for organic products hindered the development of the domestic market. The organic products demand a price that is 15 to 20 percent above similar non-organic products. More than 90 percent of the organic grains and other organic products are exported. Since 2007, there has been a slow but steady increase in organic products coming to the Market.

Genetically engineered products (GMO) are banned in Hungary. The European Commission has tried unsuccessfully to have the ban lifted. However, the Hungarian parliament has twice upheld the moratorium, in 2007 and again in 2009. There are no GMO products in the markets in Hungary.

Viktualienmarkt | Munich, Germany

Four hundred years ago, the Rhine River was the source of trade from the north through Germany to the south. Trading posts were set up along the banks of the river for the wool from Ireland, tapestries from Belgium, and tobacco from Scotland. From the Mediterranean came olive oil and citrus fruits, spices from Asia and coffee from Africa. The wares were sold and bartered from these trading posts.

By the 1700s, the main farmers' market in Munich was located at the Marienplatz, where grains, animals and produce were sold. As the town grew, so did the market and soon it was too congested to meet the needs of shoppers and farmers. In May 1807, King Maximilian decreed a new market would be established near the plaza. It was called Viktualienmarkt from the Latin word "victuals," meaning food or groceries.

The market was severely damaged during World War II. Following the war, there was some concern about the need to rebuild it. However, the Munich administrators decided the city needed a centrally located open Market. Today, the Market is run by the City of Munich.

The outdoor Market grew and today boasts one hundred and forty canopy-covered stalls and, of course, includes an outdoor beer garden. The spacious beer garden, with at least seven hundred seats, is a gathering place for tourists and local shoppers. One area allows for self-service and another smaller area is served by waitresses who carry huge trays of filled beer steins. The beer garden is especially busy on the days of a Market festival or concert. The shoppers have a wide selection of traditional foods, gourmet specialties and imported fruits, wines and seafood.

The fruit and vegetables stands are well stocked with beautiful greens: kale,

spinach, parsley, endive, red tip lettuce, bibb lettuce, green cabbage. Herbs are also plentiful with large bunches of basil, dill, thyme, sage and more. The shoppers seemed to be very careful in selecting the herbs they buy. The stands were selling long green beans, fresh peas, green onions with some of the garden dirt on the ends, pure white cauliflower, piles of red tomatoes and elongated white radishes. A large stall, run by a family from the Middle East, not only had fresh vegetables but also had several large cloth bags with dried beans, peas, rice and grains.

Those stands selling fruit displayed large red cherries, peaches with a blush of red on the skin, red grapes, strawberries and apples. Pineapples and mangos were two of the imported fruits on the counters.

The many butchers in the Market sold all parts of the animals, including tripe, brains, testicles, heart, lung, sweetbreads and feet. Wild boar was sold at several butcher shops. I had my first taste of wild boar at a prepared food stand in the Market. I was pleasantly surprised by the taste. Other game meats for sale were venison and elk.

The butcher shops in the Market had displays of beef, pork and lamb on refrigerated, stainless-steel counters. I also saw fresh, dark-red horse meat at one of the shops. The Gefluegel Poerre Poultry Company had whole dressed chickens, ducks and rabbits for sale.

Germany is noted for its excellent bread. The dark, heavy rye and multigrain breads were available unwrapped on the counters for all the shoppers to see, feel and smell. The aroma was great. Some bakeries had lebkuchen, stollen, gingerbread and peppernut cookies for sale.

Germany produces several types of fresh, cured and smoked cheeses, and these were for sale at the Toiler Kais Laden's cheese shop. I was told by a smartly dressed, friendly, young shopper that the stall also imports cheese from France and Italy. Unfortunately, they were not giving out samples of their products.

At the far end of the Market were several flower stalls. The tall, slender, gray-haired lady was busy trimming dried leaves from her potted plants. Cut flowers were sold from the buckets that held them.

The Market has mostly organic foods, known in Germany as "bio-foods." I learned the organic agriculture movement originated in Germany in the 1920s. The largest organic food trade show, known as "Bio-Fach," is held in Nuremberg each year with more than three thousand exhibitors.

Hala Mirowska | Warsaw, Poland

In the oldest area of Warsaw and near the ghettos is the Hala Mirowska Market. The two long, narrow brick buildings were constructed between 1899 and 1901 under the authorization of Russian Mayor Nikolai Babikov. Although a great deal of Old Town was destroyed by German bombs in World War II, the market buildings survived and functioned as a market until the uprising in 1944. In retaliation to the civilian population, the Hala Mirowska was destroyed by flame throwers from the German military. All that remained of the buildings were the outside brick walls. The bullet holes from the battles are still visible.

Following the war and during the Communist occupation, the Polish people rebuilt the market using materials found in the piles of debris. However, there was no surplus food for sale. In the 1950s, the buildings were used for a bus depot. My guide, Gregory, told me the Communist government had offices in the building.

With the end of Communism in 1989, foodstuffs were once again obtainable.

Hala Mirowska Market came back to life. The two long, red brick buildings were restored. The fascias are ornate, with darker bricks forming the design on the lighter brown bricks. Along the street side of the building are small windows.

Hala Mirowska Market is state-owned. The vendors must buy a license to sell their wares at the Market. The Market is run with strict regulations on sanitation and in accordance with trading regulations so that meat, fish and dairy products can be purchased without a health concern.

The two long buildings now house supermarkets. These markets sell everything, more like a general merchandise store. They are not as well-organized or as neat as most large supermarkets.

To the left of the entrance is a busy coffee bar. Farther on is an area of individual kiosks selling a wide assortment of products such as jewelry, rugs, shoes, dishes and appliances.

On the other side of the buildings from the street are the permanent stalls for the sale of fruits, vegetables, nuts, breads, fish and meat. Another smaller building also contains shops for these same products.

I was aware of the aroma of fresh baked bread before I found the bakery stand. The fresh bread and rolls in molded plastic containers were not wrapped and available for the customers to pick up, inspect and purchase or not. There were light rye, dark rye, braided egg, whole grain and crusty white breads in several of the containers.

Every vegetable stand had large beautiful red, green and golden peppers. The red peppers are called paprika. The colors of the peppers were as beautiful as the flower bouquets. Another unusual product at the vegetable stands was the bouquet of soup vegetables. Most bouquets contained carrots, parsnips, leek, celery and some with celery root. Other bunches had not only these vegetables but also fresh herbs such as flat leaf parsley, chives and basil.

Many of the fruit stands had a variety of apples. It was fall, and the apple season was in full swing. I saw Fuji, Gala, Delicious and Greening apples for sale. There are many orchards around

Warsaw. The apple trees are pruned to stand straight and narrow. The branches do not spread out into the aisles, making the rows between the trees quite wide. This facilitates picking of the ripe fruit. Poland exports about 90 percent of its apple crop each year as fresh fruit or as apple juice concentrate.

The Market had several types of mushrooms for sale. The brown caps with greenish-stems of the porcini were the most popular. Some shiitake and portobello mushrooms were also for sale. A mushroom called "puff" is grown in the woods in Poland. It can grow to be as large as a soccer ball.

I met Albert at his fruit and vegetable stand. He did not speak English so my guide, Gregory, translated for me. Albert told me that his parents had owned the stall at the Market for several years as he was growing up. Now he owns the stall and has for the past five years. He said, "I buy my produce from several farmers, and I have many women who supply me with wild mushrooms." They find the wild mushrooms in the woods.

The meat shops sold well-trimmed pork, large slabs of salt pork and some pork bellies for the fat. A few stalls specialized in sausages. These, in various colors, sizes and shapes, were in glass-enclosed cases. Pork is a popular meat in Poland, often served with sauerkraut or cabbage or cooked with root vegetables. Kolduny, a meat dumpling, and zrazy, a stuffed beef roast, are also favorites. Large sections of bright red, lean beef were stacked on carts. The butcher would cut the meat into roasts or steaks as the customer desired.

The amount and types of fish in the Market were limited. This was not surprising since Warsaw is not near the ocean. One vendor sold only pickled fish, and most of his containers were empty. I don't know if they had been full at the start of the Market day. Carp was being sold at the other fish market. Two other types of fresh water fish were in water tanks in this stall. There were no shellfish for sale at the Market.

Along the street adjacent to the buildings were street vendors with foods, flowers and some clothes. These women did not have stalls or booths but set up their wares on the sidewalk or sold them from the back of a van or truck. They were dressed in their housedresses, well-worn jackets and kerchiefs or scarves. Many were older ladies and men who travel from outside Warsaw early every morning to try to sell their produce of fresh herbs, fresh eggs, homemade jams, honey and wildflowers.

At the end of the block, behind the last large building, was the great flower market. Most of the stands were selling roses of many different shapes and colors, including the silver lavender rose. The white calla lilies and the colorful bouquets of dahlias and asters were a rainbow of colors. Poland exports flowers all over the world. Many of the tulip bulbs from Holland are raised in Poland. The flowers at the Hala Mirowska Market are much less expensive that those sold in florist shops.

The middle-aged, nicely dressed shoppers at the Market appeared to be office workers from the nearby buildings. A few older women from the nearby apartment complex had brought their own shopping carts.

Rynek Glowny | Krakow, Poland

The main market square in old town Krakow is known as Rynek Glowny and also as Rynek Krakowski. It is the largest medieval town square in Europe, dating back to the thirteenth century. Its layout was drawn up in 1257 after the town was granted its charter by Duke Boleslaw V Wstyaliwy. The square was designed in its current layout, with each side repeating a pattern of three evenly spaced streets set at right angles to the square. The exception is Grodzka Street, which is much older and connects the Main Square with the Wawel Castle.

Originally, the square was filled with low market stalls and administrative buildings. King Casimer III the Great built the first Cloth Hall and Town Hall that filled nearly a quarter of the square.

The square has been more than just a marketplace. It has staged many important events in Poland, including coronations, regal ceremonies and royal funerals. The less festive of these were the public execution of prisoners held in the Town Hall. During the occupation of Poland by Nazi Germany, the Main Square was renamed Adolf Hitler Plaza.

The historical monuments and commemorative plaques were taken from the building in the Market Square.

During the Communist government rule and until 1989, there was a scarcity of food in the market. Only a few stalls with a limited quantity of products were seen on market days.

Today, the Main Square Market is lively and crowded at all seasons of the year. Festivals and celebrations are frequent public events in the square. The New Year's Eve party in Rynek Glowny is said to be the biggest and best in Poland. In December 2005, Krakow's Rynek Glowny was voted the World's Best Square by the Project for Public Spaces.

The open food Market covers about one-half of the square. The center of the open Market has tables displaying mostly fruits and vegetables. Around the perimeter of the open area are the enclosed shops selling meats, breads and bakery goods. The meat and poultry are displayed in refrigerated cases and in the windows adjacent to the walkway to the open market. To purchase these products, one needs to enter the shop. The selection

of fresh meats includes beef, pork, lamb and a variety of sausages. The smoked and hard sausages are hung over the counters. Several of the meat shops sell mounds of white pork belly fat or lard.

Outside the shop, I saw an elderly woman holding a fresh dressed chicken. She was trying to sell the chicken that she had brought from her yard to the Market.

The fruit and vegetable stands in the center of the Square were overflowing with produce. Fresh sweet corn was in season and the neat rows of kernels on the ears were blemish-free. The most outstanding and plentiful products were mushrooms. Several different types of mushrooms filled the bins at the vegetable stands. The large, brown portobello mushrooms were the size of a dinner plate. In each display, some of the large mushrooms were sliced in half, exposing their creamy white centers. The fruit stands held several varieties of melons, bananas, berries, apples, peaches and pears.

Celery roots with their stems and leaves were laid in neat rows in one stall while the other stalls displayed the round, brown, rough roots with no stem. The roots were quite large, about the size of a baseball. Potatoes, carrots and parsnips were displayed at the stalls. Salad greens and freshly washed leaf spinach, with the clean yellow roots still on the stalks, were in plastic tubs.

One long, U-shaped table was manned by at least twelve to fifteen ladies wearing housedresses and aprons, and some had scarves over their blond hair. They were chatting with all the customers and seemed very friendly and happy. They were selling their home-produced chesses. Most had creamy white soft cheese in large round or rectangular mounds, much like cream cheese. Along with the cheese, some of the ladies were selling butter and a soft yogurt. It seemed that many of the people buying yogurt had brought their own jars to fill with the creamy yogurt from the large crocks.

Along the other side of the tables was a variety of other cheeses. A friendly, neatly dressed blond lady gave me a taste of smoked cheese that she had made. It had a strong smoky flavor.

The table with a fairly large spice display was close to the Market building. The spices, such as curry, paprika and several others, were in small plastic bags.

In the square near the Market stands were two middle-aged ladies dressed in black and selling flowers. Their supply of daisies and mums was small. I think the flowers were from their own flower gardens.

The shoppers at the Market were mostly housewives dressed in cotton dresses or skirts and blouses. Several had kerchiefs on their head. Poland has a large Catholic population so it was not surprising to see several Catholic nuns, dressed in their habits, shopping at the Market. Very few men were at the Market.

Outside the entrance to the Market were several middle-aged or older women holding garments. They were not part of the Market and seemed nervous about being there. They were selling these garments that had apparently come from their home closets.

Naschmarkt | Vienna, Austria

The Naschmarkt is the oldest, largest and most popular market in Vienna. It has been in existence since the sixteenth century. The first fruit and vegetable market was located at Freyung in the city center. When it arrived, the location was being used by a local milk market.

Just before entering the Market proper, I was greeted by a large display of flowers. The stall owner was selling large golden sunflowers, fragrant lilies, delicate orchids, bright red birds of paradise, many daisies and roses. This was a great introduction to the large Market.

As I entered from Operngasse, I found a small café selling fresh fish and seafood from refrigerated counters. The customers would select the seafood they desired. They had a choice to take the fish home or to ask the chef to prepare it for their

meal. The café had a few tables with chairs but most of the diners were sitting on stools around the counter. All the fishmongers in the Market had their products in glass-enclosed, refrigerated display cases. The fish and crustaceans were on crushed ice. One very busy operator had a tank of water with several large, dark live fish swimming in circles in their small pond. They looked like carp. The assortment of fresh fish and sea-

food was extensive at several stalls. I saw salmon, trout, red snapper, tuna, swordfish and others. There were several kinds and sizes of shrimp for sale. The vendors also offered squid, octopus, oysters, lobster, clams and mussels. These were displayed in round white plastic bowls. Other fish vendors had the seafood in rectangular trays in their cold counters. Interestingly, there was no fish smell around the shops.

The fruit and vegetable stands were open onto the aisles. The colors, patterns and shapes of the fruits and vegetables presented a kaleidoscopic view. Of the one hundred stalls at the Market, at least one-third were for produce, each more interesting than the last. The handsome young clerk working in the fruit stand offered several kinds of grapes: blue Concord, seedless white and the large red Tokay grapes. The counters also held oranges, tangerines, kumquats, limes, clementines and lemons. I learned

that the fruit came from many different countries. The next fruit stand had five varieties of pears for sale. The fresh blueberries were the size of shooter marbles and strawberries as large as Ping-Pong balls. However, to me, the most amazing fruit display was a large white plastic tub full of pomegranate seeds. I had never before or since seen just the pomegranate seeds for sale. Several of the produce stalls held tropical fruits: papaya, mangos, guava, persimmons, kiwi, coconut and cherimoya. A fruit new to me was the pitahaya with a bright orange-red skin in an elongated shape and about the size of my fist. Several were cut in half revealing a white flesh filled with tiny black seeds about the size of poppy seeds. Martha, the stall holder, offered me a sample. I found its taste similar to a cherimoya, only a little tarter. Another fruit from Thailand and Australia was the durian, an ugly, green-brown fruit about the size of large pineapple and covered with pointed thorns. This fruit, when sliced, has a terrible aroma but tastes heavenly. I also saw fresh lychees, star fruit and small pineapples the size of baseballs that are known to be very sweet. Two stands were selling fresh dates and fresh figs from Egypt, Israel and the Sahara. I seldom see these fruits at the markets.

I found stands selling dried fruits and nuts. The variety was extensive with mango, kiwi, apricots, papaya, peaches, raisins, pears and currants. The nuts could be purchased in the shell or shelled.

Dried vegetables, such as beans, lentils and peas, were displayed in cloth bags.

The vegetable stands were as beautiful and as interesting as the fruit stands. The white and green asparagus stalks were tied in small bundles and were positioned to stand tall on their cut ends. Clusters of red cherry tomatoes on the stem were an unusually bright color. This stand also had okra, artichokes, snow peas and red and yellow peppers for sale. At the end of one aisle, I saw cabbages piled three feet high on a counter that was at least six feet square. Cabbage is used to make sauerkraut and is popular in Austria. Nearby was a shop selling shredded cabbage in four different wooden tubs. The shop owner, Fredrick, told me each tub of cabbage was at a different stage of fermentation to become sauerkraut. Some customers prefer the less sour cabbage and buy from the appropriate barrel. Fredrick was generous with samples to any prospective customer. I preferred the middle stage of fermentation. Pickled vegetables in glass jars, as well as wooden barrels containing sour pickles, were available.

One of the stands offered root vegetables: light-skinned sweet potatoes, cassava, turnips, parsnips, red and white potatoes, and daikon. Squash and gourds were in season and added color to the produce stands. One of the large stands had faces drawn on several of the pumpkins. Another creative stall holder had placed his gourds in woven baskets and included some bright red bittersweet.

The meat shops were not in the open but in shops with glass-enclosed refrigerated counters. The fresh meat was cut and arranged as roasts, chops or steaks. Several butchers displayed an assortment of cuts of lamb, sheep and goat, as well as beef and pork. Veal is popular in Austria and was available in roasts, steaks, cubes, ground and boned, rolled and tied roasts. The whole skinned carcasses of lamb and goats were hung in the back of the work area so the butcher had them available for cutting a desired piece for a customer. Some of the meat shops had smoked meats and sausages hung on rods above

the counters and along the back walls of the shops.

Poultry of all types was available in a few shops. Whole dressed chicken, squab, turkey, quail, duck and pigeon were for sale. Chicken and turkey parts were also on trays in the meat case. I saw only one vendor selling eggs, and he had only brown eggs. Later, in a specialty shop, I did see quail and ostrich eggs for sale.

I do enjoy the taste of cheese and was excited to find several shops selling cheese at the Market. The large wheels of Swiss, Vorarlberger and Grjka cheese were placed on a marble slab for cutting. Other soft and semi-soft cheeses were in refrigerated cases. The cheeses came to the Market from all around the world. Some of the innovative workers had molded the soft cheese into cone shapes and decorated the cones with parsley, cilantro and black olives. Yogurt also was sold at the stands.

Teas from around the world and a wide selection of various coffees were sold at the Kaffee Shop. The Austrians developed a taste for Turkish coffee after the retreating Turks in the nineteenth century left behind bags of coffee beans. Spices packaged in small plastic bags filled an entire stand. The delightful aroma of the spices filled the air in this part of the Market.

Vienna is known for its wonderful pastries, and there were counters loaded with delicious looking sweet rolls, fruit tarts, custard-filled cakes and chocolate tortes. The bakery shops in the Market promoted every size and shape of bread. The round loaves were as large as a dishpan. It was possible to purchase half loaves of bread, if desired. The breads were made from different grains, and some had seeds and nuts in or on the crusts.

The Naschmarkt in Vienna is one of my favorite markets. It was large but not overwhelming, with a marvelous array of foods. I enjoyed learning about the new and unusual products. I also was impressed with the friendly vendors who were happy to educate me about their products.

Naplavka Market | Prague, Czech Republic

The Vltava River has for centuries been the means of transporting supplies and materials to the towns and villages along the river. Trading posts were set up for the exchange, barter and sale of products from other countries. The first market-places were along the river banks.

The most centrally located Market in Prague is Naplavka Market, held each Saturday on the banks of the Vltava River, next to the Palackeho Bridge. The translation of Naplavka is "at the river-bank," and that is an accurate name for this Market. The forty or more vendors sell homemade cheeses, sausages, organic meats, fresh fruits and vegetables, bakery goods and pastries, dried mushrooms, pickled cabbage, a freshly grilled zancler (a perch-like fish), beer, wine, and pre-pared foods.

It was the season for cucumbers, and all the vendors were hawking theirs as the best. The cucumbers were separated into boxes by their size. The tiny ones would be used for sweet gherkins, the

medium-sized cucumbers would be used for dill pickles, and the largest ones would probably become bread and butter pickles. The merchants wisely sold garlic, dill and other herbs used in making pickles. A small, neat stall was busy selling

canning supplies of jars, covers, steamers and other utensils.

When I visited the Market, it was the beginning of the plum harvest. The shoppers, mostly middle-aged women in housedresses, flat shoes and carrying large woven baskets, were in queues to buy the beautiful blue to black ripe plums. The fresh plums were not only available for sale at the produce stands, but the kitchen equipment stand and the leather goods stand each had cardboard boxes sitting right in front of their stand full of fresh plums for sale.

A small stand hidden away from the active shopping line was selling spices in small plastic bags. The selection was lim-ited. I was surprised that he had only one kind of paprika, a sweet paprika.

The Market boasts several meat markets. The Rybnik Organic Farm stand was selling aged organic beef and mutton from their glass-enclosed cases. The other butcher shops had a wide selection of smoked meats and sausages.

The bakery stands were scattered throughout the Market. Petite France was selling baguettes, croissants and French bread. Flatbreads and flaxseed pancakes were a novelty to me. At the Opatovsky Bread Shop, an attractive, tall, young saleslady had her hair restrained in a pale blue kerchief. She told me they did not make cakes, cookies or other pastries, only bread and rolls. Several bakeries specialized in pastries, cupcakes and cookies. Kolaches and tarts were on display in Votre Plaisir Bake Shop.

One would not go thirsty at the Market. I found several stands selling not only fruit juice and cider but also promoting carrot, beet and even cabbage juice. Some of the best beer in Europe is made in the Czech Republic, and the Market provided a wide selection. Wine from five wineries was available to consume at the Market or to buy and take home. One of the most unusual was the honey wine, much like mead. The stall featured twenty-five types of honey wine.

The Market is open on Saturday and is very busy with local shoppers and tourists. The young and old come to the Market on a sunny summer day. Many families with small children in strollers move along the aisles and the walkways along the river.

Havelske Trziste | Prague, Czech Republic

arkets were one of the first signs of a settlement, called a town. By the tenth century, several markets were set up in Prague. Hradcany Square in front of the historic Prague Castle was the site for a large market as far back as 937 A.D. At about that same time, on the site of today's Lesser Side Square, there was a marketplace, which along with the surrounding buildings constituted a settlement. The importance of this central space of the settlement grew when, during the reign of the King Otakar II, the settlement was granted official status as a town.

Charles Square, the largest square in Prague, was originally called the Livestock Market. Before the thirteenth century, all types of livestock were sold in this square.

The Havelske Trziste Market is centrally located near Wenceslaus Boulevard. It is one of the oldest markets in Prague and has been operating (off and on) since 1274. The Market is situated in the center of a wide boulevard for foot traffic only. It is approximately one-and-a-half blocks long. The stalls are in the center of the street, with access to both sides of the center island for the shoppers' convenience.

I first visited the Market on a weekend and was disappointed in the number of stands selling produce. Most of the stands were selling souvenirs. However, when I returned on Monday morning, I was delighted to find that many fruit and vegetable stands had replaced the trinket vendors.

The green cabbage heads were as large as a soccer ball. One entrepreneur had made sauerkraut from the green cabbage and was selling it in quart-sized plastic containers. He also had dill pickles for sale from plastic tubs sitting in front of his stand. The pickles were sold in small plastic Zip-Lock bags. Each bag contained two or three medium-sized pickles, often with dill and pieces of garlic.

Celery roots were unusually large and sold as one item. It was also possible to buy half of a celery root. Some were cut in half, exposing the creamy white flesh against the light brown outside skin.

Most of the vegetable stands had piles of peppers, labeled as paprika. Mushrooms were also in season, and the counters had piles of tan, brown and white mushrooms.

The bakery stall owned by Zclenek Sterfan was always busy. He said, "We are a family bakery with thirty employees that was inherited from our parents from their parents." They keep the old traditional recipes for the gingerbread, rolls with almonds and hand-rolled bread and rolls. The bakery is in East Bohemia, so to travel to the Market, he must leave with his baked goods at 2 o'clock in the morning to open his stall at 8 a.m. in Prague.

The Havelske Trziste Market caters to the hurried downtown shoppers. The individuals buying the products were dressed in suits and dresses. Both men and women were doing the shopping. The Trziste Market did not carry fresh meat, poultry, fish or cheese.

Nagycsarnok Market | Budapest, Hungary

The beautiful Blue Danube River bisects the city of Budapest. For centuries, the river divided the two settlements called Buda and Pest. These villages were established as far back at the second millennium B.C. The river provided a means of immigration and transport. The active trade along the Danube made the two cities prosperous. It wasn't until 1873 when the legislature unified Pest and Buda into one city that Budapest was created. The population of the capital city continued to grow and brought with it an increased demand for food markets.

The numerous street markets were disorganized, chaotic and undependable. Residents would find a street market on their corner one week, but the next week it would be a different vendor or no market at all. The Budapest City Council recognized the problem and in 1894 decided to establish five covered markets throughout the City.

The Great Market Hall, Nagycsarnok, was designed by Samu Pecz and was the most outstanding and largest of the five markets in Budapest. The location was

planned next to the Danube River. A tunnel from the river bank to the lower level of the Market Hall made delivery of products from the boats to the stalls convenient. The construction of the large structure covering 10,500 square meters with three levels began in 1894 and was completed in 1896. The Great Market Hall was officially opened in March 1896. At that time, it was the most modern and up-to-date Market in Europe,

with modern lighting, refrigeration for storage and adequate ventilation.

During World War I, the Market was not damaged. However, World War II was disastrous to the Market. The Nazi army installed rigid rules, and most of the food went to supply the military. The Great Market Hall remained open, but

supplies were scarce and expensive. After the death of Stalin and the collapse of the Soviet Union, the Market gradually made a recovery.

Between 1991 and 1994, the Great Market Hall underwent a total remodeling and modernization. The large roof structure was completely covered with Zsolnay tile produced especially for this enormous roof by the Zsolnay Porcelain Company. The decorative wrought iron works for the stairs and the third-level railings were completely redone and reinstalled.

When I walked into the Great Market Hall, I was impressed by the large size of the building and was surprised by the numerous colorful stalls selling Hungarian paprika. All the stalls were beautifully decorated. Some had rings and strings of the red peppers hanging on the sides of the stands; others had made a full circle of the dried peppers around and over the stand. One of the stands looked like the front of a small cottage, and others were decorated to look more rustic. Often the ladies attending the shops were dressed in the traditional Hungarian costumes with a white embroidered blouse, black skirt covered with a white apron lined with red and green embroidery, reflecting the colors

of the Hungarian flag, white, red and green. The large varieties of paprikas were packaged in bottles, jars, plastic packages, cloth and paper bags, and some paprika was even in a paste form and sold in a tube. It was available in mild, moderate, spicy and very spicy forms. The darker brown smoked paprika also was being sold in various degrees of intensity.

The central area of the Market is the home for the shops selling meat. The stalls not only have every kind of fresh meat but also numerous kinds of sausages. I met Martin, a sturdy, middle-aged man in a blue T-shirt and a large white apron, who was eager for me to see all of the meat products in his shop. He told me that he sells a lot of pork. I saw the whole skinned heads of several pigs along the back counters of his meat cases. In the cases were pigs' feet, pigs' tails, pigs' bellies and other parts I did not recognize. Martin was very friendly, and the shoppers seemed to enjoy talking with him.

The long strings of sausages were draped over the top rail of the booth and were so long they touched the counter. They varied in thickness from 1/2-inch thick to 4 inches in diameter and in many different colors, from bright red, pale pink, dark brown, dark red flaked with white, and some with black peppercorns throughout the smoked meat. While standing at one shop, I counted thirteen different types of sausages and salami. The meat cases were loaded with the sausages in casings of short tubes. White mold on the Teliszalami, hard sausage, told the age of the product. Liver pâté, liver sausage, as well as head cheese, were available at several of the meat stands. I learned that

the dark brown sausage was called Veres Hurka and was similar to black pudding or blood pudding that is also popular in England and Ireland.

Henry, the stall holder, was selling poultry. What I found interesting is that he was selling all parts of the chicken, including the cleaned chicken feet.

The bakery shop had round, oval and elongated loaves. Several different grains were used in the preparation of the bread and rolls. Some of the fresh bread was wrapped.

The fresh produce stands held bright, colorful displays of fruits and vegetables. The fresh radishes with their leaves still on looked as if they had just arrived from the garden. The bright, variegated green heads of cabbage varied in size from that of a baseball to a large basketball. The cabbage stacked next to purple eggplant and red onions made an attractive picture. Every produce stand had a large selection of red, green, yellow, orange, and large to small peppers. A counter holding a large display of cauliflower, with the outside leaf surrounding the creamy white head, took up most of the space on the front table. Several of the stands had carrots and beets with the full

stem of leaves attached. Other vegetables on display were tomatoes, turnips, baking potatoes, white and yellow onions, garlic, and many different greens for salads. White potatoes were available, and these are used for potato dumplings, a Hungarian favorite. Mushrooms were popular and several stands were selling oyster and shiitake mushrooms.

The fruit on the displays were of fine quality with no blemishes or bruises. This was the season for tree fruit, and each stand had large yellow peaches with a ruby blush, apricots, pears, apples and three kinds of plums—blue, red and green. The pears were uniform in shape and color and were arranged in a wooden tray like the formation of a marching band. If one would remove a pear the band would be out of formation. The signs with the names and prices were, of course, in Hungarian. I was interested in the varieties of apples and asked the lady selling the fruit, who did speak some English, for the translation of the varieties of apples. She told me the Hungarian names and tried to find the English translations, but the Hungarian words did not translate. I counted seven varieties of fresh apples at this stand.

Grapes were also for sale. The large, round blue grapes had some moisture on the clusters and glistened in the light. The green grapes, and the smaller, elongated,

seedless red grapes, were being sold at several stands. Fresh plump figs, bright yellow lemons, limes, several bins of oranges and grapefruits were available. I did not see any indication that the produce was organic.

Honey is popular in Hungary, and it was for sale at several of the shops. The golden Acacia honey is the most desired.

I saw only one cheese stall, but cheese was being sold at some of the meat and spice stands. A cheerful lady, who must have been in her 60s, showed me the two Hungarian cheeses: Trappist and Palpusztai. I sampled tiny bits of each, and they were delicious. She also had fresh cheese called Turo and ewe's milk cheese called Juhturo.

The fish shops were located in the lower level of the Great Market Hall as well as several pickle stands and a well-stocked supermarket. The refrigerated cases at the fish stands were attractively arranged, with both fresh and smoked fish. The cod and whitefish were used for a spicy fisherman soup called Halaszle. The spice in the soup is from the paprika.

It seemed as if every kind of pickled vegetable was available at the several stands selling pickles. Of course, cucumbers of all sizes were made into sweet, dill, sour, bread and butter, salty, spicy, garlicky and mild pickles. I found onions, peppers, cauliflower, tomatoes, asparagus, green beans and garlic pickled. Many of the pickles were sold in bulk by the kilo.

The third floor of the Market was the place to find the most beautiful linens. The tablecloths were of every size, with the simplest to the most elaborate embroidery. This is also the place to find fancy decorated blouses and scarves.

Scattered throughout the area were arts and craft items. I am sure most of the items on display are purchased by tourists.

I must mention the array of prepared food stands. Several sit-down cafes were located along the wall. The menus listed foods for a full breakfast, baked pastries, and traditional Hungarian dishes such as stuffed cabbage rolls, goulash, stuffed peppers called Taltott, and Szekelijgutyas, a stew made with three different meats. I found the Hungarian pastries and desserts were divine and available at these small restaurants.

Recipes | Eastern European Markets

Lubkuchen, Viktualienmarkt, Munich

Lubkuchen is a Christmas cookie that is cut into the shape of angels or bells and decorated with frosting and candies. German tradition was for a young lady to give a lubkuchen or a small bag of these cookies to the man of her choice.

1 cup butter
1 cup sugar
1 egg
1 cup honey
1 cup buttermilk
6 cups all-purpose flour
1-1/2 teaspoons baking powder
1/2 teaspoon salt
1 teaspoon ground ginger
1/2 teaspoon mace
1 tablespoon cinnamon

Preheat oven to 375 degrees.

Place butter and sugar in mixer bowl. Cream until light and fluffy. Add egg and beat. Add honey and buttermilk and beat to blend. Gradually add flour, baking powder, salt, ginger, mace and cinnamon. Mix to blend. Refrigerate dough for one hour. Roll dough to 1/4-inch thickness and cut into desired shapes. Place on ungreased baking sheet, and bake for 6 to 8 minutes. Cool and decorate

Yield: 48 or more cookies, depending on size of cutters

Red Cabbage Slaw, Viktualienmarkt, Munich

The large piles of red cabbage in the market-place were neatly arranged. The recipe for Red Cabbage Slaw makes an attractive, delicious salad for any meal.

4 cups shredded red cabbage
1 cup chopped apple, Honey Crisp or Granny Smith
1/2 cup finely chopped fennel
1/2 teaspoon salt
1/4 teaspoon pepper
2 tablespoons balsamic vinegar
2 teaspoons honey
2 tablespoons olive oil

Combine cabbage, apples and fennel in a bowl. In small bowl, combine salt, pepper, vinegar, honey and oil. Whisk to blend. Add to vegetables and toss. Chill before serving.

Yield: 6 servings

Gingersnaps, Viktualienmarkt, Munich

The bakeries at the Viktualienmarkt Market in Munich had gingersnaps and molasses cookies for sale. The gingersnaps were cut and decorated into the shape of gingerbreadmen. They were the children's favorite.

3/4 cup butter or margarine
3/4 cup sugar
1/4 cup brown sugar
1/3 cup dark molasses
1 egg
2-1/4 cups all-purpose flour
2 teaspoons baking soda
1/2 teaspoon salt
1/2 teaspoon ground ginger
1/2 teaspoon ground cinnamon
1/4 teaspoon ground cloves
Sugar for coating dough balls

Preheat oven to 375 degrees. Grease baking sheets with shortening.

Combine butter, sugar, brown sugar, molasses and egg in large mixing bowl. Beat on medium speed for 2 minutes until fluffy. With the beater on slow, add remaining ingredients. Mix for 2 minutes. Chill dough for 30 minutes for easier handling. Shape dough into 1-inch balls. Roll in sugar. Place on baking sheet approximately 2 inches apart. Bake for 10 minutes. Cool on baking sheet for a few minutes for easier handling.

Yield: 36 cookies

Green Beans with Pears and Bacon, Viktualienmarkt, Munich

The green beans, pears and bacon are an unusual combination but results in a delicious dish.

8 slices double smoked bacon, cut into 1-inch pieces
1/2 cup water
1/2 teaspoon salt
1 pound fresh green beans, tips removed and cut into
   1-inch lengths
1 pound fresh pears, cored and sliced into 1/4-inch thick
   slices
1/4 teaspoon dried leaf thyme
1/4 teaspoon marjoram
1/4 teaspoon black pepper

Place bacon in skillet and cook until part of the fat is rendered. Do not cook until crisp. Place bacon on paper towel. Place water and salt in a saucepan and bring to a boil. Reduce heat to low. Add beans. Layer pears on top of beans, and place bacon on top of pears. Sprinkle with thyme, marjoram and pepper. Cover and simmer on low for 45 minutes. Stir and place in serving bowl.

Yield: 6 servings

Spaetzle, Viktualienmarkt, Munich

Spaetzle has been called German pasta and is often served in place of potatoes. The small droplets of dough can be cooked in water or broth. Spaetzle is most often served with meat stews or gravy-rich ragouts.

1-1/4 cups sifted all-purpose flour
1/8 teaspoon grated nutmeg
1/2 teaspoon salt
1 extra large egg
1/3 cup milk
1/4 cup melted butter
Boiling water or broth

Combine the flour, nutmeg and salt in a bowl. Make a well in the center of the flour. Whisk egg and milk together and pour into well of dry ingredients. Place mixture in food processor and pulse until bubbly and elastic, about 3 to 4 one-minute pulses. Push the batter through a spaetzle maker or colander or simply pinch off small pieces of batter and drop into boiling water or broth. Cook uncovered for 8 minutes. Remove with a slotted spoon and place in ice water. Continue cooking remaining spaetzle dough. Drain spaetzle well in a colander. Warm in melted butter for 4 to 5 minutes.

Yield: 4 servings

Sauerbraten, Viktualienmarkt, Munich

Sauerbraten was originally made with horse meat, but today it is most often prepared with beef or pork. Wild boar, venison or other game prepared as sauerbraten has less of a wild taste due to the seasoning and spices. The addition of gingersnaps in the gravy was made popular in the United States after the publication of *Liuchow's German Cookbook* in 1952.

Marinade

1 cup red wine
1 cup apple cider vinegar
2 cups water
1 lemon sliced
6 whole cloves
2 bay leaves
10 whole peppercorns
1 tablespoon sugar
1 cup diced onion
3 cloves garlic, chopped
2 medium carrots, sliced
1 rib celery, chopped

Meat

4 pounds boneless wild boar roast, or beef roast
1/2 cup all-purpose flour
1 teaspoon salt
1/4 teaspoon ground black pepper
1/4 cup vegetable oil

Gravy

10 gingersnaps
1 tablespoon currant jelly (optional)

Place all marinade ingredients in large kettle and bring to a boil. Reduce heat and cook for 5 minutes. Cool marinade. Place meat in marinade. Cover and refrigerate for 3 days, turning the meat daily. Remove meat and dry on paper towel. Combine flour, salt and pepper. Coat meat with flour mixture. Heat oil in heavy skillet. Brown meat on all sides. Place in a slow cooker or Dutch oven. Heat marinade to boiling. Pour hot marinade over roast, cover and simmer for 3-1/2 to 4 hours. Remove meat from marinade. Strain marinade and return to pot. Add gingersnaps and, if desired, currant jelly. Stir and bring to a boil. Slice meat into 1/2-inch slices. Serve with gingersnap gravy.

Yield: 8 to 10 servings

Beer Bread, Viktualienmarkt, Munich

The Germans have the reputation of brewing good beer. The yeast in the beer acts as the leavening agent in beer bread. Herbs, such as garlic, rosemary, dill, dried oregano, parsley, chives and basil, and cheeses, such as grated asiago, sharp cheddar, feta and other hard cheeses, can be added, if desired.

3 cups all-purpose flour
3 tablespoons sugar
1 teaspoon salt
1 tablespoon baking powder
1 can (12 ounces) beer
1/2 cup melted butter, divided
1/2 cup shredded cheddar cheese

Preheat oven to 375 degrees.

Place flour, sugar, salt and baking powder in bowl. Add beer and 1/4 cup butter. Add cheese. Mix to moisten dry ingredients. Pour into a greased 8-inch loaf pan. Pour remaining butter over top of loaf. Bake for 1 hour or until wooden pick inserted in center comes out clean. Cool in pan on rack for 10 minutes. Remove from pan and cool for 15 minutes before slicing.

Yield: 1 loaf

Green Bean, Beet and Tomato Salad, Hala Mirowska, Warsaw

The Green Bean, Beet and Tomato Salad recipe calls for golden beets. If these are not available in your market, the ruby red beets can be substituted.

1/2 pound fresh green beans, trimmed
2 medium golden beets, cooked, peeled
4 medium tomatoes, quartered
1/2 large red onion, sliced
Vinegar and oil salad dressing

Steam green beans for 5 to 6 minutes in microwave, until crisp tender. Cool beans. Slice each beet into 4 slices about 1/4-inch thick and cut each slice in half to have 16 half slices. Arrange 4 salad bowls with 4 slices of beets, 4 quarters of tomatoes, 4 cooked whole green beans. Add rings of red onion on top. Serve cold with vinegar and oil dressing.

Yield: 4 servings

Green Herb Dumplings, Hala Mirowska, Warsaw

Steamed or deep fried dumplings are popular in most Eastern European countries. The dumpling dough can be made with various grains such as soy, buckwheat, millet and wheat. The dumplings are most often steamed but can be deep fat fried. The fillings for the dumplings are of pork, shrimp or other seafood, chicken, sprouts, and other vegetables.

Herb Sauce

1 cup chives, packed to measure
1 cup fresh parsley, packed to measure
2 tablespoons diced fresh basil
1 tablespoon diced fresh oregano
1/4 cup crème fraiche or thick cream
1/4 cup sour cream
1/4 teaspoon sea salt
1/8 teaspoon black pepper

Place all ingredients in a blender and blend until smooth. Set aside.

Dumplings

2 whole eggs
1 egg yolk
1/8 teaspoon nutmeg
1-1/2 cups all-purpose flour
1/8 teaspoon white pepper
2 tablespoons butter
3 tablespoons chicken broth
1 tablespoon black truffle oil (optional)

Beat eggs in mixing bowl. Add half of herb sauce. Add nutmeg, flour and pepper. Bring a large pot of salted water to a boil. Drop dough, using a teaspoon, into the boiling water. Do not crowd the dumplings in the water. When the dumplings float to the top, remove them using a strainer or sieve. Place in colander. Run cold water over the dumplings to stop the cooking. Place 2 tablespoons butter in large skillet. Heat butter until it turns light brown. Place dumplings in hot butter and sauté until the edges are brown. Add 3 tablespoons chicken broth and remaining herb sauce. Cook to heat sauce, about 2 minutes. Divide dumplings onto 4 dishes. Drizzle each serving with truffle oil.

Yield: 4 servings

Sautéed Mushrooms, Rynek Glowny, Krakow

Throughout Eastern Europe, wild mushrooms are hunted in the woods and sold at farmers' markets. There seems to be a large variety but that does vary with the seasons.

2 tablespoons butter
2 tablespoons chopped white onion
2 cloves garlic, minced
1 pound fresh mushrooms (shiitake, button, portobello and chanterelle), sliced
1/2 teaspoon sweet paprika
2 tablespoons crème fraiche
1/2 teaspoon sea salt
1/4 teaspoon fresh ground black pepper

Melt butter in a large skillet. Sauté onions and garlic until tender but not brown. Add mushrooms and cook for 6 to 7 minutes until tender and juicy. Remove from heat and strain juice into a bowl. Add paprika to skillet and heat. Add crème fraiche, salt and pepper. Add juice from mushrooms to skillet and stir to blend. Return mushrooms to skillet and heat. Stir to blend flavors.

Yield: 4 servings

Beef Stroganoff, Hala Mirowska, Warsaw

Beef Stroganoff is a dish that is served on special occasions and on Sunday in Poland and in Eastern Europe. The sour cream and mushrooms, that are used in the recipe are traditional foods found in most Polish markets. The Stroganoff is often served over noodles or dumplings.

1-1/2 pounds beef round, cut into strips 1x3 inches
1/2 cup all-purpose flour
1 teaspoon salt
1/2 teaspoon black pepper
1/4 cup vegetable oil
1-1/2 cups beef broth, divided
3 cloves garlic, minced
2 tablespoons tomato paste
1 tablespoon Worcestershire sauce
2 cups sliced fresh mushrooms
1 cup sour cream
1/3 cup sherry wine

Place beef in large plastic bag. Add flour, salt and pepper. Shake to coat meat. Heat oil in heavy large skillet or Dutch oven. Add meat and brown on all sides. Place remaining flour mixture into 1/2 cup beef broth. Stir to dissolve flour. Add to meat in skillet and stir to prevent lumping. Add remaining 1 cup of broth, garlic, tomato paste, Worcestershire sauce and mushrooms. Bring mixture to boil and reduce to a simmer. Cover and cook for 30 minutes. Add sour cream and sherry wine. Stir to blend.

Yield: 6 servings

Gingerbread, Hala Mirowska, Warsaw

Gingerbread has been baked and served in Warsaw for centuries. It is believed the crusaders returning from wars in the eastern Mediterranean brought ginger and gingerbread to Europe in the eleventh century. The gingerbread can vary from a soft, delicately spiced cake to a crisp cookie. The thin, flat cookie is often cut into different shapes before baking, gingerbread men being the most common shape.

Warm gingerbread is often served topped with whip cream or a fruit sauce.

1-1/2 cups all-purpose flour
1 teaspoon cinnamon
3/4 teaspoon ground ginger
1/2 teaspoon allspice
1/4 teaspoon ground cloves
1 teaspoon baking soda
3/4 teaspoon baking powder
1/2 cup brown sugar, packed
1/2 cup (1 stick) butter, softened
1/2 cup molasses
1/2 cup hot water
1 egg

Preheat oven to 350 degrees. Grease 8- or 9-inch square pan.

In a mixing bowl, place flour, cinnamon, ginger, allspice, cloves, baking soda, baking powder and sugar. Mix on low to blend. Add butter, molasses and water. Beat until smooth. Add egg and continue beating to blend. Pour batter into prepared pan. Bake for 30 to 35 minutes. Serve warm with brandy sauce or other sauce as desired.

Yield: 8 to 9 servings

Celery Root and Apple Soup, Hala Mirowska, Warsaw

Celery root, also known as celeriac, is a rather ugly, round, rough, ball-shaped vegetable that is used more often in Eastern Europe than in the United States. It can be used in soups, stews, as a steamed vegetable, pureed and added to mashed potatoes or pureed and flavored with truffle oil. Celery root can be enjoyed raw when grated or shredded and added to salads. When I visited the markets in Poland, celery root was available with the stems or just as the root.

4 ounces (1 stick) butter
1 large celery root, peeled and cut into cubes
    (about 3 cups)
3 cups peeled and chopped apple such as Granny Smith
    or Honey Crisp
1 cup chopped onion
4 cups chicken broth
Salt and pepper to taste
Celery leaves for garnish

Melt butter in a large pot over medium heat. Add celery root, apples and onions. Simmer until celery root and apples are translucent, stirring to prevent browning, about 15 minutes. Add chicken broth, cover and simmer for 30 minutes. Remove from heat and cool slightly. Working in batches, puree soup in blender until smooth. Add more broth if mixture is too thick.

Place puree back into the pot and heat. Season with salt and pepper. Garnish with celery leaves.

Yield: 6 to 8 servings

Roasted Red Pepper Spread, Rynek Glowny, Krakow

Red peppers are plentiful in the Market in downtown Krakow. The peppers can be roasted in the oven under the broiler until charred and placed in a bag for 8 to 10 minutes and then peeled. The smoky flavor is present in the spread.

1/2 cup mayonnaise
1/2 cup sour cream
3 large roasted red bell peppers or 1 jar
    (6 ounces) roasted red peppers
1 teaspoon dried basil
1 teaspoon garlic, minced, or less, if
    desired
1/4 teaspoon sea salt

In a food processor, blend all ingredients until smooth. Refrigerate for 1 hour before serving.

Yield: 2 cups

Sacher Torte, Naschmarkt, Vienna

This delightful chocolate torte has an interesting history dating back to 1830. The origin of the cake, as well as the name of the creator, has been a matter for debate for many years and even resulted in a seven-year lawsuit. There are several stories to choose from. The one I enjoy most is that the Emperor of Austria, Franz Josef, asked his pastry chef, Edward Sacher, to create a less filling cake than the usual whipped cream-filled cakes that were popular in Vienna at that time. Sacher was working as a pastry chef at the Demers Pastry Shop in Vienna where he created for the emperor the jam-filled chocolate cake known as the Sacher Torte.

5 ounces bitter chocolate, chopped
1/2 cup plus 2 tablespoons unsalted butter, room temperature
1/2 cup powdered sugar
1/2 teaspoon vanilla extract
6 large eggs, separated
3/4 cup plus 2 tablespoons sugar
1-1/4 cups all-purpose flour
2 cups apricot jam

Preheat oven to 350 degrees. Butter and flour an 8-inch cake pan. Line the bottom with parchment paper cut to fit the pan.

Place the chopped chocolate in a bowl or the top of a double boiler. Place the bowl over simmering water. Do not place the bowl in the water. Stir the chocolate until it is melted. In an electric mixer bowl with the paddle attachment, beat the butter and powdered sugar until fluffy, 4 to 5 minutes. Add the vanilla extract. Separate the eggs. Add the yolks, beating one at a time, to butter mixture. Stir in the melted chocolate. Set aside.

In a clean electric mixing bowl, with the whip attachment, beat the egg whites until foamy. Gradually add the sugar and whip until soft peaks form. Stir a small amount of the egg whites into the chocolate mixture. Gently fold in the remaining egg whites. Use a whip or spatula to prevent deflating. Fold in the flour. Pour into the prepared cake pan. Spread the batter close to the edge so the cake looks slightly concave. Bake for 55 minutes until a toothpick test comes out clean. Run a knife around the edge of cake and turn out onto a rack. Place the jam in a small saucepan and bring to a simmer. Cook for 2 minutes until jam is hot. Let jam cool to warm. When the cake is cool, split in half horizontally so there are two rounds. Place a cake layer on a cut round piece of cardboard the size of the cake. Spread the cake rounds with jam. Place the second layer on top of fruit jam. Repeat with the remaining layer. Spread jam on top and around sides of cake. Cover with chocolate glaze. Use a wet palette knife under the torte to release it and place on a cake plate. Serve with whipped cream.

Chocolate Glaze

3/4 cup plus 2 tablespoons sugar
1/3 cup water
5 ounces bittersweet chocolate, chopped

Place the sugar in a saucepan with the water. Bring to a boil to dissolve the sugar. Add the chocolate and cook until a candy thermometer reaches 350 degrees. Strain the chocolate mixture through a fine mesh strainer set over a bowl. Immediately pour 1 cup of the glaze onto a metal baking sheet. Stir the remaining chocolate. Using a long metal spatula, stir the chocolate on the baking sheet until it cools slightly. Scrape the chocolate back into the bowl and stir. Pour another cup onto the metal baking sheet and stir to cool. It is important to keep the chocolate moving so it does not harden. Continue this process until the glaze is sticky and slightly thickened. Immediately pour the glaze evenly over the cake. Let cool until the chocolate glaze hardens.

Yield: 6 servings

Latkes (Potato Pancakes), Rynek Glowny, Krakow

Potato pancakes, known in Polish as *placki ziemniaczane z gulaszem na ostro* are often served topped with meat sauce, pork crisps or goulash, as well as sour cream, applesauce, mushroom sauce, cottage cheese or sheep's cheese or even fruit syrup. Their popularity is closely associated with the historic presence of one of the largest Jewish communities in the world flourishing in Poland in the nineteenth century. In times of economic difficulty during the foreign partitions, potato pancakes often replaced missing bread among the peasants. Potatoes are plentiful and inexpensive in the markets in Poland.

2 large baking potatoes
1 tablespoon all-purpose flour
1/4 teaspoon baking powder
1 large egg
1/4 cup milk
1/2 teaspoon salt
1/4 teaspoon white pepper
1/4 cup chopped onions
3 tablespoons chopped fresh basil or 1 tablespoon
   dried basil
1/4 cup finely ground cornmeal or matzo meal
1/2 cup oil for frying

Heat oven to 400 degrees.

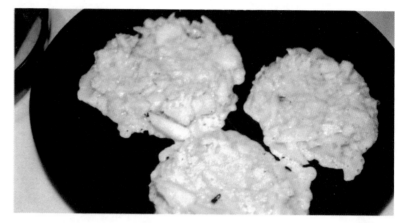

Peel potatoes and place in food processor, pulse until coarsely chopped. Place in large bowl. Add flour and baking powder to potatoes. Place egg in small bowl and add milk to egg. Beat egg mixture and add to potatoes. Combine potatoes, egg mixture, salt, pepper, onions, basil and cornmeal. Stir to blend. Heat a large griddle or skillet over medium high heat until hot. Add oil to coat bottom of griddle. Pour 2 tablespoons potato mixture onto hot griddle for each latke. Flatten each slightly with the spoon. Cook until golden and gently turn each latke to cook the other side. Remove from griddle and place on paper towel. Repeat process until all latkes are cooked. Place latkes on non-stick baking pan and place in oven to crisp for 8 minutes. Serve hot with desired sauce.

Yield: 4 servings

Smoked Sausage Country Style, Rynek Glowny, Krakow

Pork is the main meat eaten in Poland and is used in the preparation of sausages. The sausages are made with spices, apples, herbs and combinations of meats. The sausages in the markets vary from pale gray to dark red, thus make an interesting picture as they are piled high on trays in the meat cases. The sausages are often cooked with vegetables such as cabbage, sauerkraut or potatoes.

1-1/2 cups chicken broth
1 tablespoon prepared stone ground mustard
1 pound sweet potatoes, peeled and cut into 1-inch cubes
1/2 cup chopped onion
1 pound smoked sausage, cut into 1-inch pieces
6 cups chopped green cabbage
1 tablespoon orange zest
1/2 cup fresh orange juice
1/2 teaspoon sea salt
1/8 teaspoon pepper

In a large skillet, heat chicken broth and mustard to hot. Add sweet potatoes and onions. Cook for 10 minutes until potatoes are tender. Add sausage, cabbage, orange zest, orange juice, salt and pepper. Cover and cook for 15 to 20 minutes, stirring twice during cooking.

Yield: 6 servings

Apple Strudel, Naschmarkt, Vienna

While in Vienna, I had the good fortune to be present for a demonstration of making apple strudel conducted at the palace. An energetic, chubby, short, twenty-year-old lady with long blond hair, wearing a white chef's jacket, gave us directions while she was rolling the dough. The tabletop holding the dough was a large marble slab at least 3 feet square. Our teacher rolled the dough very thin so it covered the entire slab. She vigorously buttered the sheet, folded it over and rolled it thin again. She repeated the rolling and but-

tering several times. The apples were sliced and coated with sugar and flour ready to fill the strudel dough. When the strudel was ready for the oven, it fit neatly on a baking sheet. The finished product was beautiful.

1/2 cup golden raisins
1/4 cup apple juice or hard apple cider
3 large tart apples as Granny Smith, peeled and
   sliced
1 teaspoon lemon zest
2 tablespoons lemon juice
1 teaspoon cinnamon
1/2 cup brown sugar
3/4 cup bread crumbs, or crushed vanilla wafers
2 tablespoons butter, cut into small pieces
1/4 cup pecans, chopped
6 sheets phyllo dough, thawed
3 tablespoons butter, melted, for phyllo dough

Preheat oven to 375 degrees.

Place the raisins in the apple juice for 15 minutes. In a large bowl, combine the apples, lemon zest, lemon juice, cinnamon, sugar, bread crumbs, butter pieces and nuts. Add raisins and apple juice. Remove the phyllo dough from the box and unroll 6 sheets. Cover with a damp towel to prevent them from hardening. Roll 1 sheet onto work surface and brush with melted butter. Repeat with the remaining sheets placing each on top of the other. Place the apple mixture on the third of the dough closest to you, leaving two inches on the edges clear. Fold in the edges and roll the dough jellyroll style. With the seal under the roll, gently place it on the baking sheet. Brush the top with melted butter and sprinkle with sugar. Bake for 30 minutes. Brush the top again with butter and sprinkled sugar. Continue baking for 20 to 25 more minutes. Let the strudel cool for 10 minutes before cutting.

Yield: 8 servings

Veal Schnitzel, Naschmarkt, Vienna

Veal Schnitzel is always served with lemon slices. Sometimes grated Parmigianino Reggiano cheese is added to the flour for coating the cutlet before cooking. Chicken or pork cutlets also can be prepared in this method although the veal cutlet is most often used in the cuisine of Eastern Europe. Veal Schnitzel is sometimes served with a poached egg resting on top of the cutlet.

1/2 teaspoon salt
1/4 teaspoon black pepper
1/2 teaspoon sweet paprika
1/8 teaspoon nutmeg
3/4 cup all-purpose flour
2 eggs, beaten
3/4 cup bread crumbs
4 veal cutlets, 4 to 6 ounces each
Vegetable oil for cooking
Lemon wedges for garnish

In mixing bowl, combine salt, pepper, paprika, nutmeg and flour. Place well-beaten eggs in bowl for dipping. Place breadcrumbs in another bowl. Place each veal cutlet between wax paper and flatten cutlets to 1/4-inch thickness. Coat cutlets in flour mixture. Dip into beaten eggs. Roll each cutlet in bread crumbs. In a large skillet, brown the cutlets in hot oil until golden. Turn and cook for 5 to 6 minutes until golden. Serve with lemon wedge.

Yield: 4 servings

Dill Gherkins, Naplavka Market, Prague

The stalls at the Naplavka Market in Prague were busy selling cucumbers of various sizes to be made into pickles. Some of the vendors were giving samples of the sour, dill, sweet and garlic dill pickles. I enjoyed all types.

4 pounds small cucumbers, no more than 3 inches long
1 bunch fresh dill
2 quarts water
2-1/2 tablespoons salt
1 slice white bread

Wash cucumbers and cut off ends. Puncture peel with a fork. Place half of dill in 1 gallon crock. Add cucumbers. Pour water into saucepan. Add salt and bring to a boil. Pour hot salt water over cucumbers in crock. Place remaining dill and bread on top. Cover with plastic. Place a plate or weight on top of the cucumbers and let stand at room temperature for 4 to 5 days. Remove the bread and dill from crock. Place gherkins into sterilized jars. Strain liquid from crock. Heat to hot and pour over gherkins in jars. Seal jar covers tightly. Refrigerate.

Yield: 4 pint jars

Scrambled Eggs with Portobello Mushrooms, Naschmarkt, Vienna

The large, brown portobello mushrooms were displayed in boxes and crates at the Naschmarkt Market in Vienna. Some were the size of a dinner plate. One mushroom would serve several people.

1 large portobello mushroom
1 tablespoon butter
4 eggs, slightly beaten
1 tablespoon milk
1/4 teaspoon salt
1/8 teaspoon pepper

Clean mushrooms. Remove stem and slice into bite-sized pieces. Heat butter in non-stick skillet to hot. Add mushrooms and sauté until light brown. Beat eggs with milk, salt and pepper. Add to mushrooms in skillet. Sauté, stirring occasionally until desired firmest.

Yield: 4 servings

Quail with Pomegranate, Naschmarkt, Vienna

Quail is a game bird that is raised domestically for the specialty market. Pomegranate seeds and juice, when added to meat, acts as a tenderizer. Recently, pomegranate juice has become available on the market; however, it has been used with meat for many years in the near East. I was amazed at the large bins of pomegranate seeds on display in the Market in Vienna. I wondered how long it would take a farmer to fill one of the bins with pomegranate seeds.

1 cup pomegranate seeds
1/2 cup pomegranate juice
1/2 cup orange juice
1/2 cup Marsala wine
2 tablespoons chopped fresh mint
4 quails, dressed
1/2 teaspoon salt
1/4 teaspoon fresh ground black pepper
4 slices pancetta or lightly smoked bacon
2 tablespoons olive oil
1 cup mandarin orange segments, canned or fresh
1/2 cup pomegranate seeds for garnish

In a large bowl, combine the pomegranate seeds, pomegranate juice, orange juice, wine and mint. Place the quail in the mixture and coat the birds with the marinade. Cover and marinate at room temperature for 2 hours. Remove the quail from the marinade, pat dry and season the inside and outside with salt and pepper. Strain the marinade; save the liquid. Stuff the quail with the pomegranate seeds from the marinade. In a large skillet, heat the oil to medium hot. Cook quail until golden on all sides. Cool enough to wrap with pancetta. Place quail in roasting pan in a single layer. Pour the reserved marinade in the skillet the quail was cooked in. Bring to a boil; reduce heat and simmer to reduce liquid by half, about 10 minutes. Pour sauce over quail in roasting pan. Bake at 400 degrees for 20 to 25 minutes, until meat thermometer reads 160 degrees. Place quail on serving platter. Cover to keep warm. Pour pan sauce back into the skillet. Add orange segments and bring sauce to a boil. Cook for 3 minutes. Add more pomegranate juice, if needed. Pour the sauce and orange segments over quail. Garnish with pomegranate seeds.

Yield: 4 servings

Spring Greens and Herb Salad, Naschmarkt, Vienna

The Market in Vienna sold various kinds of greens and herbs. The combination of the different greens adds interest to the salad.

6 ounces spring greens
1 cup watercress, stems removed
1 cup arugula, torn into bite-sized pieces
1 cup fresh basil leaves
1/2 cup shaved Parmesan cheese

Combine greens, watercress, arugula and basil in large bowl.
Just before serving, add dressing and toss. Arrange greens on serving dishes.
Top with cheese.

Yield: 8 servings

Dressing

1/2 cup olive oil
1/4 cup raspberry vinegar
1/4 cup fresh orange juice
1/2 teaspoon salt
1/2 teaspoon cracked pepper

Combine all ingredients in a jar and shake to blend.

Yield: 1 cup

Weiner Schnitzel, Naschmarkt, Vienna

Weiner Schnitzel is often served with a poached egg on top of the cutlet. The lemon slices add an interesting flavor to the meat.

1/2 teaspoon salt
1/4 teaspoon black pepper
1/2 teaspoon sweet paprika
1/8 teaspoon nutmeg
1/4 cup Reggiano cheese
3/4 cup all-purpose flour
2 eggs, beaten
3/4 cup bread crumbs
4 veal cutlets, 4 to 6 ounces each
Vegetable oil for cooking
4 large eggs for poaching
Lemon wedges for garnish

In mixing bowl, combine salt, pepper, paprika, nutmeg, cheese and flour. Place well-beaten eggs in bowl for dipping. Place breadcrumbs in another bowl. Place each veal cutlet between wax paper and flatten cutlets to 1/4-inch thickness. Coat cutlets in flour mixture. Dip into beaten eggs. Cover each cutlet in bread crumbs. In a large skillet, brown the cutlets in hot oil until golden. Turn and cook for 5 to 6 minutes until golden. Place eggs in poacher and cook until the yolk is becoming firm. Place cutlets on serving plates and top each with a poached egg. Serve with lemon wedge.

Yield: 4 servings

Savory Cabbage, Naplavka Market, Prague

Every market in Prague had cabbage for sale. There were piles of green, savoy and red cabbage available. Cabbage is, indeed, a popular vegetable and is used in many different recipes.

2 cups potatoes, sliced medium thick
6 to 8 cups shredded savoy cabbage
1 tablespoon minced onion
1/2 teaspoon salt
1/4 teaspoon pepper
1/2 teaspoon paprika
2 teaspoons caraway seed
2-1/2 cups water or only enough to cover vegetables
1/4 cup butter
3 tablespoons chopped onions
3 tablespoons all-purpose flour
2 cups cubed salami

Place sliced potatoes in large pot. Add cabbage on top of potatoes. Add 1 tablespoon minced onions, salt, paprika and caraway seed. Add enough water to cover vegetables. Cover and cook for 20 minutes until tender. Drain and save liquid. Cover to keep warm. In a large skillet, heat butter to hot; do not brown. Sauté chopped onions. Add flour and stir to cook. Add liquid from potato-cabbage pot to skillet. Bring to a boil, stirring to prevent lumps. Add salami and simmer for 5 minutes. Pour mixture over potato and cabbage. Gently stir to blend. Serve with sour cream if desired.

Yield: 6 to 8 servings

Roast Duck, Naplavka Market, Prague

The farmers in the Czech Republic often raised ducks and chickens for the family meals. Today, most of the poultry at the Market is raised specifically for sale. The farmer will slaughter and dress the birds before coming to the Market. The ducks and chickens were kept in coolers at the Naplavka Market.

1 duck, approximately 4 to 5 pounds
1 teaspoon kosher salt
2 cloves garlic, minced
1 apple, cored and quartered
1/2 cup water or apple juice

Preheat oven to 500 degrees.

Wash dressed duck. Pat dry. Remove all visible fat from duck. With a sharp fork, pierce duck skin to release fat and to crisp the skin while roasting. Rub inside and outside with salt and garlic. Place apple in duck cavity. Place in roasting pan. Roast at 500 degrees for 30 minutes. Remove from pan and drain off fat. Reduce oven temperature to 375 degrees. Return duck to roasting pan. Add water or apple juice. Roast for 1-1/2 hours until internal temperature reaches 180 degrees. If the duck skin becomes brown, cover the duck with foil and continues the roasting until the desired temperature is reached. Cover and let duck rest for 10 minutes before slicing.

Yield: 4 to 6 servings

Pork Goulash, Naplavka Market, Prague

Goulash is a popular dish throughout Eastern Europe. The recipe will vary depending on the area and the products available. Pork is most often used in preparing the goulash.

1/4 cup lard or shorting
1 cup chopped onions
1 cup chopped celery
1/2 cup all-purpose flour
1 teaspoon salt
1/2 teaspoon black pepper
1 teaspoon sweet paprika
1-1/2 pounds pork shoulder, cut into bite-sized cubes
1 tablespoon caraway seeds
1 cup tomato juice
1 cup water

In a large pot, heat lard or shortening to hot. Add onions and celery. Sauté for 4 to 5 minutes until tender. Remove from pot. Combine flour, salt, pepper and paprika. Place pork cubes into flour mixture to coat meat. Place meat in hot pot and stir to brown, about 8 minutes. Add 2 tablespoons of flour mixture to pot. Stir to cook flour. Add cooked vegetables to pot. Add caraway seeds, tomato juice and water. Stir to blend. Cover and simmer for 30 minutes.

Yield: 6 servings

Kolaches, Naplavka Market, Prague

Kolaches are a traditional Czech sweet roll. Wherever there is a Czech bakery, one will find kolaches. In some Czech settlements, they have Kolache Festivals and the ladies from the community gather, generally in a church basement kitchen, and make dozens of kolaches. Each roll has a filling that might be apricot, cherry, apple, blueberry or pineapple jams or prune puree or a favorite poppy seed filling. Years ago, the mothers would not let their children eat the poppy seed-filled kolaches because they did not want them to acquire the opium habit.

2 packages dry yeast
1/4 cup lukewarm water
1 tablespoon sugar
1 cup butter or margarine
2 cups milk
1/2 cup sugar
2 whole eggs, beaten
4 egg yolks, beaten
1/2 teaspoon mace
1 teaspoon salt
5 to 6 cups all-purpose flour (plus extra flour for kneading)
Butter for top of baked rolls

Dissolve yeast in lukewarm water and 1 tablespoon sugar. Combine butter and milk. Heat to hot but do not boil. Cool milk to lukewarm. Add 1/2 cup sugar, eggs, egg yolks, and yeast. Add mace and salt. Mix well and add 3 cups flour, one at a time. Gradually stir in remaining flour, enough to make soft dough. Place dough on lightly floured surface and knead until smooth and shiny. Add more flour as needed. Place dough into well-greased bowl and let rise until double in bulk. Place dough on lightly floured surface and divide into balls about 2 inches diameter. Place on greased cookie sheet. Let rise until almost double. Press center of each with thumb and fill with filling. Let rise again until light. Bake at 400 degrees for 15 to 20 minutes until lightly brown. Remove from oven and brush top of each kolache with butter. Place on a rack to cool.

Yield: 6 dozen

Cherry Filling

1 cup sugar
6 tablespoons cornstarch
1/4 teaspoon salt
2 cans (15 ounces each) red sour cherries, drained (reserve juice)
1 teaspoon red food color
1/2 teaspoon almond extract

In a large saucepan, combine sugar, cornstarch and salt. Add the juice from the cherries. Bring the mixture to a boil. Reduce heat and cook until thick. Add remaining ingredients. Stir to blend. Cool before filling kolaches.

Yield: 4 cups

Poppy Seed Filling

1/2 pound ground poppy seeds
1 cup water
1 cup milk
1 tablespoon butter
1 teaspoon vanilla extract
1/2 teaspoon cinnamon
1 cup sugar
1/2 cup graham crackers, crushed into crumbs

In saucepan, combine poppy seeds and water. Cook until thickened. Add milk and cook slowly for 10 minutes, stirring. Add butter, vanilla, cinnamon and sugar. Continue cooking for 5 minutes. Add graham cracker crumbs and stir to blend. Remove from heat and cool to lukewarm for filling kolaches.

Yield: 4 cups

Plum Dumplings, Naplavka Market, Prague

Fresh plums were in season when I visited the Naplavka Market in Prague and several stands had boxes of the shiny, dark blue plums for sale. The vendors had picked the ripe plums from their own trees.

2 cups all-purpose flour
3 tablespoons butter or margarine
2 cups mashed potatoes
1 teaspoon salt
2 eggs, slightly beaten
8 plums cut in half, pit removed
1/3 cup sugar
Water for cooking

Place flour in large bowl. Cut butter into flour to form a course meal. Add mashed potatoes, salt and eggs. Mix until smooth. Place dough onto floured surface and roll to 1/4-inch thickness. Use extra flour as needed. Cut dough into squares of 4 inches each. Place cut plums in microwave-safe dish. Sprinkle sugar over plums. Microwave for 1 minute. Place plum half onto dough square. Wrap dough around plum, completely covering the plum. Gently place the dumplings into slow boiling water. Do not allow the water to boil rapidly. Cook in batches so dumplings are not crowded. Cook for 15 minutes. Remove from water with strainer. Continue to cook the remaining dumplings in the water. Serve with plum sauce and/or sugar, cinnamon and melted butter.

Yield: 16 dumplings

Eggplant Stuffed with Mushrooms, Havelske Trziste Market, Prague

Mushrooms grow wild in the woods around Prague, and the women gather the fresh fungi early in the morning on the Market days. Different mushrooms appear at different seasons. In the spring, the morel mushrooms are hunted, whereas in the fall, chicken or hen mushrooms can be found at the base of some old oak trees. These can grow to be the size of a washtub. In the Czech Republic, I saw white puff mushrooms with a reputation of growing very large and exploding when very old.

4 Italian eggplants (2-1/2 pounds)
1 teaspoon salt
4 tablespoons olive oil, divided
1/4 cup water
4 thick slices baguette, diced into 1/2-inch pieces
1/2 cup dry red wine
1 pound mushrooms, sliced lengthwise, 1/4-inch thick
5 cloves garlic, minced
1 medium red onion, diced
2 tablespoons butter, divided
2 ounces diced Pecorino Romano cheese
3/4 cup vegetable broth
Salt and pepper to taste
2 tablespoons chopped parsley

Preheat oven to 350 degrees.

Halve the eggplants lengthwise and cut out the pulp, leaving 1/4-inch around the shells. Chop the pulp into 1/2-inch pieces. Coat shells with 1 teaspoon salt and let marinate for 30 minutes. Pat dry and rub with 1 tablespoon oil. Place them cut side down on baking sheet. Add 1/4 cup water and bake for 45 minutes. Soak bread cubes in red wine.

In a large skillet, heat 1 tablespoon oil. Add mushrooms, salt and pepper. Cover and simmer for 5 to 7 minutes until mushrooms are tender. Place in a bowl. Add 1 tablespoon oil to skillet. Add eggplant pulp, cook for 3 or 4 minutes stirring until golden. Add to the bowl of mushrooms. Place in large skillet 1 tablespoon oil, 1 tablespoon butter, garlic and onion. Sauté for 2 minutes. Add mushroom, eggplant, wine-soaked bread, cheese, broth, salt and pepper to skillet. Increase oven temperature to 425 degrees. Fill the eggplant shells with the mushroom mixture. Top with remaining 1 tablespoon butter. Bake at 425 degrees for 10 to 15 minutes. Garnish with parsley.

Yield: 4 servings

Sour-Cherry Soup, Havelske Trziste Market, Prague

The fresh red cherries flood the markets in July. They are used in desserts, salads, jams, jellies and even in a soup. The fruit soup is generally served cold in the summer and warm in the winter. The sour cream in this recipe gives it a creamy texture.

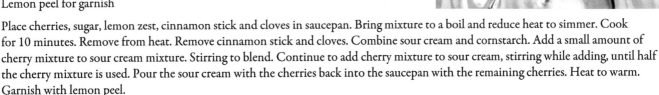

2 cups pitted red sour-cherries or 1 can (16 ounces) pitted red unsweetened cherries
1/2 cup sugar
1 teaspoon lemon zest
1 cinnamon stick
2 whole cloves
3/4 cup sour cream
1 tablespoon cornstarch
Lemon peel for garnish

Place cherries, sugar, lemon zest, cinnamon stick and cloves in saucepan. Bring mixture to a boil and reduce heat to simmer. Cook for 10 minutes. Remove from heat. Remove cinnamon stick and cloves. Combine sour cream and cornstarch. Add a small amount of cherry mixture to sour cream mixture. Stirring to blend. Continue to add cherry mixture to sour cream, stirring while adding, until half the cherry mixture is used. Pour the sour cream with the cherries back into the saucepan with the remaining cherries. Heat to warm. Garnish with lemon peel.

Yield: 4 servings

Stuffed Cabbage, Rynek Glowny, Krakow

Cabbage is one vegetable that is available at the farmers' markets throughout Poland. It is a staple in the Polish diet. During World War II, a time of scarcity of food in Poland, and then under Communist rule, cabbage could mean the difference between starvation and survival.

8 large cabbage leaves
2 tablespoons olive oil
4 garlic cloves, minced
1/2 cup chopped onions
1/2 pound lean ground beef
1/3 pound ground pork
3/4 cup cooked long grain rice
2 tablespoons chopped parsley
1/2 cup tomato sauce
1 large egg, slightly beaten
1 teaspoon sea salt
1/8 teaspoon black pepper
1 teaspoon sweet paprika
2 cups spicy tomato sauce

Gently remove the outer leaves from the cabbage head. Place the leaves in a large pot of boiling salted water. Cook for 5 to 6 minutes. Drain and cool leaves. In a saucepan, heat oil over medium heat. Add garlic and onions and cook for 3 minutes. Remove from saucepan and cool. In a large bowl, combine garlic, onions, ground beef, ground pork, rice, parsley, tomato sauce, egg, salt, pepper and paprika. Stir to blend well. Flatten each cabbage leaf and remove any hard stems. Place 1/4 cup filling onto each leaf. Fold the bottom of the leaf over the filling and fold in the sides toward the center. Roll tightly into a bundle. Place seam side down in a casserole dish. Arrange cabbage rolls tightly in dish. Ladle spicy tomato sauce (see below) over cabbage. Cover the casserole. Bake at 350 degrees for 1-1/2 hours

Yield: 8 rolls

Spicy Tomato Sauce

1 can (14 ounces) tomato sauce   1/4 teaspoon onion powder
1/2 teaspoon garlic powder   1/8 teaspoon red pepper flakes

Combine all ingredients. Mix well.

Yield: 2 cups

Braised Chicken with Apples, Havelske Trziste Market, Prague

Chicken and apples are a delicious combination. The apples add a sweet-tangy taste to the dish. In the markets in Prague it was possible to buy a dozen different varieties of apples. I did not recognize the names of the apples. However, the appearance of the apples was common enough for me to recognize some. Tart apples such as the Honey Crisp are desirable for use in this recipe.

3 tablespoons olive oil
1 chicken (approximately 3-1/2 pounds), cut into 8 pieces
1 teaspoon salt
1/4 teaspoon ground black pepper
3 fresh tart apples, peeled, cored and cut into quarters
1 cup apple cider (alcoholic cider can be used, if desired)
1-1/2 cups half-and-half cream
1/4 teaspoon nutmeg

Add oil to large skillet and heat to high. Rub chicken pieces with salt and pepper. Place in hot skillet with the skin side down and reduce heat to medium high. Cover and cook until browned on underside about 10 minutes. Turn chicken and cook for another 5 minutes; remove the chicken from the skillet. Cover with foil to keep warm. Add the quartered apples and sauté until tender crisp but not soft. Remove from skillet and set aside. Return chicken pieces to the skillet. Add apple cider, and simmer for 20 minutes until most of the liquid has evaporated. Add cream and nutmeg and simmer for 5 minutes. Add apples and continue to cook for 5 minutes to warm. Do not boil.

Yield: 6 to 8 servings

Sweet and Sour Red Cabbage, Havelske Trziste Market, Prague

A sour cabbage dish such as sauerkraut is popular throughout Eastern Europe. The recipe for Sweet Sour Cabbage provides a sweet-tangy sour cabbage without the fermentation found in sauerkraut. The ingredients: red cabbage, onions and apples are common, inexpensive foods found in the markets in Prague.

2 tablespoons butter
4 cups shredded red cabbage
1/2 cup chopped red onion
1 tart apple, cored and chopped
1/3 cup brown sugar
1/4 cup balsamic vinegar
1/2 cup red wine
1/2 teaspoon sea salt
1/4 teaspoon black pepper
1/8 teaspoon ground cinnamon
1/8 teaspoon ground cloves

Melt the butter in a large pot. Add the shredded cabbage, onion and apple. Sauté for 8 to 10 minutes until vegetables are soft. Add sugar, vinegar and wine. Cover and simmer for 30 minutes, stirring occasionally. Season with salt, pepper, cinnamon and cloves.

Yield: 6 servings

Sauerkraut Salad, Havelske Trziste Market, Prague

Both the Havelske Trziste and the Naplavka Markets in Prague were selling bulk sauerkraut from plastic buckets. It was possible to buy sauerkraut in different stages of fermentation. Sauerkraut is often served with dumplings.

2 cups or 1 can (14.5 ounces) sauerkraut
1 red pepper, chopped
1 green pepper, chopped
1/2 cup chopped onion
1 tablespoon extra virgin olive oil

Drain sauerkraut. (For less salt, place sauerkraut in a sieve and rinse with cold water.) Combine sauerkraut, red pepper, green pepper and onion. Drizzle with olive oil. Toss to blend. Refrigerate before serving.

Yield: 6 servings

Duckling ala Orange, Nagycsarnok Market, Budapest

The flaming Duckling ala Orange is a special entrée served at parties or celebrations.

1 duckling, about 4 to 5 pounds
1 teaspoon salt
1/8 teaspoon black pepper
2 oranges, unpeeled and quartered
1 sprig fresh thyme
1 sprig fresh rosemary
1/2 cup orange marmalade

Preheat oven to 475 degrees.

Wash duck inside and out and pat dry. Prick the duck skin in several places. Combine the salt and pepper and rub inside of duck with mixture. Place oranges in duck cavity. Place the thyme and rosemary in duck cavity. Place duck in roasting pan. Roast duck in 475 degrees oven for 45 minutes. Remove from oven and drain off all fat that has accumulated. Return duck to oven and reduce temperature to 350 degrees and roast for 2 hours. Remove duck and coat with orange marmalade. Return duck to oven and roast for 15 minutes or until thermometer in duck breast registers 180 degrees. Remove from oven and cover with foil to rest for 15 minutes. Serve flaming with orange sauce.

Yield: 4 to 6 servings

Orange Sauce

3/4 cup orange juice
1 tablespoon cornstarch
1/4 cup water
1/4 cup pan drippings
1 tablespoon orange zest
1/2 cup Grand Marnier® or Cointreau®

Place orange juice in saucepan. Dissolve cornstarch in water and add to orange juice. Add pan drippings and bring to a boil. Continue cooking and stirring until thickened. Add orange zest and liquor. Light the sauce with a kitchen torch or long match. Pour over duck. The marmalade on the duck will enhance the flame. When the flame dies, slice duck and serve.

Halaszle (Hungarian Fish Soup), Nagycsarnok Market, Budapest

Hungary does not have an ocean coast but does have fresh water lakes and rivers. Lake Balaton and the Danube River and the Tisza River supply a variety of fresh fish for Hungarian cuisine. The carp, catfish, perch, pike and sturgeon are prized for the traditional fish soup Halaszle. The recipe for the fish soup varies with the area of the country and with the available ingredients. It is a bright red, hot soup prepared with generous amounts of hot paprika, onions, and green peppers. The fish is sliced in large pieces and simmered in the fish stock and vegetables. After the fish is added, the soup is not stirred so the fish does not fall apart. The fish bouillon is prepared with the fish trimmings, head, bones, skin and fins, and boiled with onions and peppers for a rich flavor. It is strained before adding to the soup.

The soup is served with white bread, pickled salads and red wine. Traditionally, pasta mixed with sour cream and cottage cheese is served as a main course following the soup. To be really authentic, the soup should be cooked in a narrow-bottomed black kettle hung on a tripod over an open fire.

6 cups fish stock, strained (or 2 cups bottled clam broth and 4 cups chicken stock)
1 teaspoon sweet paprika
1 teaspoon hot paprika
1 teaspoon smoked paprika
1 red bell peppers, chopped
1 green bell pepper, chopped
1 jalapeño, chopped fine
1/2 large onion, chopped
1 large tomato, peeled, sliced
1/2 teaspoon salt
1/4 teaspoon black pepper
1-1/2 pounds freshwater fish fillets
Garnish with sliced green bell pepper and sliced hot peppers on the side.

In a large pot, bring the fish stock to a boil. Add paprikas and simmer for 2 minutes. Add red pepper, green pepper, jalapeño pepper, onion, tomato, salt and pepper. Cook for 5 minutes. Add fish fillets and simmer for 15 minutes. Garnish with green bell pepper and sliced hot pepper.

Yield: 4 to 6 servings

Bohemian Cabbage with Sausage, Nagycsarnok Market, Budapest

Cabbage and sausage are traditional foods of Hungary. Every market has a selection of green, red and white cabbage as well a savory cabbage. The meat section in the Great Market Hall had long red ropes of sausages draped over the railings and across the counters in the Market.

4 medium-sized red potatoes, peeled
2 fresh pork sausages, 8 ounces each
1 tablespoon vegetable oil
3 cups shredded green cabbage
1 medium onion, chopped (about 1 cup)
2 tablespoons Italian salad dressing
1/2 cup sour cream
1/2 teaspoon caraway seeds
1/2 teaspoon coarse salt
1/8 teaspoon pepper

Place potatoes in saucepan. Add water and salt. Boil until tender. Remove from heat and cut in half.
Cut each sausage into 6 pieces. In a large skillet over medium heat, sauté the sausages until browned, about 10 minutes. Remove from skillet. Add oil to skillet. Add cabbage and onions. Cover and simmer for 10 minutes until tender, stirring occasionally. Add salad dressing, sour cream, caraway seeds, salt and pepper. Stir to blend. Add cooked potatoes and sausage and heat to serve.

Yield: 4 servings

Hungarian Potato Dumplings, Nagycsarnok Market, Budapest

There are two types of dumplings with many variations in each type. The potato dumplings, which I had in Hungary, were shaped like a slice of bread with no crust and were very moist. This type of dumpling is steamed over boiling water or broth. The other type of dumpling, that I am aware of, is shaped into walnut-sized dough that is dropped into boiling water or chicken broth.

1-1/2 cups (2 large) baking potatoes, grated
3/4 cup all-purpose flour
1/2 teaspoon salt
3 strips smoked bacon, cooked crisp and crumbled
Bacon drippings
4 ounces Swiss cheese, shredded
2 tablespoons fresh parsley, chopped

In a large pot, bring 4 quarts salted water to boil. Peel and grate potatoes. In mixing bowl, combine potatoes, flour and salt. Using a sharp tablespoon, scoop dough into the spoon to about the size of a walnut and drop into the boiling salted water. Cook for 10 minutes. Remove dumplings with a slotted spoon and place in a colander. Rinse with cold water to stop cooking. Drain. Place bacon drippings and dumplings in a large skillet. Add cheese and heat until the cheese is melted, stirring gently so as not to break the dumplings. Garnish with crumbled bacon and parsley.

Yield: 6 servings

Celery Root and Mashed Potatoes, Nagycsarnok Market, Budapest

Celery root is a knobby, brown root of the celery plant that is about the size of a baseball. The white flesh of the root has a strong celery taste. When eaten raw, it has the texture similar to a crisp apple. The celery root has been part of the cuisine in Europe since ancient times. It is mentioned in Homer's *Odyssey* as selinon. Records also show that celery root was cultivated in the Middle Ages.

4 medium-sized russet potatoes, peeled and cubed
1 medium-sized celery root, peeled and sliced
2 cups chicken broth
1/3 to 1/2 cup half-and-half cream
1 tablespoon butter
Salt and white pepper to taste

Place potatoes and celery root in a saucepan. Add chicken broth and enough water to barely cover vegetables. Cook for 15 to 20 minutes until vegetables are very soft. Remove from heat and drain. Mash potatoes and celery root. Add cream and butter and mash into the vegetables until smooth. Add salt and pepper to taste.

Yield: 6 servings

Markets in the Iberian Peninsula

The Iberian Peninsula is located in the far southwest corner of Europe and includes Portugal, Spain and British Gibraltar. Over the centuries the land has been ruled by the Celts, Phoenicians, Romans, Germanic tribes and Moors. In 2000 B.C., the Celts from northern France and Germany crossed the Pyrenees and invaded Iberia from the north. They brought with them their native foods such as salted fish and various meats. The root vegetables and cabbage that they introduced to the inhabitants of northern Iberia soon became part of the local diet.

The large expanse of coastline on the Mediterranean Sea, the Atlantic Ocean and the Bay of Biscay facilitated the invasions, as well as created trade cities. Spain and Portugal have a long tradition of markets. The Phoenician merchants and Greek traders made their appearance along the coastal regions of the peninsula. Their trading connections formed a complex of merchants and markets along the coasts of Portugal and the Bay of Biscay. They traded with the inland tribes for valuable metals. Other important local products were salt, salted fish and Lusitanian horses.

The Phoenicians and Greeks are credited with bringing olive trees and viticulture to Iberia. Another very valuable product they established in Iberia is saffron. It was one of the most desired and expensive spices of ancient Greece and was popular among the Phoenician traders who carried it wherever they traveled. Today saffron is one of the most valuable exports of Spain and can be found in every Spanish market.

In 218 B.C., the Roman armies invaded and occupied Hispania, as the Romans called Iberia. With a time of peace and prosperity, the grain crops, orchards, vineyards and other food crops expanded.

Surplus grapes, olives and grains were sold and traded at local markets and overseas. Cattle and sheep were widely used for meat and dairy products. The Romans may have introduced pigs to Iberia. Soon, the hams of Pompeiopolis were bringing a good price when sold or bartered at the markets.

On July 19 in 711 A.D., an army of Muslims from northern Africa, called Moors by the Spanish, invaded Hispania and defeated the Roman king. The Moors brought many new foods to the markets. They planted rice, orange and lemon trees, melons, apples, pears, pomegranates, bananas, dates, figs, quince and sugar cane. The Moors enjoyed spices such as cinnamon and nutmeg in their food and imported these fine spices. At that time, cinnamon and cloves were about the same price as gold. During this time, the open air markets flourished, with vegetables, fruits, grains and animals for sale.

The Moors lived and prospered in Iberia for seven hundred years although not always in peace.

The discovery of the Americas changed Spain and all of Europe. The government of Spain regulated trade, and all products from the New World came only to Spain. Traders from all corners of Europe flocked to the markets in Spain for new foods and seeds.

Agriculture and the production of food varied with the various rulers and the financial resources of the country. Markets, to a large extent, were established as a means of trade or barter. A money economy was developed in the fifteenth century to pay workers in currency. This soon became part of the market transactions. In 1755, a large

earthquake destroyed the cities and villages in Portugal and eliminated the markets. It wasn't until one hundred years later that market halls were being built in Lisbon. The large Mercado de Ribeira was built in 1882 and the La Boqueria in Barcelonia was constructed in 1850. Now every village in Portugal and Spain, has some type of street or farmers' market. The large cities have numerous markets.

The conversion to organic farming has not been difficult for some farmers in Iberia because they already were fulfilling many of the requirements for organic certification. In the olive groves of northern and central Portugal and southern Spain, traditional care approximates organic farming. Olive groves account for the bulk of the organic farm area. Many of the farms are small and ideal for raising organic vegetables.

The Ministry of Agriculture reported in the early twenty-first century that there were 564 registered organic products being produced. The distribution of organic food in Portugal and Spain is not well-organized. There are only one or two fully organic markets in Lisbon.

Some supermarkets are carrying a limited supply of organic vegetables and olive oil. The organic farmers also sell their products directly to the consumers, who come to the farm and to cooperatives. Mercado Biologico is an organic food market. The Ecological Market in Lisbon, which sells natural products, is held the first Sunday of the month.

Lagos Market | Lagos, Portugal

Lagos is a city and a municipality situated at the mouth of the Bensafrim River where it empties into the Atlantic Ocean. The harbor provides one of the closest European ports to North America. It is near Lisbon in the southwestern region of Algarve.

For more than two thousand years, trade has flourished along the coast, and sailing vessels looked to the harbor at Lagos on their return trips from Africa, Asia and the New World.

The captains of the sailing ships brought back riches and new foods, such as spices from Asia; tomatoes, corn, chocolate, and potatoes from South America; sugar cane and tobacco from the New World; and slaves from Africa. Business of trade was booming. Trading houses and market halls were facilitators in introducing new products to Portugal and all of Europe.

I arrived in July when the gardens were at their peak of production. My goals were to visit a farmers' market. I did not know where to find the market, but I was aware that Lagos did have a Farmers' Market. I later learned Lagos had three markets. The Farmers' Market is held every Saturday from 8 a.m. until noon or 1 p.m.

On my first morning in Lagos, I awoke around 6 a.m. When I walked onto the balcony of my room, I saw it was a beautiful, clear, bright day. While taking in the view from my vantage point, I glanced down to the parking lot adjacent to the hotel. I noticed some small pick-up trucks and older vans driving into the parking area and stopping. I watched as the men and women got out of their vehicles and carried boxes, baskets and bags into the large covered pavilion. It finally dawned on me that this was the Farmers' Market.

I dressed in a hurry and went to the parking lot to watch the merchants unload their products and arrange the area on the cement where they would sell their goods. This was truly a Farmers' Market. Everyone setting up their area had raised or caught the items they were selling. The boxes and crates of fruits were set on the cement floor. The vegetables that were not in boxes, such as carrots, greens and turnips, were placed on the cement next to the crates of vegetables and fruit.

Most of the vendors had a balance scale for selling their products by the kilo. The merchant would place a weight on one side of the scale and the product being purchased on the other side. When the two sides were evenly balanced, the sale was completed.

The Market soon became quite busy with local shoppers. It had a relaxed atmosphere. The vendors were not shouting to get the customers to come to their stalls.

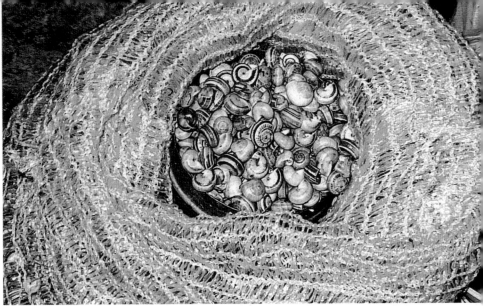

It appeared the customers were aquainted with the vendors.

I found the people selling the food to be as interesting as the products being sold. An elderly lady dressed all in black except for a wonderful, floppy white hat, had arrived at the Market with her granddaughter. The granddaughter spoke some English and told me her grandmother had lived in the region all her seventy-six years. Her deceased husband had been a fisherman. They had collected a large woven mesh basket full of live snails that they brought to the Market for sale. The brown and tan striped tiny snails were moving around in the mesh.

Another elderly lady wearing a full apron and a kerchief on her head was sitting on a metal stool by her vegetables. She had long green beans, kale, garlic, onions and small potatoes for sale. In a small wire cage, she had two red-feathered chickens for sale. Other vegetables such as tomatoes, cauliflower, turnips, lettuce, greens,

radishes and carrots were available in the Market.

Wonderful smelling peaches, pears, apples and grapes were the fruit at the Market. I could smell the wonderful aroma before I even reached the boxes of fruit. A stand selling small plastic containers full of large, shiny blackberries was quite busy. This was the only stand with berries for sale so it provided a special treat for the customer.

A tall, slender farmer was selling rice, dried beans and lentils from woven straw baskets. He used a tin cup to measure the amount the customer ordered.

Along the back part of the Market, a lady had two chickens and a duck in separate cages. She also had fresh brown eggs for sale as well as lettuce, cabbage and beans.

There was no meat or fish for sale at this market.

Mercado da Ribeira | Lisbon, Portugal

Mercado da Ribeira is located in the historical part of Lisbon close to the Tagus River. The original market hall was built in 1882. In 1930, the new hall was constructed for the market. At this time the area had become run down and developed a bad reputation with sleazy clubs, brothels and thieves. The city made a determined effort to clean up the area. In 2000, the wholesale market for fruits, vegetables and flowers was moved farther out of the city, and Mercado de Ribeira became the largest and busiest food market in Lisbon.

The ground floor is devoted to the sale of meat, fish, vegetables, nuts, cheese and dairy products, fresh and dried fruits, bread and pastries. The first floor has

cafes, coffee shops, prepared food stands and flowers.

Fish and seafood reign supreme at the Market. The long Atlantic coast line and the access to the Mediterranean Sea have always been a source of food for the people of Portugal. Throughout the Market, numerous fish stalls sell an unending selection of fish and seafood. The display of fresh fish on crushed ice includes swordfish, mackerel, sea bass, cod, sardines, hake, anchovies and others. Stone bass, wreckfish, dorado, corvina, besugo and pargo are generally cooked whole. The stands are full of shellfish: clams, oysters, mussels, periwinkles, scallops, crab, squid, octopus barnacles, goose barnacles, shrimp, giant prawns, eel, ray fish, cuttlefish, lobster and spiny lobster.

Salted, dried cod is very popular in Portugal, and each region has its own recipe for the dish called bacalhau. It is said there are 365 different recipes to make bacalhau, one for each day of the year. Unfortunately, the fish has a strong, undesirable odor when it is being cooked and tends to cause newcomers to reject the product.

The fresh sardines and anchovies are not at all like what we find in the can. The silvery fish range from 5 inches to 10 inches in length. Grilled sardines are very popular and are always served on saint feast days in June.

The produce stands are bright and colorful with the light from the large open pavilion. The deep purple eggplants; large, small and medium-sized red and yellow tomatoes; dark green kale leaves with pink striped veins; all shades of

Chicken, turkey, ducklings, squab, pigeon, whole dressed and cut into quarters, fillets and pieces, were being sold in a stall separate from the meat section.

Portugal is noted for the cheese made from the milk of goats and sheep. The Queljo da Serra made from ewe's milk in the Serra da Estrela is traditionally made in winter and is coagulated with a rennet from thistle *(flor do cardo)*. Monte, another fast-selling cheese from the northern Portugal area, is a soft, creamy cheese made with both ewe's and cow's milk. Most of the cheese and yogurt stalls were staffed by middle-aged ladies wearing white smocks and white hairnets.

The bakery stands sold several types of bread and pastries. Some of the bread was unleavened and is believed to have been introduced by the Jewish population way back in the fifteenth century. Several types of sweet breads were moving off the counter to eager customers. Bread is eaten at every meal and, at one time, each homemaker had a favorite bread recipe. Today, they come to the market for their bread.

A popular dessert found in Mercado da Ribeira and other markets' pastry shops and stands is the custard-filled tart called Belem or Bola de Belem. Many of the desserts have a custard base of egg, milk and sugar. Cinnamon also is used in desserts. One stand was selling an array of spices, cinnamon, nutmeg, saffron, ginger, peppercorns, curries and many others.

The demand for organic products from the market has increased over the past few years with a growth in consumers' health awareness. The financial aid from the European Union to the farmers has become an incentive for the conversion of land to organic farms.

green greens; pure white heads of cauliflower, large basketball-sized heads of cabbage; white, brown and purple striped garlic; beets and carrots with their long, firm leafy tops still attached; red, white, green and yellow onions—all add to the colorful mosaic of the stands.

Fresh fruit from a to z is also available. All the fruit stands feature citrus—several kinds of oranges, lemons, tangerines, grapefruit and limes. Several types of melons were for sale at the stands. A few stalls did have some organically raised produce.

Meat was once the staple of the Portuguese nobleman's diet and was only available to the wealthy. Although fish is the most popular entrée, beef, pork and chicken are sold at several stands in the Market. The butcher will tell you the best beef is from northern Portugal and the best pork is from the region south of Lisbon. The black pig of the Alentejo region has a very distinct taste due to the acorns

that they eat. It is said that at one time in Algarva, fish was fed to pigs and the meat had a fishy taste. A holdover from that time is seen in a dish that is served in the southern region combining pork and clams. Some of the meat merchants sell tripe. Tripe may have become part of the Portuguese diet as far back as the fourteenth century when Lisbon was under attack by the Castilians and food was scarce. Since the seventeenth century, people from Porto have been called "tripetros," or tripe eaters. Liver and other organ meats were for sale at these stands.

La Boqueria Market | Barcelona, Spain

The largest and most well-known market in Barcelona is the La Boqueria Market located on the Rambla Boulevard. The earliest records of La Boqueria are dated 1301 and concern the passing of a by-law prohibiting the sale of meat in Barcelona anywhere other than around La Boqueria. For centuries, farmers from the surrounding country-side sold their fresh fruits and vegetables alongside the meat butcher and fishwives' spot on Rambla Boulevard. The market along the street could be identified by the aroma long before it came into view.

By the late eighteenth century, the selling of a particular product had its own loca-tion. Fish were sold behind the Palacio de la Virreyna; game, poultry and meat were for sale by the convent de San Jose. Fruit and vegetables blocked the main thoroughfare and made traffic move-ment difficult. The horse-drawn wagons and the numerous carts coming to the

area loaded with produce and the large number of shoppers checking out all the produce clogged Rambla Boulevard.

On market day, traffic movement came to a halt. By the mid-eighteen-hundreds, it became necessary for the government to impose regulations for the placement of the stalls and to establish sanitary standards.

The Mercado de la Boqueria was origi-nally planned as a portico quadrangle in the style of the traditional Spanish Plaza Mayor in Madrid or Main Square. The plans were to have balconies on all sides that would be supported by Ionic columns. However, arguments over the size and the area required delayed the construction. Several new designs were submitted between 1836 and 1846, but all caused passionate disagreements among the city architects. The design that was finally approved with modifications was by an engineer, Miguel de Bergue. The plan was for a large, covered pavilion divided into five bays and supported by a basic structure of iron columns, but-tresses and arches. Cast-iron architecture was all the rage in Europe in the 1800s. Construction of the Market was started in 1850 on the site that was occupied by San Jose Convent, which explains why La Boqueria's sub-title is Mercado de San Jose.

Stalls with similar food items are grouped together. The fish and seafood are in the center oval of the Market. This is one of the Market's liveliest sections. The wives of the fisherman shout out about their products. They sing the praises of the sea bass and sea bream, shout about their fresh anchovies and boast of selling the best seafood from the Mediterranean. One might hear "They're alive, hand-some and cheap" or "Buy it, darling—it's straight off the boat" or "I'm selling lob-ster for the price of codfish."

The codfish and bacalao—dried, salted and cut into large pieces, strips, chopped or crumbled—are sold from other nearby stalls. Barcelona is near the coast of the Mediterranean Sea supplying the Market with freshly caught fish: cuttlefish,

anchovies, sardines, salmon, sea bream, mussels, prawns and lobster. The fishing boats arrive in the harbor very early in the morning, and the fish are in the Market by 9 a.m. and on the dinner table at noon. I loved the way the smoked sardines were displayed in a round wooden basket like spokes in a wheel.

Many of the stalls have been run by the same family for years. Blar's meat market has been at La Boqueria for more than eighty years. Similar to the other meat shops, Blar's meat cases contained beef, pork, veal and lamb. Over the counter were several large cured Iberia hams and Serrano hams in mesh bags. In the meat bay Carniceria Orte are the butchers who sell exclusively fighting bulls' meat from Barcelona's Plaza Monumental Bullring.

Separate from the meat shops were those selling dressed poultry. I talked with Leon, the owner, who told me in clear English, "The chickens are raised on a farm where they eat grain that makes the meat taste good. They are not organic but are free-range." I saw only chickens and turkeys in the refrigerated case. However, Leon told me he has geese, ducks, quail

and squab for sale at different times. At Christmas and the holidays, he sells more than a thousand birds.

One of the oldest stalls is Soley Fruits and Vegetables, dating back to 1888. This stall, as well as the many other colorful produce stands, held arrays of green beans, peppers of red, green, gold and purple, lettuce, onions, melons, pineapple, apples and citrus fruits. This does not cover all the kinds of produce available. A

show stopper was the counter piled high with bright red, tart cherries.

The dark green, brownish "Haas" avocados were lined up on the table like soldiers. Avocados are not native to Spain although there is some evidence they were brought to Spain from Central America around 1520. The trees were raised in monasteries, and the avocados

were not used as an edible fruit. The mild climate with fertile soil was ideal for the growth of avocado. Spain is now the largest producer of avocados in Europe and grows sixty thousand tons of the fruit for home consumption and thirty thousand tons for export yearly.

Other stalls that boast of being more thanone hundred years old are Rosells, selling a wide variety of Spanish olives, and Vidal Pons, which specializes in preserved, dried and fresh fruits. Near the Vidal Pons stand was a large counter ten feet long with dried fruits such as apricots, cherries, apples, figs, and mangos. The stand also sold shelled almonds, cashews, hazelnuts and chestnuts.

The candy displays in the Market are as creative and beautiful as a work by Gaudi. I had never before or since seen a candy showcase as fascinating and dramatic as the one near the entrance to the Market. Fifty to sixty one-foot square plastic containers, each filled with a different candy, were stacked one on top of the other vertically extending up for five to six feet above the countertop.

Located toward the back and in the center of the Market is a coffee shop that opens at six in the morning for the shop keepers, delivery men, maintenance personnel and those all-night celebrants who are just now returning home. The shoppers and tourists, as well as some local office workers, fill the stools during the rest of the day.

Mercado Central | Valencia, Spain

Valencia, the third largest city in Spain, is located on the Mediterranean Coast and on the dry Tura riverbed. Its harbor welcomed traders from foreign ports as early as two hundred B.C. It has long been a center of trade. During the time of Spain's exploration and conquest of the New World, the harbor of Valencia was busy with shipping. Spanish ships left for the Americas from this port and returned with their riches to Valencia. Today, Valencia's port is the biggest on the Mediterranean western coast and first in Spain's container traffic.

In the third and forth centuries, the Moors were ruling Spain. However, they experienced discrimination because of the growing Catholic population. Records show that in the 1200s the Moorish archiepiscopal palace was the site of a grain market.

More than five hundred years ago, an active market existed on the same site the Mercado Central occupies today. The construction of the present market pavilion was started in 1910 and in 1928 King Alfonso XII officially inaugurated the building and opened the market.

The architects of this magnificent structure were Francesc Guardia and Alexandre Soler. They studied in Barcelona and collaborated with the famous architect Domenech I Montaner.

The huge hall of eight thousand square meters, with thirteen hundred stalls, is one of the busiest markeplaces in Spain. The entrance to the building has three arched doorways and the front of the market building is decorated with ceramic tiles in mosaic patterns. The Valencia coat of arms—colorful tiles and with orange branches surrounding the two letters—is prominent. The inner walls are also decorated with the Valencia coat of arms. In the center of the cavernous hall is a high dome ceiling with beautiful clear and stained glass. Many of the large windows throughout the market also have stained glass, allowing the daylight and rainbow colors of light to enter the building. The Central Market looks more like a cathedral than a hub of commerce. It ranks as one of the oldest and largest covered markets in Europe. The number of stalls in the market varies from one thousand to thirteen hundred, depending on the seasons and products available.

The mild climate and irrigation have made the city an agricultural center and the market the site of global produce sales.

I was overwhelmed in the section of fruit stands in the center of the market. The fruit stalls were piled high with the famous locally grown Valencia oranges plus lemons, limes, grapefruit, mandarin oranges, kumquats, tangerines, blood oranges and clementines.

One fruit stand was featuring pummelos, the giant grapefruit-type fruit, and the "ugly" fruit, which is like grapefruit, only sweeter and with a bright red pulp.

It seemed to me that Mercado Central had more tropical fruit than the other markets in Spain. The fruit stands had counters of mangos in shades of green to pink and several varieties of bananas from tiny, brown-skinned ones to the large clusters of bright yellow fruit. Some even had the full stalk of bananas reaching three feet tall standing on the counter. Large papayas could be purchased whole or sliced in half. The bright orange flesh and the tiny black seeds in the cavity of the papaya made for an attractive picture. Pineapple of various sizes was also on display.

Another fruit that we seldom classify as a fruit is the olive. To find olives in a Spanish market is not surprising for

Spain is the world leader in the production and export of olives.

Olives have been used as a food for six thousand years. There are more than three hundred varieties of olives grown in Spain.

The olives in Mercado Central varied from green to purple to black, according to their level of ripeness. Green olives must be processed before eating for they are very hard and bitter, with an unpleasant taste when raw.

I learned from the vendors the manzanilla fina variety are the most desired olives and are often the favorite for stuffing. The pitted stuffed olives I saw in the market were stuffed with anchovy paste, (Spanish favorite) pimento, red pepper paste, lemon, hazelnut, garlic, almonds, chili peppers, capers and cheese.

The black olives in the large plastic tubs were dressed with different ingredients for seasoning. Some of the additions were mint, orange rind, cinnamon, lemon rind, chives, aniseed and honey. I am sure there are others that I missed. I enjoyed

sampling the olives that the vendor very graciously served one at a time ladled from the bulk bins with a long wooden spoon.

The vegetable stands were well-stocked with every kind of vegetable known. Some of the stands carried herbs and spices. Throughout the produce market, I saw many stands with braided ropes of garlic hanging from the rods at the top of the stalls. The La Mancha garlic is called "stinking rose." I saw pure white, purple and the striped garlic at the produce stalls. Garlic is used in many Spanish dishes. I did not taste the garlic at the market.

I was looking for the precious spice, saffron, at each of the markets I visited in Spain, the home of exquisite Spanish Saffron. At the spice stall in Mercado Central in Valencia, the proprietor of the spice shop was anxious to tell me about his saffron. When the Moors came to Spain in the eighth century, they brought

saffron with them. When planted in the rich soil of Spain, the stringy bulbs grew well and produced a purple crocus flower. The flower has three stigmas, which are handpicked from the blossom, dried and permitted to ferment slightly to produce saffron. It takes about fourteen thousand stigmas to produce one ounce of saffron. No wonder it is so expensive.

Saffron is an essential ingredient in paella, bouillabaisse and chartreuse

liqueur, giving a distinct flavor, color and aroma to the products.

Because Valencia is on the coast, the seafood found in the Market is the freshest available. The fishing boats arrive before dawn to unload their catch. The fish are at the market a few hours later. The large area devoted to fish and crustaceans had stalls around the edge of the market. I noticed an aroma of the ocean, maybe seaweed but not a fishy odor, when walking along the aisles. The selection and variety of fish and seafood was endless. I think everything that lives in the ocean was for sale here. This was also the noisiest part of the market. The vendors were talking loudly to potential customers.

Like other markets in Spain, the meat shops featured the Serrano ham and jamon Iberico. Several types of sausage were for sale. At a fairly large meat shop, a tall man in his fifties with dark brown hair and bright brown eyes was wearing a blue cotton work coat and spoke to me in English. He was proud of his sausage. He told me the ingredients varies in each type and that some were smoked and others not. Pimento and the smoked pimento were used in some of the sausages to add color and flavor. He said, "Everyone has a favorite sausage to use in the making of paella."

At the Market, all the ingredients for the traditional dish paella—rice, meat, seafood, saffron, chicken and vegetables—were available. Paella is said to have been created in Valencia. This famous dish is often served for Sunday lunch.

Rice is an essential ingredient in paella and is raised around Valencia. Several stands were selling rice, chickpeas, lentils and other grains.

Valencia's main festival, Las Fallas held in March, honors paella. Valencians will have many versions of the dish, and the varieties can be purchased in the Mercado Central or from street vendors.

In and near the Mercado Central were cafes, tapas bars, restaurants and coffee shops, all using the products from the Market in their prepared foods.

Mercado de Triana | Seville, Spain

The Mercado de Triana has a long history, as does the neighborhood of Triana. Triana is physically separated from Seville by the Guadalquivir River whose two branches reach out on both sides of the neighborhood. The residents are independent and strongly identify with the characteristic of the neighborhood of Triana. In the nineteenth century and early twentieth century, the city was known for bullfighters, gypsies, flamenco dancers and troubadours and boasted a Bohemian atmosphere.

With the discovery of the New World by Columbus, both Seville and Triana profited as all the goods imported from the New World had to pass through the Casa de Contracton before being distributed throughout Europe. The Guadalquivir River was a highway for ships bringing riches from the New World. The government awarded the royal monopoly for trade with the expanding Spanish colonies in the Americas to the port of

Seville. Sailing ships leaving and returning to this port with valuable cargo brought on the golden age of commerce and trade. Merchants from Europe and other trade centers traveled to Seville to acquire the desired goods. The population of Seville grew to nearly a million people by the sixteenth century. Street markets were set up to meet the needs of the expanding population.

From the fifteenth century until the middle of the eighteenth century, the Castello de San Jorge was the site of the Spanish Inquisition. It was abandoned and suffered from frequent flooding by the Guadalquivir River. The neglect caused the structure to be in a dilapidated condition. The Castello de San Jorge remained empty until 1823 when it became a marketplace and was designated as Market Square.

In 1992, the Market was in need of updating, reconstruction and modernizing for the upcoming exhibition.

The new Mercado de Triana was built in a traditional Moorish Revival style and opened in 2005. It is located just across the Puente Isabel II Bridge in Triana. The two story building is a golden color with the name on a large tile plaque near the entrance. Using the tile for the name was keeping in tradition of the neighborhood

for in the nineteenth century several ceramic and tile factories flourished near the site of the Castillo San Jorge.

I arrived at the Market fairly early in the morning, walked down a few steps to the entrance and discovered the Market did not open until 10 o'clock. I returned to the Mercado de Triana around 9:30 and was surprised to find the door unlocked. The Market was not officially open except for the delivery men and the vendors actively moving boxes, crates, tubs and carts filled with products for this market day. I was happy to witness the stands being made ready for the shoppers. At

10 o'clock, the customers started to arrive and the stalls opened for business.

The Market held several stalls for fresh fish and seafood. The fresh whole and cut fish were placed on crushed ice. The first stand I came upon had several large ugly carp staring at me with their glassy eyes and gaping open mouths. The carp come from the Guadalquivir River.

Some of the fish at the Market are caught as they migrate up the river from the sea and ocean. The fishing boats can dock and unload their catch practically at the doorsteps of the Mercado de Triana. Fish farms help to supply the vendors with a constant source of grey mullet and shrimp. Inland reservoirs are fished for sea bass, corvine and gilt-head bream. Other fish I saw in the Market were Atlantic salmon, anchovies, sturgeon, shad, tuna, shark and sole. One stand had live eel in a plastic bucket sitting on the floor next to the counter. Red shrimp in white plastic tubs and mussels and clams in mesh bags were on ice on the crowded counters.

The ladies selling fish were wearing white uniforms and covering their hair in a white cap to prevent any hair from falling into the customers' fish.

I watched the butcher cut a large sturgeon to the desired size for customer needs. My great surprise at Mercado de Triana was the quantity of La Caracoles, snails at two stalls. Each had several large black and blue plastic tubs filled to overflowing with shell-on brown snails,

snails of pale tan with brown stripes and other tubs of just the snails. Snails are small, and it must have taken thousands to fill these tubs. I always think of snails as gourmet; however, they are a common item on the family menu in Seville.

The meat shop was decorated with a row of hanging Iberia hams. He also had long ropes of red sausages hanging from the rail over the meat counter. Various types of sausages were in the refrigerated meat case.

The fruit and vegetable stalls were arranged with shelves for products in front of the stand and along the back wall. The shelves and racks on the back wall reached up four or five feet tall. A metal rod on the very top was loaded

with hanging bunches of leeks, kale, bananas, carrots and braided strings of garlic. Another produce stall had both onions and garlic hanging in long braided strings from the top railing.

Columbus brought peppers to Spain from the New World, and Spain brought peppers to the rest of Europe. Peppers and tomatoes were for sale at every produce stand to meet the need for many Spanish recipes.

The bakery displayed long oval and round loaves of bread, as well as large rolls. I did not see pastries at the Market.

Portuguese Chicken with Chorizo and Scallops, Lagos Market, Lagos

The combination of chicken and clams did not sound tasty to me, but I learned it is a popular dish in Portugal. At the markets in Lagos and in Lisbon, all the ingredients for this dish were available. And indeed the chicken, chorizo and scallops are Portugal's bounty of the land and the sea. The recipe can be prepared without the chorizo but must have the chicken and scallops. The dish is often served with the delicious crusty bread.

4 whole chicken legs, or 4 thighs and 4 drumsticks
1 tablespoon smoked paprika
1 tablespoon sweet paprika
1 teaspoon coarse salt
1/4 teaspoon black pepper
2 tablespoons vegetable oil
1 pound Spanish style chorizo, sliced
3 medium potatoes, diced
1 cup white onion, sliced
3 cloves garlic, minced

2 roasted red peppers cut into strips
1/2 cup white wine
1/2 pound sea scallops
1 cup packed chopped spinach or kale leaves
1/4 cup chopped parsley
1/2 cup chopped fresh cilantro
1/4 cup chopped fresh basil
1/4 cup chopped chives, for garnish
Olive oil for drizzling after cooking

Preheat oven to 350 degrees.

Place washed and patted dry chicken into large bowl. Add smoked paprika, sweet paprika, salt, pepper and mix well. Coat chicken with spice mix. In a large saucepan or heavy pot, heat the oil to high. Add chicken and cook until crispy on all sides, about 5 minutes. Remove chicken from pan and place into baking pan. Add chorizo to pot and cook for 2 more minutes. Add potatoes, onions, garlic and red peppers to pot and cook for 3 minutes. Remove from pot and place into baking pan with chicken. Pour wine into hot pot and deglaze pot. Pour deglaze into baking dish with chicken. Cover and place in oven. Bake for 30 minutes until chicken is tender. Remove from oven and add scallops and chopped greens. Cover and return to oven for 10 minutes. Remove from oven. Garnish with chopped chives. Drizzle with olive oil and serve.

Yield: 6 to 8 servings

Portuguese Cornbread, Lagos Market, Lagos

Broa, traditional Portuguese bread, is one of the staples in the Portuguese diet. It is smooth, almost like a pound cake in texture. The bread made with ground yellow cornmeal, broa, can be kept for weeks in a dry cupboard. The bread is available at the bakery stand in the Market and sells rapidly to the local shoppers who no longer make their bread at home.

1 cup yellow cornmeal plus 1 more cup for kneading
1 tablespoon salt
1 tablespoon sugar
3 cups boiling water
1 tablespoon active dry yeast
1 cup warm water
2 tablespoons olive oil
4 cups all-purpose flour

Combine 1 cup cornmeal, salt and sugar in a large bowl. Make a hollow in the center of the cornmeal. Add boiling water and mix to a paste. Cool slightly. Add yeast to 1 cup warm water and stir. Allow to sit for 5 minutes. Add yeast mixture and olive oil to cornmeal. Mix with dough paddle of electric mixer or with hands. Add flour a little at a time, mixing all the while. Transfer dough to an oiled bowl turning to coat all sides of dough ball with oil. Cover the bowl with a damp cloth and let rise in a warm place until doubled in volume. Oil a baking sheet and sprinkle with cornmeal. Turn dough onto surface and shape into a round loaf. Place on baking sheet and let rise for 45 minutes to double in volume. Reshape the dough into a ball. Cut the top of the loaf with a sharp knife into a criss-cross pattern. Bake at 400 degrees for 10 minutes. Reduce heat to 350 degrees and continue baking for 60 minutes and the loaf sounds hollow when tapped. Transfer to a rack to cool.

Yield: 1 loaf

Kale Soup (Caldo Verde), Lagos Market, Lagos

The ladies from around Lagos pick the kale and other greens early on the morning they come to the Market. Some of the leaves still sparkled with dew drops. Kale is used in a popular soup *Caldo Verde* by the poor farmers and is served at the most fancy restaurants in the capital city. It is often the main dish at the noon meal or served for a light supper along with the crusty bread. The basic ingredient in the soup is kale. The other vegetables and spices added to the soup depend on what is in the kitchen or the whim of the cook.

2 tablespoons olive oil
1 large white potato (Yukon Gold), peeled and diced
1 medium onion, chopped
4 cloves garlic, minced
1/2 red bell pepper, chopped
1 bunch green kale, coarsely chopped
1 can (15 ounces) garbanzo beans, drained and rinsed
1/2 cup tomato paste
1/2 pound chorizo sausage, casings removed, chopped
5 cups chicken broth
1 tablespoon sugar
1/2 teaspoon smoky paprika
1/2 teaspoon kosher salt
1/4 teaspoon black pepper

Heat oil in heavy sauce pot over medium heat. Add potatoes and onions. Cover and cook for 5 minutes, stirring to prevent burning. Add garlic, red pepper and kale. Cover the pot and cook for 4 minutes to wilt kale. Add beans, tomato paste, chorizo and broth to the pot. Add sugar, paprika, salt and pepper. Bring to a full boil. Reduce heat to medium and simmer for 20 to 30 minutes until vegetables are tender. Serve with crusty bread.

Yield: 6 servings

Snails with Anise, Lagos Market, Lagos

Before cooking the snails they must be washed, blanched taken from the shell to remove the black stomach then simmered in court bouillon before they are ready for the final treatment of butter and garlic or herb sauce. The recipe for Snails with Anise is served in a toasted roll and can be an appetizer or a main course.

1/4 cup butter
8 round crusty dinner rolls
2 garlic cloves, finely chopped
2 shallots, finely chopped
2 cups crème fraiche or heavy cream
1 teaspoon aniseed

Pinch ground nutmeg
Salt and pepper
4 dozen cooked or frozen snails (washed, cleaned and cooked)
1 tablespoon Pernod or other anise-flavored liqueur
2 tablespoons parsley, chopped

Preheat oven to 350 degrees.

Melt half the butter and set aside. Cut the tops of the rolls and hollow out to make a bread shell. Brush the insides with the melted butter. Set on a baking sheet and toast in the oven until the edges are crisp and starting to brown, 10 to 12 minutes. Heat the remaining butter in a deep skillet. Sauté garlic and shallots until soft about 1 minute. Add cream, aniseed, nutmeg, salt and pepper. Simmer until sauce is reduced by about half, 10 to 15 minutes. Add snails to the sauce and simmer until very hot, 3 to 5 minutes. Add Pernod and parsley. Set the toasted bread shells on plates and spoon the snails and sauce into each roll. Serve at once.

Yield: 8 rolls

Braised Pork with Clams, Lagos Market, Lagos

A traditional dish in Portugal is made with pork and clams. These foods are always available and inexpensive in the Market. The recipe will vary from one end of Portugal to the other and is often influenced by what is in the kitchen. The dish is on the local restaurant menus. I did not think I would like the combination, but the blending of the flavors resulted in a stew that was very tasty.

2 tablespoons olive oil
1-1/2 pounds boneless pork shoulder, cut into 1-inch pieces
1 teaspoon sea salt
1/2 teaspoon ground black pepper
1/4 cup chopped onion
2 carrots, thinly sliced
2 celery ribs, thinly sliced
3 tablespoons tomato paste
1/2 cup dry white wine
4 cups chicken broth
1/2 teaspoon thyme
3 tablespoons chopped parsley
1 bay leaf
1-1/2 dozen littleneck clams, scrubbed
2 tablespoons chopped cilantro

Preheat oven to 350 degrees.

In a large ovenproof pot, heat the oil on medium high. Season the pork with salt and pepper. Place in hot oil and cook to brown meat, about 10 minutes. Remove pork from pot and cover. Place onion, carrots, and celery in the pot and cook for 5 minutes to soften. Add tomato paste, wine and broth to pot. Place pork back into pot and bring to a boil. Add thyme, parsley and bay leaf. Cover and place in the oven for 45 to 50 minutes. Remove and place on stove. Remove bay leaf. If the liquid is low, add more broth. Simmer mixture uncovered for 5 minutes. Arrange clams on liquid in the pot. Cover and cook until clams open, about 5 to 6 minutes. Serve in bowls. Garnish with cilantro.

Yield: 6 servings

Espiros, Lagos Market, Lagos

The people in Portugal tend to have a sweet tooth. They have several desserts that are a combination of sugar and eggs. One popular dessert is Sweet Egg, a combination of whole egg and sugar beaten into a fluff and baked. Espiros are similar to Sweet Egg, only these cookies are more like a meringue.

3 large eggs, room temperature
3 egg whites, room temperature
1/4 teaspoon salt
1 tablespoon frozen orange juice concentrate
2/3 cup sugar

Preheat oven to 250 degrees. Grease baking sheet.

In a large mixing bowl, combine eggs and egg whites, salt, orange concentrate and sugar. Beat on high until mixture is fluffy, thick and holds a stiff peak. Do not underbeat. For each cookie, drop a tablespoon of batter onto greased baking sheet. Bake for 25 minutes until the edge of the cookies are light brown. Allow to cool on baking sheet and carefully remove from the sheet. The cookies are very delicate.

Yield: 36 to 40 cookies

Pasteis de Belem, Mercado da Ribeira, Lisbon

The Ribeira Market is a large Market in an enclosed pavilion with numerous vendors selling all types of food, both fresh and prepared. The pastry shops all feature the traditional *Pastel de Belem*, a tart shell filled with an egg custard. The tart was created in the late seventeenth century by Catholic nuns at the Jeronimos Monastery in Belem in Lisbon. The Casa Pasteis de Belem in Lisbon was the first place outside of the convent selling the original tart. After the monastery closed in 1820, the dessert was called *pasties de Belem* after the name of the area and its famous bakery. The tart shell has several variations, and this recipe calls for puff pastry and, fortunately, that can be purchased frozen.

Custard

1 tablespoon cornstarch
1 cup half-and-half cream, divided
3 tablespoons sugar
1/8 teaspoon salt
3 large egg yolks, slightly beaten
1-1/2 inch cinnamon sticks
2 strips lemon peel, each 2 inches long and 1/2-inch thick
1/2 teaspoon vanilla extract

Place the cornstarch and 1/4 cup cream in a saucepan. Stir to dissolve cornstarch. Add sugar, salt, egg yolks and remaining cream. Whisk to blend. Add cinnamon stick and lemon peel. Cook over medium heat, stirring with a whisk constantly until thick, about 8 minutes. Remove from heat and add vanilla. Pour into a bowl and cover to cool.

Yield: 1-1/4 cups

Crust

1 package (10 ounces) puff pastry

Preheat oven to 400 degrees.

Roll cold pastry on unfloured surface into a rectangle to 1/8-inch thick. Starting with the long side, roll pastry dough into a log about 1 inch thick. Cover log with parchment paper and refrigerate for 15 minutes. Remove from refrigerator. Cut the log into 10 even pieces. Place each round into a non-stick muffin tin. Using your thumb, push the pastry into the muffin tin and shape dough into the bottom and sides of the muffin cup and slightly above the rim. Fill each pastry cup 3/4 full of custard. Bake at 400 degrees for 13 to 14 minutes. Custard will puff up. Turn oven to broil and place muffin tin under the broiler for 1 minute or until caramelized brown spots appear on the top. Watch carefully because they can burn easily.

Yield: 10 tarts

Roasted Beets and Watermelon Salad, Mercado da Ribeira, Lisbon

2 heads bib lettuce, leaves separated
1 cup watermelon, seeded and cut into cubes
1/4 cup pistachios, shelled and roasted
4 kumquats, sliced and seeded
1/3 cup strawberry poppy seed dressing
6 roasted small red beets
6 roasted small gold beets
6 roasted small Chioggia beets
1/4 cup sundried golden mulberries (or golden raisins)
1/2 cup soft goat cheese, crumbled

Tear lettuce into bite-sized pieces. In mixing bowl, toss lettuce, watermelon, pistachios and kumquats. Add 3 tablespoons salad dressing and toss. Place salad on individual salad plates. Place beets in the mixing bowl. Add remaining salad dressing to coat beets. Arrange beets around the perimeter of the salads. Top each with sundried mulberries and goat cheese.

Yield: 6 servings

Strawberry Poppy Seed Dressing

1 cup strawberries, washed and rimmed
2 tablespoons champagne vinegar
1/4 teaspoon sea salt
1 teaspoon sugar
1/4 cup almond oil or walnut oil
1 tablespoon poppy seeds

Place berries, vinegar, salt and sugar in blender. Blend until smooth. Blend on high and slowly drizzle oil into mixture until emulsified. Pour into bowl and stir in poppy seeds.

Yield: 1-1/3 cups

Glazed Meatballs, Mercado de Triana, Seville

The recipe for meatballs that are glazed with a tart red jelly is used both at home and at tapas bars. When prepared at home, the dish will vary depending on what might be in the pantry or refrigerator.

1 pound lean ground beef
1/4 cup dry bread crumbs
1 teaspoon salt
2 tablespoons chopped onions
1 egg, slightly beaten
1 tablespoon smoky paprika
1 tablespoon tomato paste
1 tablespoon olive oil
1 cup currant jelly
1/4 cup water

In a medium-sized mixing bowl, combine beef, bread crumbs, salt, onions, paprika and tomato paste. Mix well and shape into 1-inch-diameter balls. In a large skillet, heat oil to medium hot. Brown meat balls, turning occasionally. Add jelly and water to skillet. Simmer for 10 minutes to coat meatballs. Serve warm.

Yield: 16 meatballs

Fusilli with Shrimp and Arugula, Mercado da Ribeira, Lisbon

The waters surrounding Portugal supply fresh shrimp to the markets daily. Many different species and size of shrimp are for sale.

1/4 cup olive oil
1/4 cup diced shallots
1 tablespoon minced garlic
1/4 teaspoon red pepper flakes
1 cup sherry wine
2 ripe tomatoes, cut into small wedges
1 pound large raw shrimp, peeled and deveined
12 ounces fusilli pasta
3 cups packed fresh arugula, torn into bite-sized pieces
1/2 teaspoon sea salt
1/8 teaspoon coarse black pepper

Heat oil in large, heavy skillet. Add shallots and garlic. Sauté for 2 minutes until translucent. Add red pepper flakes, wine and tomatoes. Simmer uncovered for 5 minutes to reduce liquid by about half. Add shrimp and cook only until they are pink, about 2 minutes. Do not overcook. Remove from heat. Cook the pasta in boiling salted water until al dente tender, about 8 to 10 minutes. Drain and add to skillet. Add arugula, salt and pepper and toss to coat and wilt arugula. Serve immediately.

Yield: 6 servings

Portuguese Sweet Bread, Mercado da Ribeira, Lisbon

The bakeries in the Market carried many varieties of breads. The shelves held loaves that were round, flat, long oval, and square. One of the pretties was the Portuguese Sweet Bread. This large, round, golden bread is often prepared for the Easter holiday and, for that celebration, a whole egg in the shell is baked in the loaf. Although this bread is easy to make, most of the home-makers buy the bread at the Market

1-1/2 cups lukewarm milk, divided
2 packages active yeast
1 cup plus 1 teaspoon sugar
1/2 cup butter, softened
1/2 teaspoon salt
4 eggs, beaten
5 to 6 cups all-purpose flour

Dissolve yeast in 1/2 cup warm milk with 1 teaspoon sugar. Let stand for 8 to 10 minutes. In an electric mixing bowl with the paddle attachment, combine 1 cup sugar, remaining milk, butter, and salt. In a separate bowl, beat eggs until foamy. Add eggs and yeast mixture to milk and sugar mixture. With the beater on slow speed, gradually add 5 cups of flour until soft dough forms. Change to dough hook and kneed for 5 to 8 minutes. If dough is too sticky, add more flour to form a soft ball. Turn onto work surface and knead by hand for 2 to 3 minutes, adding flour as needed. Oil the inside of a plastic or glass bowl. Place dough into bowl and cover. Place in a warm place to rise about 1-1/2 hours until double in bulk. Punch down the dough and shape into one large round loaf. Place on greased baking sheet. Cover and let rise until light, about 30 minutes. Preheat oven to 350 degrees. Bake loaf for 45 minutes. Cool on rack.

Yield: 12 servings

Shrimp and Spinach Soufflé, Mercado da Ribeira, Lisbon

Two of the outstanding products in the Ribeira Market were the greens of every shade at the produce stands and the large variety of fresh-caught seafood. The fish and seafood stalls were immaculate, with no fish odor. I was delighted to see the variety of shrimp available. Some of the shrimp were being sold with heads, shell and tails; others had the head removed, and still others were cooked and coral colored. The ingredients for the recipe Shrimp and Spinach Soufflé were available at the stands.

2 tablespoons butter, divided
3 tablespoons grated Parmesan cheese
12 large raw shrimp, peeled and deveined
1 tablespoon all-purpose flour
1 tablespoon tomato paste
1/2 cup half-and-half cream
2 tablespoons brandy or orange juice
2 tablespoons fresh lemon juice
1/2 teaspoon sea salt
1/8 teaspoon white pepper

Coat 4 soufflé cups with 1 tablespoon butter. Sprinkle each with Parmesan cheese to coat bottom and sides. Divide shrimp into the 4 prepared cups. In a small saucepan, melt 1 tablespoon butter. Add flour and cook for 1 minute. Add tomato paste and cream, stirring constantly until thickened. Add brandy, lemon juice, salt, and pepper. Simmer for 2 minutes. Pour over shrimp in soufflé cups.

Soufflé

1 tablespoon butter
1/2 cup onions, finely chopped
2 tablespoons garlic, minced
2 cups fresh spinach leaves, chopped
1/2 teaspoon dried thyme
1/4 teaspoon ground nutmeg
3 egg yolks, slightly beaten, room temperature
3 egg whites, room temperature
1/8 teaspoon cream of tartar

Preheat oven to 375 degrees. In a medium-sized saucepan, heat butter and sauté onions and garlic. Add spinach, thyme and nutmeg. Cook until spinach wilts. Add egg yolks, stirring constantly for 2 minutes. Remove from heat and cool. Beat egg whites and cream of tartar until stiff peaks form. Fold 1/3 of egg whites into spinach mixture. Fold in remaining egg whites. Pour batter over shrimp mixture in prepared dishes. Bake for 30 minutes until test skewer comes out clean. Invert soufflé cups and serve warm.

Yield: 4 servings

Pineapple in Port, Mercado da Ribeira, Lisbon

Fresh pineapple in the Portuguese markets comes mainly from the Philippines. The addition of the local port wine makes for an attractive and interesting dessert. Some variations for the dish are to serve it in a sherbet dish with coconut ice cream or a favorite sherbet or with Greek yogurt sweetened with honey.

1 fresh pineapple, about 3-1/2 pounds
1 cup red port wine
1/4 cup fresh mint, minced
Mint sprig for garnish

Slice the top and the bottom from the pineapple to stand on one end. Peel pineapple, removing all prickly eyes. Cut lengthwise into 8 wedges. Remove core. Slice the wedges into 1/2-inch thick slices. Place the pineapple slices in large non-metallic bowl. Add port and toss to mix. Cover and chill for 3 to 4 hours. Add minced mint and chill another 30 minutes. Serve in stem glasses and garnish with mint sprig.

Yield: 6 servings

Orange Salad with Avocado and Blue Cheese, Mercado Central, Valencia

Valencia is the home of the Valencia oranges that are said to have come to Spain from India and Persia in the twelfth century. The oranges became popular for their sweet juice and tart taste. The tree-ripe fruit is available in the summer months. The climate in the south of Spain is ideal for the orange groves. I have not been in Valencia when the orange trees are in bloom but the fragrance of the groves in bloom must be a sensual experience.

The mild climate in southwest Spain along the Costa del Sol is ideal for the production of avocados. Spain has become the largest avocado grower in Europe. The avocado arrived in Spain with the Spanish conquistadores from Central America and South America, where avocados grew abundantly. The avocados are picked near the markets in Valencia.

The Cabrales cheese is a salty and intensely flavored cheese that is popular throughout Spain.

4 large oranges
1 large ripe avocado, peeled and sliced
1/2 cup black pitted kalmaria olives
1/4 cup extra virgin olive oil
1 tablespoon fresh lemon juice
1/4 cup crumbled blue cheese (Cabrales cheese is an excellent Spanish
　　blue cheese)
Lettuce leaves for liners on salad plates

Peel oranges and remove white pith beneath the peel. Section oranges by cutting between segments. In a medium-sized bowl, place orange segments, avocado and olives. In a small bowl, add lemon juice to olive oil, whisk together and drizzle over orange mixture. Divide among 4 leaf-lined salad plates. Sprinkle blue cheese over each salad.

Yield: 4 servings

Magdalena Muffins, Mercado Central, Valencia

The Mercado Central in Valencia is a showplace for citrus fruit that grows abundantly in the region. The large lemons and limes are used in the preparation of many Spanish dishes. Magdalenas are small, sweet cupcakes with a lemon flavor. They are most often served at breakfast with *café con leche*.

1 cup sugar, divided
4 eggs
1/2 cup butter, melted and cooled to room temperature
Zest of 1 lemon
1 tablespoon fresh lemon juice
1-2/3 cups all-purpose flour
1 tablespoon baking powder

Preheat oven to 375 degrees.

Measure sugar and set 1/4 cup aside. Place eggs and 3/4 cup sugar in mixing bowl and beat until light and fluffy. Slowly add melted butter to egg mixture with the beater running. Add lemon zest and lemon juice. In a separate bowl, combine flour and baking powder. Gradually add flour mixture to egg mixture with mixer on low speed. Dough will be thick. Place paper liners in muffin pan. Using a large serving spoon, fill muffin cups half full of batter. Sprinkle reserved sugar on top of each cupcake. Place muffin tin on the middle shelf of oven. Bake for 18 to 20 minutes, until magdalenas have turned a golden color. Remove from oven and cool in pan for 5 minutes.

Yield: 18 muffins

Crab-Stuffed Mushrooms Bienville, Mercado Central, Valencia

The variety of mushrooms at the Market varies with the seasons. The people in the small towns and countryside still look forward to hunting for mushrooms in the woods. Today, because the demand is large, mushrooms are raised commercially. This allows for a more constant supply to the Spanish markets. Stuffed mushrooms are popular and seen frequently at tapas bars. The Crab-Stuffed Mushrooms Bienville can be served as a luncheon dish as well as an appetizer.

20 large mushrooms
1 can (6 ounces) jumbo lump crabmeat, flaked
1/2 cup green onions sliced
1 green bell pepper, chopped
1 red bell pepper, chopped
1/3 cup chopped red onion
3 cloves garlic, minced
1 cup unsalted butter
1/2 cup sherry wine
1 teaspoon salt
1 teaspoon coarsely ground black pepper
1/2 teaspoon cayenne pepper
1 cup all-purpose flour
2 cups heavy cream
2 ounces mozzarella cheese, shredded
2 ounce provolone cheese, shredded

Wash and separate stems from mushroom caps. Place caps on baking sheet lined with parchment paper. Place a teaspoon of crabmeat on each cap. In medium saucepan, melt butter over medium heat. Add vegetables and cook until vegetables are tender, about 8 minutes. Add wine, salt, pepper and cayenne. Cook 2 minutes. Add flour. Continue cooking and stirring until mixture forms a dough with the vegetables. Add cream and mix into vegetable mixture. Cook, stirring constantly, until stuffing no longer sticks to the side of the saucepan. Transfer to flat pan to cool. Using a tablespoon, cover crabmeat with stuffing, leaving top slightly rounded. Mix cheeses and sprinkle on top of mushroom stuffing. Bake at 400 degrees for 15 to 20 minutes until cheese is slightly brown.

Yield: 20 stuffed mushrooms

Migas, Mercado Central, Valencia

Migas have been a peasant food of Spain for centuries and are still enjoyed by the people of Spain. The dish is traditionally made using dry bread, some sausage meat and the local foods that are in season or available. Because the ingredients vary, the recipe is only a suggested combination of flavors. The basic foods generally found in Migas are olive oil, chorizo sausage and garlic. The dish is often served with grapes or pimientos. In Andalucía, Migas are often eaten the morning of the *matanza,* the day of butchery of a goat, pig or sheep, and are served with a stew that includes curdled blood, liver, kidneys and other offal.

2 teaspoons smoked paprika
1/2 cup extra virgin olive oil
4 cloves garlic, minced
1/2 cup diced bacon
1/2 cup chorizo, thinly sliced
1 cup chopped onion
1/2 teaspoon salt
6 to 8 cups dry bread, cubed
2 cups chicken stock or water

Preheat oven to 350 degrees.

Place paprika in a large ovenproof skillet and heat until paprika is hot, about 2 minutes. Remove from skillet. Place olive oil in skillet, heat to medium hot. Add garlic, sauté for 1 minute. Add bacon and cook until fat is rendered. Drain fat from skillet. Add chorizo, onion, salt and the paprika to the skillet. Cook for 2 minutes. Add dry bread cubes and continue stirring while cubes absorb flavors. Add 1 cup broth and toss. Add remaining broth and cover skillet. Bake for 20 minutes. Remove cover, stir and continue to bake for 10 more minutes until dish becomes crisp on top.

Yield: 4 servings

Spanish Chicken, Mercado Central, Valencia

The Mercado Central in Valencia has every product produced in Spain on display. The chickens available varied from the large stewing hens to the free-range birds, great for frying. The Spanish Chicken recipe uses many of the products Spain is known for: olive oil, peppers, lemons, olives, wine and the best chicken in Europe. The sherry wine adds a bit of sweetness to counteract the lemon juice. The Spanish Chicken recipe is an excellent luncheon dish, even on the second day.

1/4 cup olive oil, divided
6 cloves garlic, thinly sliced, divided
4 cups Italian bread, cut into cubes
1 pound skinless, boneless chicken meat, cut into 1-inch
    pieces
1 teaspoon kosher salt
1/4 teaspoon black pepper
1 teaspoon smoked paprika
1 red, 1 green and 1 yellow bell pepper, cut into thin strips
3 tablespoons, chopped shallots
1/2 cup sherry wine
1 cup sliced mushrooms
1 cup chopped fresh tomatoes
2 tablespoons lemon juice
1/2 cup sliced green olives
2 tablespoons chopped fresh parsley

In a large non-stick skillet, heat 2 tablespoons oil over medium heat. Add 3 cloves garlic and cook for 1 minute. Add bread and cook 5 to 6 minutes until golden brown and crisp, stirring often. Place bread cubes and garlic on a large platter or serving bowl. Coat chicken with salt, pepper and paprika. Add remaining oil to skillet and heat on medium high. Add chicken to hot oil and cook, stirring to brown on all sides. Remove chicken from skillet. Reduce heat to medium. Add peppers and cook for 2 to 3 minutes until peppers are soft. Add shallots and remaining garlic. Cook 4 minutes. Add wine and scrape bits from bottom of pan. Add mushrooms and tomatoes. Continue cooking for 2 minutes. Return chicken to skillet with vegetables. Cook for 8 to 10 minutes, stirring to blend flavors. Remove skillet from heat and pour mixture over bread croutons. Drizzle lemon juice over chicken dish. Sprinkle top with olives and parsley.

Yield: 6 servings

Prosciutto-Wrapped Melon, Mercado Central, Valencia

The Spanish melon is a member of the muskmelon family. It is a large, egg-shaped melon with a green ribbed skin and a pale green flesh. It is a sweet juicy melon, much like the crenshaw melon, Persian melon, or the honeydew melon. The melons are present in the markets throughout Spain from July through November. They are used for appetizers, tapas, salads and desserts. This recipe combines the sweet melon with the tart vinegar and the salty ham for a wonderful taste sensation

2 cups Spanish melon, cut into 1-inch chunks
1 tablespoon balsamic vinegar
1/2 pound prosciutto, thinly sliced in 5-inch-long and 1-inch-wide strips

Place cut melon in a bowl. Drizzle with balsamic vinegar and toss to coat. Thread water-soaked wooden skewers with prosciutto, then melon. Wrap prosciutto strips around melon. Place another melon piece on skewer and wrap prosciutto over the second slice of melon.

Yield: 8 skewers

Clementine Salad, Mercado Central, Valencia

Spain is the largest producer of clementines in the world. From October through March, the Spanish markets glow with the piles of bright orange clementines. The peak season for the fruit is December and it is often called "Christmas orange." It is believed the clementine originated in China, and it is sometimes called the Mandarin orange. The clementine is prized for its sweet taste and limited seeds. The membranes separate easily and are nutritious and delicious used in salads, desserts and snacks.

2 cups romaine lettuce
2 cups baby spinach
2 cups arugula
6 green onions, sliced
4 clementines, peeled and sectioned or
   1 can (16 ounces) mandarin oranges,
   drained
1/4 cup dried cranberries
1/4 cup sweet-sour dressing
1/2 cup sugar coated almonds, sliced

Tear lettuce, spinach and arugula into bite-sized pieces. Place in salad bowl. Add green onions, clementines and cranberries. Add dressing and toss to coat vegetables. Sprinkle with almonds just before serving.

Yield: 4 to 6 servings

Sweet-Sour Dressing

1/4 cup rice wine vinegar
3 tablespoons sugar
2 tablespoons chopped fresh basil
1 clove garlic, minced
1/2 teaspoon sea salt
1/8 teaspoon black pepper
1/2 cup extra virgin olive oil (blood orange olive oil is great for this dressing)

In blender, combine vinegar, sugar, basil, garlic, salt and pepper. With blender running, pour oil into blender to emulsify. Chill dressing for 2 to 4 hours before serving to blend flavors. Shake before using.

Yield: 1 cup

Grilled Sardines, La Boqueria Market, Barcelona

The schools of sardines off the coast of Spain look like flashes of silver as they swim in and out of the sunshine. They are caught in nets by the fishermen each day and brought to the market fresh and still wiggling. They are sold whole or can be purchased gutted and scaled. In the Market in Barcelona the silver six-inch-long sardines were displayed on piles of crushed ice. The small sardines are a staple in the Spanish diet. They are deep fried in Spanish olive oil or grilled over a wood fire for a smoky flavor or cooked on a gas grill in the backyard.

1 pound sardines, cleaned and scaled
1/4 cup extra virgin olive oil
Coarse sea salt
1 lemon, cut into wedges

Rub sardines with enough oil to make them slick, and sprinkle with salt. Place on grill over hot fire. Cook for 3 to 4 minutes, turn and cook the other side for 3 minutes. When done, carefully remove from grill with a spatula. Drizzle more olive oil over the sardines. Sprinkle with salt. Serve with lemon wedges.

Yield: 4 servings

Fresh Peach Crisp, La Boqueria Market, Barcelona

The fresh peaches in the La Boqueria Market were displayed in beautiful arrangements; some were piled like a pyramid, others were in neat rows. At the large produce stand near the entrance of the Market, an attractive, dark-eyed young lady was handing out juicy samples of the peaches they were selling. She told me, in quite good English, the peach orchards were near Barcelona.

5 to 6 ripe peaches, sliced
1/2 cup sugar
1/4 cup all-purpose flour
1 teaspoon cinnamon

Topping

1/2 cup all purpose flour
1/3 cup sugar
3/4 cup shredded cheddar cheese
5 tablespoons melted butter

Preheat oven to 400 degrees. Grease baking dish with butter.

Place sliced peaches in a large bowl. Combine sugar, flour and cinnamon in the bowl. Pour flour mixture over peaches and gently stir to coat slices. Pour into baking dish. For topping, combine flour, sugar and cheese and stir to blend. Sprinkle over peaches. Pour melted butter over topping. Bake for 40 minutes.

Yield: 6 to 8 servings

Roasted Olives, La Boqueria Market, Barcelona

Olives are one of the world's earliest cultivated fruits, and traces of them have been found dating back thirty-five hundred years. They have always been popular in Spain, where there are three hundred varieties of olives, many of them stemming from a single type that adapted to different grow-ing conditions or resulted from grafting. Spain has the reputation of being the largest producer of olives in the world. Spanish olives are exported to all parts of the world. At the La Boqueria Market in Barcelona, the selec-tion of olives is endless. They are served as tapas and displayed in tubs, trays, pans, and wooden containers. A Spanish table is naked without olives.

1 roasted red bell pepper
4 cups assorted olives with pits (Kalamata, Nicoise, Aerbequina, Cerignola,
    Picholine and oil-cured black olives, drained and patted dry)
2 tablespoons crushed fresh thyme
2 tablespoons crushed fresh rosemary
1/4 teaspoon red pepper flakes
Zest of one orange
1/4 cup red wine vinegar
1/4 cup sherry wine vinegar
3/4 cup extra virgin olive oil

Preheat oven to 425 degrees.

Cut roasted red pepper into strips. In a large mixing bowl, combine all ingredients except the olive oil. Spread the olives on a shallow baking pan. Roast at 425 degrees for 35 to 40 minutes until tender, stirring frequently. Remove from the oven and let olives cool on the pan. Before serving, drizzle with the olive oil. Stir and serve at room temperature.

Yield: 4 cups

Spanish Frittata, La Boqueria Market, Barcelona

The Spanish Frittata is eaten for breakfast, lunch, and as a snack and even as tapas in the afternoon. It is simple to make and uses the fresh foods from the Market. The home chef will vary the recipe, according to the foods in the pantry and refrigerator, so the recipe can vary a great deal but is always delicious.

2 medium-sized potatoes, peeled and sliced 1/4-inch thick
3 tablespoons vegetable oil, divided
1/4 cup chopped white onion
1/2 cup chopped red pepper
4 button mushrooms, sliced
6 eggs, beaten
2 tablespoons milk
1/2 teaspoon salt
1/8 teaspoon white pepper
1/4 cup shredded Parmesan cheese
1 tablespoon chopped parsley for garnish

Preheat broiler to 500 degrees.

Place potatoes in a small amount of salted water and cook for 3 to 5 minutes. Do not overcook. Drain and set aside. Heat 1 tablespoon oil in a large skillet. Sauté the onions for 3 minutes. Add the red pepper and sauté for 2 minutes. Add the mushrooms and sauté for an additional 2 minutes. Remove from heat and place in a bowl to keep warm. Heat 2 tablespoon oil in the large skillet to hot. Place the potatoes in the skillet and cook for 2 minutes. Turn potatoes. Pour onions, red pepper and mushrooms on top of potatoes. Whip eggs in a bowl. Add salt and pepper. Pour over vegetables in the skillet. Cook for 5 minutes until eggs are set around edges. Sprinkle with cheese and place under the broiled for 5 to 7 minutes to finish cooking and melt the cheese. Remove from broiler. Place a large plate over the top of the skillet. Flip the skillet so the frittata is on the plate with the golden brown underside now on top. Garnish with parsley.

Yield: 4 servings

Sangria, La Boqueria Market, Barcelona

Sangria is a refreshing wine, fruit juice and fruit combination that is enjoyed for lunch, afternoon refreshment and in the evening. The fruits and fruit juices available at the La Boqueria Market add to the joy of making this beverage and the enjoyment of drinking it. Red wine is usually included as an ingredient. However, I did find a recipe for Sangria using white wine. The fruit for the Sangria is what is in season in the Market. Stone fruit, such as peaches, apricots and nectarines, all add flavor and interest to the beverage. When they are in season, strawberries, blueberries and raspberries add a completely different flavor to the wine.

1 bottle red wine (cabernet sauvignon, merlot, rioja reds, zinfandel, shiraz)
1/4 cup fresh lemon juice (juice from 1 lemon)
1 cup orange juice
1 ounce brandy
1 large fresh peach, sliced
2 cups ginger ale or lemon-lime soda

Pour wine into a large pitcher. Squeeze lemon juice into wine. Add orange juice, brandy and peach slices. Refrigerate for 1 hour. Add ginger ale or soda and stir. Serve over ice.

Yield: a good time, 8 to 10 servings

Grilled Summer Vegetables, La Bogueria Market, Barcelona

The La Bogueria Market in Barcelona was overflowing with beautiful colorful summer vegetables. The eggplants of every shape and size filled the display counters. The color of the eggplants ranged from dark purple, almost black, to lavender, striped white and purple and the tiny, pure white, round vegetable. The zucchinis were arranged in rows, with flowers on some of the plants. Most of the bright green and yellow zucchinis were small, only 6 inches long. The large displays of red, green and yellow peppers added to the decoration of the Market.

1 eggplant, peeled and sliced 1/2-inch thick
1 red bell pepper, seeded and cut in half
1 yellow bell pepper, seeded and cut in half
1 large zucchini, cut into 1-inch slices
3 tablespoons olive oil
2 cloves garlic, minced
1/2 teaspoon salt
1 large tomato, cut in half

Heat grill to hot. Place the eggplant, peppers and zucchini over the direct heat. Combine olive oil, garlic and salt. Brush vegetables with oil mixture. Grill for 15 minutes, turn vegetables and continue cooking. Add tomato to hot grill and cook for 5 minutes. Remove all vegetables. Place peppers in paper bag to "sweat" for 10 minutes. Place remaining vegetables in a bowl. Peel blackened skin from peppers and cut into 1-inch sections. Add to vegetable bowl. Drizzle oil mixture over vegetables. Add salt as needed. Toss to coat.

Yield: 6 servings

Pan de Orno, Spanish Bread, Mercado de Triana, Seville

Bread is served at every meal in a Spanish household. As seen in the Market, there are many varieties, shapes and sizes of loaves. Rye and cornmeal are often used in making bread. Nuts, raisins and other dried fruits are added to sweet breads and breakfast rolls. The Pan de Orno is a sweet roll that sometimes has cinnamon in the filling, but most often white sugar and butter are the only added ingredients for the filling. Traditionally, the Spanish homemaker would use her hands to blend the ingredients to make the dough. A dough hook of an electric mixer works well, as does a large mixing spoon. The texture is created by the kneading.

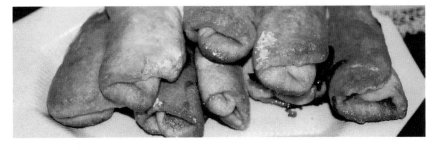

2 tablespoons active dry yeast
3 cups lukewarm water, divided
1 teaspoon sugar
7 cups all-purpose flour
2 teaspoons salt
1/4 cup olive oil
Butter
White or brown sugar
1 egg white for egg wash

Place the yeast and 1 teaspoon sugar in 1-1/2 cups lukewarm water and let stand for 10 minutes. Stir to dissolve. Sift flour into a large mixing bowl, saving some for the surface to knead the dough. Add salt. Add yeast mixture to flour. Gradually stir in the remaining water to form firm dough. Add olive oil and mix into the dough. Turn dough onto flat surface sprinkled with flour. Knead for 5 to 6 minutes until dough becomes firm and elastic. Grease a bowl and place dough in bowl, turning it so the grease covers the dough surface. Cover and let rise in a warm place until double in volume. Place dough on floured surface and knead for 5 to 10 minutes and the dough feels smooth. Let dough rest for 10 minutes. Divide dough into 8 balls. Using a rolling pin, roll each ball to the size of a large, rectangular hot dog bun. Coat the dough with soft butter. Sprinkle the dough with white or brown sugar. Roll the dough, starting with the short side, into a log. Seal the end and place on a greased baking sheet with the seam side down. Cover the baking sheet and place in a warm place to rise for 30 minutes. Brush top of rolls with egg wash. Preheat oven to 425 degrees and bake rolls for 30 minutes until the tops are golden. Remove from pan onto wire rack.

Yield: 8 rolls

Chicken Liver Pâté, Mercado de Triana, Seville

Tapas are small servings of tasty bites of many different foods. Chicken liver pâté is one kind available at the tapas bars in the Market in Seville. Barbecued chicken wings, chicken curry and chicken tenders also are served as tapas. The following recipe is a Jewish dish and may have been introduced into the cuisine of Spain by the Moors during their presence in Iberia.

1 pound chicken livers, cleaned and patted dry
1/2 teaspoon salt
1 tablespoon chicken fat, melted, or 1 tablespoon butter, melted
2 tablespoons chopped onion
2 eggs, hard cooked, diced
1/8 teaspoon black pepper
1/8 teaspoon nutmeg
Salt, to taste

Place cleaned livers in a saucepan. Cover with salted water and bring to a boil. Reduce heat and simmer for 15 minutes. Drain livers and cool. Remove any connective tissue, if present. Place livers in food processor and pulse to mash. Add melted chicken fat and onions. Blend. Remove from food processor and add diced, hard-cooked eggs. Season with pepper, nutmeg and salt to taste.

Yield: 2 cups

Gazpacho, Mercado de Triana, Seville

Every region has its own distinct cuisine and specialties. Gazpacho comes from Andalucía in southern Spain. Traditionally, a special bowl called a dornillo was used to pound the ingredients by hand, but modern Spanish cooks use a blender. The ingredients in gazpacho will vary from one region to another depending on the vegetables in that area.

6 large fresh tomatoes or 1 can (28 ounces) whole
   tomatoes with liquid
1 medium green pepper, cut into pieces
1 white onion, peeled and cut into pieces
1 large seedless cucumber, peeled and cut into
   pieces
1/4 cup red wine vinegar
1/4 teaspoon dried tarragon
2 teaspoons sugar
3 cloves garlic, peeled and chopped
1/8 teaspoon red pepper flakes
1 slice dry bread, crust removed
1/2 cup ice water
Garnish of avocado, cucumber and croutons

In a large bowl, combine all ingredients except bread and ice water. Soak the bread in a small amount of water (2 tablespoons) for 10 minutes. Gently remove and squeeze extra water out of bread. Add to ingredients in bowl. In batches, place mixture in blender and puree until smooth. Cover the bowl of pureed vegetables and refrigerate for several hours or overnight to blend flavor. Just before serving, add ice water and stir. Serve cold with garnish of diced cucumber, diced avocado and croutons.

Yield: 6 to 8 servings

Spanish Rice, Mercado de Triana, Seville

The Spanish rice used for paella and other rice recipes is a round, medium-short grain. This variety of rice absorbs the flavors of the ingredients that are cooked with it. The Bomba variety of rice is cultivated in the southeast region of Albacete and is prized for cooking in dishes with more liquid (caldosa) because it does not open up or "flower" and become mushy. Rice is a staple in the Spanish diet.

1 tablespoon olive oil
1/4 cup chopped green pepper
1 tablespoon finely chopped jalapeño pepper
1/2 cup chopped onion
1 teaspoon salt
1/8 teaspoon black pepper
2 cups water
1 cup uncooked short-grain rice
1 can (15 ounces) diced tomatoes, undrained

Heat oil in skillet. Add peppers and onion and cook for 3 minutes until vegetables become soft. Add salt and pepper. Place water in saucepan. Add rice, peppers, onions and tomatoes. Stir mixture. Cover and simmer for 30 to 45 minutes until the liquid is absorbed and the rice is tender.

Yield: 6 servings

Bonito del Norte, Mercado de Triana, Seville

The fishmongers in the Mercado de Triana Market in Seville sold many varieties of fish and crustaceans. Although Seville is not on the coast of Spain, the fish arrive fresh daily from the waters surrounding Spain. Tuna is sold as steaks and in large pieces for baking. The tuna canned in Spain is the very best quality.

1 small can tuna in oil, drained
1/2 large roasted red bell pepper, sliced into strips
1/4 cup sliced thin green onions
1 teaspoon capers, drained
1/2 teaspoon lemon zest
1 tablespoon lemon juice
1 tablespoon chopped cilantro
1/4 cup aioli mayonnaise
1/4 teaspoon sea salt
1/8 teaspoon coarse ground black pepper

Place tuna in medium mixing bowl and flake with a fork. Add pepper, onions, capers, lemon zest, lemon juice and cilantro. Mix gently. Add mayonnaise, salt and pepper to taste. Place in a round mold. Cover and refrigerate for 1 hour or more before serving. Unmold the tuna onto a lettuce-lined serving plate.

Yield: 1-1/2 cups

Paella a la Valenciana, Mercado Central, Valencia

Paella is a national dish of Spain and is said to have originated in Valencia. Valencia sits next to the Mediterranean Sea and is a fishing port. After the fisherman had sold their catch, the remaining fish and seafood were brought home for the main meal of the day. The creative housewife would use the daily staple rice, the leftover seafood, saffron and other ingredients that happened to be in the pantry to make paella. It was cooked in a large, round flat pan, often over an open wood fire.

1/2 teaspoon saffron threads
6 cups chicken broth, divided
1/2 teaspoon smoked Spanish paprika
4 tablespoons olive oil, divided
2 boneless chicken breasts, cut into 6 pieces
2 chicken legs, deboned and cut into 4 pieces.
1/4 pound chorizo (Spanish sausage), cut into 1/2
  inch pieces
1/4 pound jamon serrano ham, cubed
2 medium onions, chopped
8 cloves garlic, chopped
2 roasted red peppers, peeled, cut into strips
1 green bell pepper, chopped
1/2 teaspoon dried thyme
1/2 teaspoon dried basil
1/4 teaspoon ground cumin
1 bay leaf
3 cups short grain rice (such as Spanish Calasparra)
1/2 cup dry white wine
1 teaspoon salt
1/4 teaspoon pepper
3 Roma tomatoes, sliced
1 cup fresh or frozen peas
1 pound jumbo raw shrimp, peeled and deveined
6 king crab claws (optional)
12 clams or mussels, cleaned
Lemon wedges and parsley for garnish

Place saffron threads in 1 cup chicken broth. Set aside. Heat 2 tablespoons oil in paella pan or heavy skillet. Brown the chicken meat in hot pan for 7 to 8 minutes until golden. Remove from pan and set aside. Add 1 tablespoon oil to pan and cook chorizo until browned. Remove from pan. Add ham to pan and cook for 5 minutes; remove from pan. Add 2 tablespoons oil to pan and heat to hot. Cook onions, garlic, peppers, and spices for 4 minutes until tender. Move to edge of pan. Add rice and sauté for 3 or 4 minutes in the hot pan. Heat chicken broth to very hot. Add chicken broth and wine to pan with the rice. Add saffron broth. Return chicken, chorizo, ham, and salt and pepper to pan with cooked vegetables. Cook for 10 minutes. Add tomatoes, peas, shrimp, crab and clams or mussels to rice mixture. Cook for 15 to 20 minutes until shrimp are pink and clam shells are open. Discard any shells that are not open. Garnish with parsley and lemon wedges.

Yield: 8 servings

Markets in Italy

Many of the villages and hamlets in Italy grew up around the castle and shortly thereafter the marketplace appeared. The day for the market was established by the lord of the castle and on that day the farmers would rise before dawn and load their horse or donkey-drawn carts with the wares they planned to sell at the market. The Mediterranean Sea and the Adriatic Sea for centuries has provided all types of seafood and fish to the market. The climate from the north to the tip of the boot makes it possible to produce a large range of grains, vegetables and fruits for sale at the marketplace. Grapes and other fruits have been a continuous crop since before the time of the Romans.

The piazza and the forum in the towns and villages were gathering places where the people came to hear the news, to socialize and to shop from the farmers' carts. By the third century B.C., the open-air Marcellum Market located at the north end of the Fori Romani in Rome was busy supplying food to the neighborhood.

The first known indoor market was built at the time of Emperor Augustus by the military hero Agrippa in the flat land between the Capitoline and Palantine hills of Rome. The large structure held not only vegetables, fruit, meat, fish, and cheese markets but also shops for leather goods, armament, weapons and even offices. In the second century A.D., Emperor Trajan restructured the building to accommodate more commercial businesses. It was called Mercati di Traiano and can be seen today in the excavations and museums.

By the seventeenth and early eighteenth century, Rome's government provided places and scheduled times for the market to function. For the past three centuries, the market has been a stable enmity in the towns throughout Italy. The city or regional governments are the managers and regulators of the markets.

During the past thirty years, there has been a significant growth of supermarkets and mega-supermarkets throughout Italy. Fast food and convenience foods have expanded with the increase in the youthful population, and this has hurt the sales at the fresh food farmers' markets. Some markets in Rome have closed.

The organic food movement started in Italy in the middle of the 1980s at about the same time as other European countries became involved. The farms in Italy are small, only a few hectares, and work well for organic crop and animal production. Italian organic standards were published by the government in 1986; however, it wasn't until 1993 when the European Union regulations were adopted that the market of organic products exploded. Cereal, vegetables, fruits, olives, olive oil, wine, cheese, dairy products and grapes are the major organic products found at the farmers' markets and in the organic section of the supermarkets.

Today, there are many small organic markets located in towns and villages where the local farmers will bring their certified organic products for sale. In the larger cities, the supermarkets are selling organic products in competition with the farmers' markets. This has had a negative effect on the price farmers can ask for their products and has caused some of them to give up the market sales.

Campo di Fiori Market | Rome, Italy

Campo di Fiori, the Field of Flowers, was the name given to the meadow during the Middle Ages and is now where the Campo di Fiori Market is located. It wasn't until the fifteenth century when the first church was built by Pope Boniface that the area became populated.

The piazza became the center for trade and business. The streets fanning out from the square like a spider web took on the names of the trades: Via dei Balestrari (crossbow maker), Via di Baullari (coffee maker), Via di Cappellari (hatmaker), Via di Chiavari (key maker) and Via di Guibbonari (tailor). The area expanded and became the major corridor between the Basilica di San Giovanni in Laterano and the Vatican. The business and trade in the piazza flourished.

The active market sold vegetables and grain from the nearby farms. The farmers brought live animals, cattle, pigs and chickens to the market where many were slaughtered on the spot when purchased. Every Monday and Saturday, a horse market was held in the piazza.

Ever since 1869, there has been a vegetable, fruit and fish market open to the public every morning except Sunday. Today, the open-air Market has white tent canopy stalls for fruits, vegetables, cheese, flowers, jewelry, scarves and leather goods, as well as stalls mainly for souvenirs the tourists buy. The meat and bakery merchants have moved into permanent shops around the square facing the outdoor market. In the early afternoon, the vendors will pack their remaining products, fold their tents and

leave the piazza. The area comes alive again, with residents and tourists coming to the square to enjoy the restaurants, bars, street music or to just "hang out" on the piazza.

I like to arrive at the Market early when the stands are just opening. The products are fresh, and the displays neatly arranged. At the Campo di Fiori Market, the vegetable and fruit stands were the most outstanding and beautiful of those I saw in Italy. One stand displaying boxes and boxes of tomatoes—red, orange, yellow and large round red balls, the oval red, the elongated red tomatoes streaked with green veins, the tiny, yellow pear-shaped, the grape-sized red and the larger cherry tomatoes—was a sight for sore eyes. The large orange tomatoes looked as bright as the sun.

I found a fairly large stand selling all types of greens. The elderly, sad-looking lady in a long green sweater selling the greens told me her son raises and picks all the salad greens on or near his farm, and she sells them at the Market. The farm has been in the family for many generations, but they had not been coming to the Market until the past several years. She told me the names of the greens in Italian, but she did not know the English names for the wild grass. I asked if she sold sprouts, and she did not know what I was talking about.

Every vegetable stall had peppers, artichokes, onions, eggplant and cabbage for sale.

The selection of fresh fruit was extensive. Some fruits were grown in Italy, but some were imported, and the Italian vendor bought those products from a large wholesale produce house. Pears, bananas, grapes, plums, apples, apricots, peaches, oranges, lemons and pineapple were available.

It was early summer when I visited the Market. At this time of year, berries were plentiful, and the stands showed every kind imaginable. Walking up to the stand was like walking into an art gallery when I saw the colorful, artistically arranged strawberries, blueberries, both red and yellow raspberries, blackberries and currants. The handsome young Italian man with black hair and sparkling dark eyes selling the berries had the most enchanting smile. I asked if the berries were organic and he said, "They are all made by nature." I could have stayed at this booth all day. Not only was the beautiful young

vendor a delight to be near, but the aroma from the berries was as fragrant as roses.

The bakeries in the shops around the piazza also had this great aroma of fresh baked bread. The bakery had an impressive display of loaves in different shapes and sizes.

The meat shops were selling fresh beef, pork and lamb in steaks, chops and roasts. Some of the meat was ground. The hard Italian sausage is popular at all the markets. The butcher shops around the piazza had salami hanging over the counters and spread on the shelves. Cheese was also for sale in the glass-enclosed cases of the shops. The assortment was quite extensive.

The shoppers at the Campo di Fiori Market were well-dressed, middle-aged ladies and some young couples. They were not in a hurry and would stop to visit with other shoppers. The merchants were also friendly and conversed with the women about the products they were selling. It was a very relaxed and comfortable environment.

Rialto Market | Venice, Italy

Venice is my second favorite city in Europe, and I think a major part of my love for Venice is the Rialto Market. It is a very old Market that has been serving the residents of Venice since 1097.

Venice always traded with the Byzantine Empire and the Muslin world extensively. By the late thirteenth century, Venice was the most prosperous city in all of Europe. After the discovery of the New World by Columbus, and after Vasco de Gama found a sea route to India, Venice lost its top position in world trade. This was especially true in its wide European market for spices. Portugal became Europe's principal intermediary in trade with the East, stirring the very foundation of Venice's great wealth. However, the Venetian empire was still a major exporter of agriculture products. Venice retained its powers of trade until the late fifteenth century, weakened by a thirty-year war with the Turks and the loss of many of its eastern Mediterranean possessions.

During the eighteenth century, the Rialto Market flourished with specialties from all over the world: chocolate, tomatoes, potatoes and corn from the New World, rugs and tapestries from Persia, seafood and fish from the Aegean Sea, the Adriatic Sea and the Mediterranean Sea, citrus fruits from the Greek Islands, dates and figs from Africa, and tea from China.

Because farmers' markets are known to open early in the morning, I was awake and dressed by 6 a.m. I left the hotel and walked the narrow, winding streets in the pale light before dawn. As I got closer to the Rialto Market, I became engulfed in a thick gray fog. It became denser as I reached the arched old historic Rialto Bridge. The lights on the bridge gave off a faint halo of light in the mist, causing an eerie illumination. I stopped in the middle of the bridge and peered off into the black water of the Grand Canal.

In the water on the Market side of the canal was a large gondola, a water bus, barely visible in the pearly gray fog. Two ghosts were unloading the boxes and wooden crates onto the pier. I realized then that the waterway must be the method of delivering products to the Market. The Market was not open. I chose to return to the hotel and come back later.

At 10 a.m., when I returned to the Rialto Market, it was a bright, gloriously sunny day. The Market is located in the heart of Venice, not far from St. Mark's Square. The Tribunal of Venice, or courthouse, is just beyond the Market. I imagine this is where Shakespeare's Shylock in *The Merchant of Venice* had his trial.

The Rialto Bridge was no longer quiet and abandoned but was crowded with small ,individual entrepreneurs selling mostly souvenirs to tourists from their kiosks.

The fruit and vegetable stands (the Erberia) were crowded with shoppers, mostly middle-aged women dressed in slacks and jackets or pant suits. Some of them were pushing shopping carts and others carried woven baskets to carry their purchases. It was difficult to tell the local shoppers from the tourists except the tourists carried plastic bags and cameras or just wandered around looking and touching the fruits and vegetables.

The Market touches one's senses. The different aromas of the citrus orange, lemons and limes were pungent and made me think of orange blossoms. The fragrance of basil or oregano or rosemary or fresh thyme awakens the taste buds. The touch of a sun-warmed peach or the crisp feel of fresh asparagus makes one fully aware of the Market. The colorful displays of fruits and vegetables are much like a painting. And the loud noise of the emptying of boxes, crates, barrels, the shouting of the vendors promoting their products, the haggling of the shoppers with the merchants, the sing-song chant from the seller of nuts and dried fruits and the chatter of visitors all enliven the soul and body.

Many of the fresh vegetables that arrive at the Market at dawn are raised on the nearby island of Sant'Erasmo so they have only a short distance to travel, leaving a small carbon footprint.

The large, musty green artichokes tinged with purple were displayed on the table tops and in crates placed on the cement floor in front of the stands. Some small white eggplants, with green and velvet purple ends, were at the back of a vegetable stand. I was impressed with the pure marble white, baseball-sized, round fennel bulbs. They were so clean that I forgot that they actually grow in dirt.

Another perfect picture was the arrangement of piles of red, green, yellow, orange and purple bell peppers. The peperoncini peppers have a sweet flavor that can range from mild to medium hot and are a favorite in Italy. Next to the peppers were mounds of garlic with long green and brown stems. The busy saleslady took time to tell me that I was to use the whole garlic, stems and all. Another stand had

wonderful lush, fern-like wild greens and large-leaf kale with blood red veins, mustard greens and tender pale green to dark green romaine lettuce. I also found wild asparagus at this stand. This is a *green* stand in color and function. The selection

of vegetables was endless: zucchini with the blossoms still intact, savory cabbage, green cabbage, red cabbage in various sizes, an endless display of red ripe tomatoes just off the vine, your choice of flat beans, green, yellow, fava, white cannellini and black beans. Portobello, straw, oyster, and shiitake mushrooms were arranged in clusters on the counters.

The vegetable stands are only outdone by the fruit stalls. As I walked past them, I was again aware of the wonderful perfume of fruit. The stone fruit—soft, tiny, fuzzy blushing peaches, rose-touched apricots, burgundy and royal purple plums, and butterscotch-yellow pears—smell sweet. The pale tan cantaloupe had a completely different aroma. I watched as the shoppers pointed to the fruit they wanted to buy and the vendor cheerfully placed it in a bag. The shopper does not touch or squeeze the fruit. The aroma of the raspberries and strawberries added to the fragrance.

Cheese is my dietary weakness, and I would not think a market complete until

I found the cheese house. At the Rialto Market, there were several cheese shops, all with a wonderful array of cheeses from all over Italy. I found cheese from ewe's, cow's and sheep's milk, fresh and aged. There was Fontini, the oldest cheese in Italy, Gorgonzola, a type of blue cheese, mascarpone, a soft creamy cheese from the Lombardy region of northern Italy with a white to straw yellow color and a mild taste, mozzarella from southern Italy that was formerly made with the milk of water buffalo but is now most often made with cow's milk. Parmigiano-Reggiano, the king of cheeses, has a hard yellow rind and comes in a large wheel. Pecorino is made of sheep's milk, and the different regions of Italy have different names for it. The provolone is an all-purpose curd cheese. Romano is one of the oldest cheeses in Italy and originally came from the Rome area. Ricotta cheese is a creamy cow's milk cheese. Several of the stalls were giving small slivers of different cheeses to taste, and I was delighted to sample each.

A short distance beyond the fresh produce Market near the Grand Canal is the pescheria, a fish market, housed in a large red brick pavilion. Although the fish

market has been in existence on this piece of land for centuries, this edifice was built in 1907 by Domenico Rupolo and Cesare Laurenti in a Gothic style. One walks through grand arches and past columns to enter the spacious open area where fishmongers are hawking their wares. Each claims theirs is "Best of the Catch." The fluorescent light and the light bulbs hanging from cords in the ceiling augment the outdoor light from the high windows. The smell of seaweed and fish is prevalent but is not objectionable. It is just part of the atmosphere of the fish market. The cement and tile floor were wet, and there seemed to be water running behind some of the stalls that was used to spray onto the fish and to wash the counters.

My first encounter at the fish market was shocking. I saw a large fisherman who looked as if he had just gotten off his boat, wearing a gray sweatshirt with sleeves rolled up, covered with a black, water-resistant apron, holding a long black eel by the neck just under the eel's head. With one well-directed cut, using a long blade knife, he slit the eel from head to tail. He gutted the creature and tossed the innards into a large plastic bucket where guts and blood were collected. He washed the cavity of the eel with water from a garden hose and then wrapped it in a wax-coated brown paper and handed the package to a neatly dressed man. I was fascinated and repulsed by this fast, efficient transaction.

The fish throughout the Market looked fresh as if it had just been caught, and the people selling the fish looked like real fishermen. The immense selection of fish included sea bass, mullet, monkfish, silver

sardines, small anchovies, snow white sole, ugly skate fish, cuttlefish, both small and large, and salt cod. Some stands sold only crustaceans such as white and pink and striped shrimp, lobster still crawling in their tanks and several types of crabs. Other merchants were selling piles of bivalves, oysters, clams, mussels and pink-

shelled scallops. Squid was available, and some places even had the bags or jars of the coal black squid ink for sale. Octopus varying in size were on crushed ice. They looked to be alive.

In Italy, one would expect to find a pasta shop in the Market. I stopped at a pasta shop just beyond the produce stands. Most of the pasta was packaged in cellophane containers. The long shelves were stacked with rows of these packages. I also saw red, green and yellow-colored pasta.

The butcher shops (macelleria) were well-stocked with all types of meats. I found shop after shop with sausages, with long strings of sausages of every size and color often draped over the railings of the stall. The wonderful prosciutto ham was being

demonstrated and served by a man in a dark gray-green business suit. Other stands had dark brown, leather-skin hams hanging above the counters. The best prosciutto comes from Italy. There were whole carcasses of sheep and some smaller animal carcasses that I found to be rabbit. The butcher had left a fluff of fur on the back legs of the rabbit as proof that it was really a rabbit instead of a cat. Apparently some butchers had been charged with selling the feline meat as rabbit. There was one stand selling poultry: chicken, yellow skin duck, pheasant, partridge, whole turkeys and small Cornish hens.

At one time, Venice was the spice market for all of Europe. For the past sixty years, the Mascari family has been supplying the Venetians with exotic spices and herbs from all around the globe. They opened the Drogheria Mascari food and spice store (speziali) in 1948 near the Rialto Market on the street Ruga dei Speziali, named for the shop. My nose gave me the first indications that I was in a spice shop with the aroma of cinnamon, basil, allspice and so many others. This oldest department store in Venice sells wild oregano, long slender cinnamon sticks, nutmegs as large as eggs, brown dried cloves and allspice berries, as well as coffees from countries all around the globe, fifty kinds of honey, thirty-year-old balsamic vinegar, candy, white truffles, large black truffles, truffle paste and a wide assortment of teas from the Far East. I could have spent all day in this fascinating store.

The Rialto Market also had prepared food available. The ready-to-bake pizza was enclosed in glass cases. The variety included Napoli, mushroom, sausage, Hawaiian, prosciutto and stagioni.

San Lorenzo Market | Orvieto, Italy

The vendors had trailers or vans built for use as stalls. The sides of the vehicles were open to the public.

The large meat stall featured boar meat. It even had the full head of a large boar with black bristly hair and ivory tusks protruding from the snout. The dark red, fresh boar meat was available in many different

It is not easy to get to the ancient town of Orvieto located on the top of very tall vertical cliffs. The old walled city of Etrurian times was deliberately built on the summit as a fortress of protection from any advancing enemy. For even more protection, a labyrinth of caves and tunnels was dug into the volcanic rock at the top of the hill leading to the flat land below affording a means of escape.

Orvieto can claim the first indoor marketplace in Italy. The Palazzo del Capitano del Popolo was a large, single-story structure built in the thirteenth century that was used as a marketplace and for meetings of the city leaders. The farmers from the surrounding land would load their horse-drawn carts or the donkeys with produce, bags of grain and animal hides to take to market up the narrow winding trail to the top of the mountain. The iron gate of the walled city would lift to allow the merchant-farmer to enter. On some market days, the farmers were allowed to bring live poultry and even drive cattle to the summit for sale and slaughter.

Sometimes when traveling, one gets an extra bonus, and this is what happened on my morning in Orvieto. Walking to the piazza and in front of the great Cathedral, I saw several people with bags of produce and wrapped bouquets of flowers. It was Saturday morning, Market Day.

I followed the path of the shoppers leaving the Marketplace. Before I reached Mercato San Lorenzo, I could smell the fragrant aroma of the flowers long before they were in view. The stalls loaded with baskets, buckets and tubs of blossoms stretched for a hundred feet along the side of a large old stone building. It was Easter time, and lilies were queen of the Market. The pearl white, trumpet-shaped blossoms of the calla lilies were at least six inches long. Oriental lilies, with pure white, star-shaped blossoms and long stems, filled numerous buckets. More candy-striped pink, straw yellow and golden lilies were on display at every stall. There were multicolored roses, carnations and gladiolas beneath towering white columns. It must be the volcanic soil that accounts for the large flowers and sturdy stems of the plants.

cuts. Sausages made with boar meat were draped across the length of the stand. Fresh meat was for sale at two other trailers. The roasts and steaks were in trays in a metal rack. I was surprised that it was not refrigerated. The third vendor had the skinned carcass of lambs, both whole and split. Another trailer-stall had a large variety of salami, sausages and cheeses hanging from hooks. The glass counter under the meat held wheels of various Italian cheeses.

The cheese vendor had his shop in a trailer on wheels, much like the ice cream

or cotton candy stands we see at a fair or an amusement park. Pecorino cheese was the most popular, according to Tony, the salesman, who had dark brown hair and bright, dancing brown eyes. Some of the wheels of cheese were very large, so Tony would slice off a chunk of the desired size for the waiting customer. This would be put into a plastic zip bag or wrapped in heavy white paper.

The bright colorful produce stands all had spring-fresh asparagus as well as a variety of fresh new lettuce greens. The ruby red, pointed and tapered heads of radicchio were in a box next to other greens.

Zucchini, with its delicate yellow blossoms, was in season and arranged in boxes waiting to be taken home and gently sautéed. Artichokes of various sizes were also available at every stand. Black knobby truffles, a special treat, were limited in quantity but still available. Red, yellow, purple and green peppers were next to eggplant at the produce stand. A nice selection of apples, oranges, lemons, grapes, peaches, apricots and pears was in a long open stand, not in a trailer.

The young-looking man in a bright sweater selling fish told me he had been a fisherman for fifteen years. When I told him he did not look old enough to have that record of fishing, he said, "All my family has been fishermen so I had to start young." He also told me that he fished almost every day and that he did not have to go far out in the sea to catch all the fish he needed for the Market. He had two kinds of shrimp with heads and shells at his stand. I watched as he sliced or filleted the fish for each shopper's desires.

The San Lorenzo Market was an "all-around"- shopping experience with clothes, shoes, house wares, electrical supplies, candles, T-shirts and souvenirs for sale.

Recipes | Italian Markets

Basil Pesto, Campo di Fiori Market, Rome

Fresh basil is added to many dishes in Italian recipes and is not only available in large, dark green fragment bunches at the markets but also is raised in pots on balconies throughout the villages and towns in Italy. During the spring and summer, the markets will sell purple basil, lemon basil and even chocolate basil. The small-leafed Genoese variety of basil is a favorite for pesto for its delicate perfume and flavor. Pesto can be frozen without the cheese. The cheese can be added after the pesto is defrosted.

3 cups packed fresh basil leaves
3 large cloves garlic, minced
1/2 cup extra virgin olive oil
1/4 cup pine nuts
1/4 teaspoon kosher salt
1/8 teaspoon ground nutmeg
1/2 cup grated Pecorino or Parmesan cheese

Place the basil leaves and garlic in a food processer. Process until smooth. Gradually add the oil with the blades running. Remove basil from processor and place in a bowl. Add pine nuts, salt and nutmeg. Heat mixture and add the cheese. Stir to blend. Top cooked pasta with pesto. Serve immediately.

Yield: 2 cups

Biscotti with Cherries, Campo di Fiori, Rome

It is believed the cookie biscotti originated at the time of Columbus, created by an Italian baker who served them with Tuscan wines. They became very popular and were ideal for sailors, soldiers and fishermen because of their long keeping qualities. Each province developed its own biscotti recipe that might include fruit, nuts, seeds, spices and different flavorings. Anise became a favorite ingredient. Chocolate coating of the biscotti is also desirable.

2-1/2 cups all-purpose flour
1-1/2 teaspoons baking powder
1/2 teaspoon baking soda
1/4 teaspoon salt
1/2 teaspoon lemon zest
2 eggs
3/4 cup sugar
2 tablespoons oil
1/2 teaspoon vanilla
1/2 cup dried cherries, cut into pieces

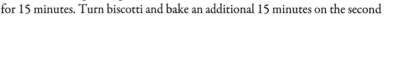

Preheat oven to 350 degrees.

In a large mixing bowl, combine flour, baking powder, baking soda, salt and lemon zest. In separate bowl, whisk eggs, sugar, oil, and vanilla together. Add dry ingredients and mix only to combine. Add cherries. Shape dough into log (approximately) 12 inches by 3 inches. Place on parchment-lined baking sheet. Bake at 350 degrees for 30 minutes until golden. Remove from oven and cool for 5 minutes. Reduce oven temperature to 300 degrees. Slice biscotti at an angle using a serrated knife to make slices about 3/4-inch wide. Place cut slices on baking sheet and bake at 300 degrees for 15 minutes. Turn biscotti and bake an additional 15 minutes on the second side. Cool on rack.

Yield: 26 biscotti

Tiramisu, Campo di Fiori Market, Rome

Tiramisu is a wonderful, creamy, delicious dessert that is said to have been created by a pastry chef called Loly Linguanotto of the restaurant Alle Beccherie in the 1960s in the town of Treviso in northern Italy. Other stories as to the creation of this dessert are abundant. The word means "pick me up" and with the addition of espresso coffee and a bit of liquor, it well may be a "picker upper." The kind of liquor used in the recipe may be a marsala wine, rum, brandy or Kahlua. Some recipes use the whipped egg whites in place of the whipped cream. However, for sanitary purposes, the egg whites should be pasteurized. I prefer the cream. One of the unique parts of the dessert is the use of ladyfingers as the structure for the dish.

6 egg yolks
1 cup superfine sugar
1/2 cup brandy
1 pound mascarpone cheese
1 cup heavy whipping cream
1/2 cup cold espresso coffee
1/2 cup crème de cocoa or Kahlua
1 pound ladyfingers (30 ladyfingers)
1/4 cup cocoa powder
1 ounce semisweet chocolate bar

In a mixing bowl, whisk the egg yolks with the sugar and brandy until creamy. Place in double boiler and cook for 10 minutes, stirring to prevent burning. Cook until creamy and thickened. Remove from heat and cool for 30 minutes. Add mascarpone cheese and beat to blend. Whip cream until stiff peaks form gently fold into egg mixture.

Combine the coffee and crème de cocoa in a flat bowl. Dip each ladyfinger quickly into the coffee mixture and place around the side of a glass bowl. Place one layer of dipped ladyfingers on bottom of dish. Spread a layer of egg and cream mixture over ladyfingers. Sprinkle with cocoa powder. Dip a second layer of ladyfingers into coffee mixture. Place ladyfingers over egg mixture. Add a second layer of egg mixture and sprinkle with cocoa powder. Repeat procedure using the remaining ladyfingers. Place in refrigerator for 8 hours. Remove from refrigerator and top with shaved chocolate.

Yield: 6 to 8 servings

Stuffed Artichokes and Tomatoes, Campo di Fiori Market, Rome

Artichokes are at every market in Italy. They are raised commercially and grow wild along the roadside. The name is derived from the northern Italian words *articiocco* and *articoclos* and has been part of the Roman diet from the time of Christ. During the sixteenth century, women were forbidden to eat the artichoke because it was deemed to be an aphrodisiac and improved the sexual power of men. Fortunately, we all can enjoy the tasty plant today.

8 precooked artichoke hearts
4 plum tomatoes, halved
1/3 cup olive oil
1/2 cup bread crumbs
1/3 cup shredded Parmesan cheese
1/3 cup shredded mozzarella cheese
4 garlic cloves, minced
1/4 cup chopped parsley
2 tablespoons minced fresh basil
1/4 teaspoon sea salt
1/8 teaspoon ground black pepper

Preheat oven to 375 degrees.

Pour 3 tablespoons olive oil into baking dish. Place artichokes hearts and tomato halves, cut side up, in baking dish. Drizzle the remaining olive oil over artichokes and tomatoes. In a medium-sized mixing bowl, combine bread crumbs, Parmesan cheese, mozzarella, garlic, parsley, basil, salt and pepper. Mix to blend. Cover vegetables with the bread crumb mixture. Bake for 25 minutes until top is golden.

Yield: 4 servings

Pasta with Seafood, Rialto Market, Venice

Pasta is believed to have originated in China and arrived in Italy from Sicily around the twelfth century. Over time, this noodle type dough, made of semolina wheat flour and water, became the staple of the Italian diet. Pasta is categorized in two basic forms: dried and fresh. Dried pasta is made without eggs and can be stored for long periods of time. There are many different shapes and sizes of pasta from the tiny penne to the large lasagna sheets. In the markets in Italy, I saw the large displays of a variety of pasta, including the colorful spaghetti and fettuccini.

1/2 pound large raw shrimp
1/2 pound large scallops
8 ounces dried tagliatelle or similar pasta
2 cups snow peas, trimmed
3 tablespoons olive oil
4 garlic cloves, diced
1/2 cup chopped scallions
1 cup diced fresh or canned tomatoes
2 tablespoons tomato paste
1/8 teaspoon red pepper flakes
Salt and pepper, to taste
1 tablespoon dried basil
1/4 cup heavy cream
1 roll (6 ounces) soft goat's milk cheese
Salt and white pepper to taste.

Remove the shell and heads of shrimp and devein. Cut scallops in half horizontally. In a large saucepan, cook pasta according to package directions. One minute before pasta is done, add snow peas to the pasta. Drain and save 1/4 cup of the cooking water. Keep pasta and snow peas warm. In a large saucepan, heat oil to hot. Add garlic and scallions and cook for 2 minutes to soften. Add tomatoes, tomato paste, red pepper flakes, salt, pepper and basil. Add cream and cheese and reserved pasta liquid. Stir to melt the cheese, cooking about 2 minutes. Add shrimp and scallops to sauce and simmer for 2 to 4 minutes to cook seafood. Add the pasta and snow peas. Cook until heated. Toss pasta to blend flavors and coat the pasta with sauce.

Yield: 4 servings

Deep-Fried Zucchini, Rialto Market, Venice

Zucchini comes in all sizes, from the 3-foot-long zucchini that I saw in an Anchorage, Alaska, market to the 2-inch long zucchini I saw in the vegetable market in Italy. Christopher Columbus is credited with bringing the squash to Italy from the New World. The Italian chefs refined and created the cuisine for zucchini as we use it today. The plant is very versatile and can be used in baked goods, stir fries, desserts and as a vegetable serving. Deep-fried zucchini is a delightful appetizers served with a dip.

2 medium-sized zucchini, thinly sliced in rings
3/4 cup all-purpose flour
2 eggs, beaten
1/2 cup Italian bread crumbs
Oil for deep frying

Pour oil into deep saucepan to the depth of about 3 inches. Heat oil in saucepan to 375 degrees. Place the flour in a flat dish; place the beaten egg in another dish and the bread crumbs in another dish. Dip the sliced zucchini into first the flour, then into the beaten eggs and next into the bread crumbs. Place zucchini slices in the hot oil and cook for 2 to 3 minutes, turning once. Remove from oil and drain on paper towels. Do not crowd the cooking zucchini in the oil. Cook in batches to prevent crowding.

Yield: 4 servings

Osso Buco, Campo di Fiori Market, Rome

The traditional recipe for Osso Buco calls for lamb shanks. However, I have seen it made with veal. The dish is generally served with gremolata, a herb and lemon mixture. In Italy, the Osso Buco is often served with pasta or risotto.

1/4 pound pancetta, diced 1/4-inch pieces
2-1/2 to 3 pounds veal shanks
1/2 cup all-purpose flour, for dusting shanks
1 teaspoon salt
1/4 teaspoon black pepper
1 large carrot, diced
2 ribs celery, diced
1 small onion, diced
4 cloves garlic, minced
6 basil leaves, chopped
1 cup white wine
2 cups chicken broth

Preheat oven to 350 degrees.

In a heavy deep kettle, cook pancetta until crisp and fat is rendered. Remove pancetta from kettle. Retain 2 tablespoons fat in the kettle. Drench veal shanks in flour. Season with salt and pepper. Heat fat in kettle to medium hot. Add veal shanks. Cook meat on all sides, turning until brown, about 5 minutes per side. Remove meat to platter and keep warm. Add carrots, celery, onions, garlic and basil to kettle. Cook until vegetables are tender, 8 to 10 minutes. Return meat to kettle. Add wine and broth. Cover and place in 350 degree oven for 1-1/2 hours until meat is very tender.

Serve with gremolata on the side.

Yield: 6 servings

Gremolata

2 tablespoons Italian parsley, chopped
1 tablespoon lemon zest
2 cloves garlic, minced

Combine all ingredients and chill.

Creamy Polenta, Rialto Market, Venice

For centuries before Columbus brought corn or maize to Italy, the Italians were making a kind of polenta with grains such as barley, millet and buckwheat, as well as chickpeas or calamine beans. The corn kernels loved the rich Italian soil and mild climate in northern Italy. The crop was well-accepted and soon became a staple in the diet, replacing bread and pasta. The residents in northern Italy were referred to as *polentoni*, polenta-eaters. Polenta was made from coarsely ground cornmeal and, in early times, was cooked in payola, a large copper cauldron that hung in an open fireplace. Today, the cornmeal is cooked in boiling salted water or in a microwave. The recipe varies from simply cooked cornmeal to the addition of herbs, vegetables and cheeses.

2 cups water or chicken broth
1/2 teaspoon salt
1/2 cup medium-grain yellow polenta
2 tablespoons butter
1/2 package (4 ounces) cream cheese

In a saucepan, heat salted water to a boil over high heat. Whisk polenta into boiling water until smooth with no lumps. Reduce heat to a simmer. Add butter and cook for 20 minutes, stirring occasionally until thick and smooth. Whip cream cheese into polenta. Heat for 3 minutes.

Yield: 4 servings

Herb Goat Cheese with Mojo Verde, Campo di Fiori Market, Rome

Each of the different regions and cultures in Italy produce their own hand-made cheese. This results in hundreds of cheeses from cow, sheep and goat milk. Many of the cheeses at the farmers' markets are produced with a combination of two or three different milks. The following recipe calls for a soft goat cheese. The herbs are added to the cheese to make a delightful combination that can be served with many different foods.

1 package (8 ounces) soft goat cheese
2 ounces cream cheese, softened
1 tablespoon chopped fresh thyme
2 tablespoons chopped fresh cilantro
1 tablespoon minced fresh rosemary
10 stem chives, chopped
1 clove garlic, minced
1/4 teaspoon salt
1/8 teaspoon coarse ground black pepper

Place the goat cheese and the cream cheese in an electric mixing bowl with a dough hook. Add herbs to cheese in mixer. Add chives, garlic, salt and pepper and beat on medium to blend. Lay a sheet of plastic wrap on a flat surface. Scrap the cheese mixture onto the plastic to make a strip about 6 inches long and 1 inch diameter. Roll the plastic wrap around the cheese mixture to make a log. Refrigerate.

Mojo Verde

1/2 cup diced green bell pepper
2 tablespoons diced red onion
4 tablespoons chopped watercress
1 tablespoon jalapeño pepper, seeded and diced
1 tablespoon white wine vinegar
1 tablespoon extra virgin olive oil
1 tablespoon lime juice
1/4 teaspoon kosher salt
1/4 teaspoon coarse ground black pepper
1 head endive leaves

In a large bowl, combine all ingredients except the endive leaves. Toss lightly. To serve, slice the Herb Goat Cheese log into 1/2-inch thick sections. Place on endive leaf. Top with 1 tablespoon or more of the Mojo Verde mixture.

Yield: 12 servings

Rabbit Cacciatore, Rialto Market, Venice

Rabbit is on the menu in Italy and Europe more often than in the United States. Live rabbits in their cages and dressed rabbits were for sale at the meat shop. The live rabbits were not butchered at the market but carried home in a wire cage or under the arm of the buyer. The rabbits were large with long ears, more like the U.S. jackrabbits. While I was viewing the meat stall, a middle-aged, plump lady ordered a dressed rabbit and had the butcher cut it into serving-sized pieces to take home.

1/2 cup all-purpose flour
1 teaspoon salt
1/2 teaspoon black pepper
1 rabbit, cut into serving-sized pieces
2 tablespoons olive oil
1-1/2 large onions, chopped
1/4 cup chopped fresh parsley
1 green bell pepper, chopped
2 sprigs chopped fresh rosemary or 1 teaspoon dried rosemary
2 tablespoons chopped fresh thyme or 1 teaspoon dried thyme
8 cloves garlic, chopped
1 large tomato, peeled and chopped
2 tablespoons chopped fresh basil or 1 tablespoon dried basil
3/4 to 1 cup white wine
Water as needed

Combine flour, salt and pepper. Coat rabbit pieces with mixture. Heat oil in large skillet. Brown rabbit meat in hot oil. Add onions, parsley and bell pepper. Cook until soft. Add rosemary, thyme and garlic. Cook for 3 minutes, stirring occasionally. Transfer rabbit and cooked herbs and vegetables to large pot. Add tomatoes and basil to rabbit. Add wine. Place 1/2-inch of water into the skillet used for cooking the rabbit. Scrape the drippings and add to the rabbit pot. Add water to cover the rabbit and mixture in the pot. Cover and simmer on top of the stove for 1 hour until rabbit is tender. Serve with pasta.

Yield: 8 servings

Risotto with Fennel, San Lorenzo Market, Orvieto

Rice arrived in Italy hundreds of years ago with the traders from India. It is used in Italian cooking from one end of Italy to the other, with the predominance in the northern regions. Italy has four types of rice: the common rice with small kernels mainly used in soups; semi-fine, medium-grain rice; the long grain or fine rice that is recommended for risotto; and the superfine, longer and rounder grains. Each type has several different varieties.

2 tablespoons olive oil
1 medium bulb fennel, about 2 cups, chopped
1/2 cup chopped onion
1 cup uncooked Arborio rice
3 cups chicken broth
1/2 cup heavy cream
3/4 cup freshly grated Parmesan cheese
1 tablespoon chopped flat leaf parsley
Freshly ground black pepper and salt, as desired

Heat oil in large, heavy saucepan. Add fennel and onions and cook for 3 minutes. Add rice and cook until toasted, stirring constantly. Heat chicken broth in microwave. Add one cup broth to rice, stirring until liquid is absorbed. Repeat this process with the remaining broth, stirring constantly for approximately 20 minutes. Stir in the cream, half the Parmesan cheese and all of the parsley. Cook until thick and creamy. Season with black pepper and salt. Place into bowls and sprinkle remaining Parmesan on top of risotto.

Yield: 6 servings

Carbonara, Rialto Market, Venice

The many different shapes of pasta lend themselves to a variety of dishes. The pasta is almost always served with a sauce that can be a tomato base or simply olive oil and cheese. Pasta is used for soups, salads, entrees or "prima plate" and even in desserts. Many of the recipes are creations from adding "what was on hand or in the pantry." This is true of the recipe for Carbonara that can be simply made with bacon, cheese and herbs or have vegetables like peas, tomatoes, carrots, onions, green beans or others.

8 ounces pasta, such as tricolor rotini
3 tablespoons extra virgin olive oil
1/4 pound pancetta (Italian bacon), chopped
1 cup fresh or frozen peas
1/2 teaspoon red pepper flakes
1 tablespoon fresh oregano, chopped
1 tablespoon fresh basil, chopped
5 cloves garlic, minced
1/2 cup white wine
2 large egg yolks
Salt and pepper
Freshly shredded Romano cheese
1/4 cup fresh flat leaf parsley, chopped for garnish

In a large saucepan, place 2 quarts of water and 1 teaspoon salt. Add spaghetti and boil until al dente, about 8 minutes. Heat a large skillet over medium heat. Add olive oil and pancetta. Cook until slightly brown, about 2 minutes. Add peas, red pepper flakes, oregano, basil and garlic and cook for 2 minutes. Add wine and stir to loosen pan drippings. In a separate bowl, beat egg yolks. Whip in 1/2 cup of pasta cooking water to eggs. Drain pasta and add to the skillet with pancetta. Pour egg mixture over pasta and toss immediately to coat pasta without cooking the egg. Remove from heat. Place in serving bowl and add salt, pepper and shredded cheese to desired taste. Garnish with parsley

Yield: 4 servings

Linguine with Black Truffles, Rialto Market, Venice

Truffles are a rare and delicious wild mushroom. Two types of truffles are found in the woods of France and Italy, the black and the white truffles. This fungus is considered a delicacy often called "the diamond of the kitchen." The black truffle is as black as coal on the outside and the inside is tan to brown. It has a stronger flavor then the white truffle. When cooked, truffles release their flavor and aroma. A small amount of thinly sliced black truffles will flavor a bowl of pasta. The addition of truffle oil adds interest to this enjoyable dish.

8 ounces uncooked linguine pasta
1/2 cup truffle oil
1-1/2 cups grated Parmesan cheese, divided
1 teaspoon sea salt
1/4 teaspoon freshly ground black pepper
1/4 cup chopped fresh chives
1 tablespoon black truffles, shaved very thin

Cook pasta according to directions on the package. Drain and return to pan to keep warm. Add truffle oil, 1 cup cheese, salt, pepper and chives to pasta and toss to coat pasta. Place in serving bowl and add remaining 1/2 cup of cheese and, if desired, more truffle oil. Shave or thinly slice black truffle. Add half of shaved black truffles to pasta and toss. Garnish the top with remaining shaved black truffles.

Yield: 4 servings

Veal Scaloppini, San Lorenzo Market, Orvieto

Veal chops, roasts, cutlets, steaks were available at the meat shops in the markets. The price of the veal was about the same as the cost of the similar cuts of beef. The meat stall in the Orvieto Market was not busy, and the young, dark, handsome butcher was happy to talk with me. He spoke English, and that was a blessing because I did not speak Italian. I learned his name was Victor. He told me the veal was from a farm only a few miles away where the calves are raised and butchered when they are only a few weeks old. The meat was a light pink and beautifully displayed in the counter. Veal Scaloppini is often served with pasta.

1/4 cup all-purpose flour
1 teaspoon salt
1/4 teaspoon black pepper
6 veal cutlets, about 5 ounces each
2 tablespoons olive oil
3 medium-sized fresh tomatoes, chopped
1 cube or teaspoon beef bouillon
1/2 cup dry white wine
6 tablespoons butter
12 ounces fresh mushrooms, sliced
1/2 cup chopped white onion
1 green bell pepper, chopped
1 garlic clove, minced

In a flat dish, combine flour, salt and pepper. Coat meat with flour mixture. In a large skillet, heat oil to hot. Brown meat in hot oil for 5 to 6 minutes, turning once. Stir in tomatoes, beef bouillon and wine. Cover and simmer for 15 minutes. In a separate large skillet, melt butter. Cook mushrooms, onion, green pepper and garlic until tender. Add vegetables to meat and simmer uncovered for 8 to 10 minutes. Stir once to blend flavors.

Yield: 6 servings

White Bean Soup, San Lorenzo Market, Orvieto

The white cannellini beans are like kidney beans and are related to navy and great northern beans. They are mild in flavor. The cannellini beans are sold dried in every Italian market. It is a very popular bean in Italy, especially in Tuscany. Cannellini beans are the reason Tuscans are referred to as "bean eaters" or "mangiafagioli." The beans are used in soups, mainly minestrone, stews, salads and in pork dishes.

2 cups dried white beans
8 cups water
1 teaspoon salt
1-1/2 cups chopped celery; or 1 cup celery and 1/2 cup
    chopped fennel bulb
1 cup chopped onion
2 cloves garlic, minced
1/4 teaspoon white pepper
1/2 teaspoon smoked paprika
Parsley for a garnish

Cover beans with water and soak overnight. Drain beans. Place beans in a large, heavy saucepan. Add water and salt. Add celery, onion and garlic. Cover and simmer for 1-1/2 to 2 hours until beans are tender. Add pepper and paprika. Remove from heat and allow soup to cool slightly. Place soup in blender and puree in batches until all the soup has been blended and is smooth. Return to pot and heat. Serve hot with parsley garnish.

Yield: 8 servings

Eggplant Parmesan, San Lorenzo Market, Orvieto

Eggplants are found in all the markets in Italy. They vary in color, from dark purple to pale creamy white, and they come in all shapes, from the small, round tennis ball shape to the thin, elongated tube.

The classic dish, Eggplant Parmesan, is Italian. However, there is confusion as to what part of Italy is the originator of the dish. There are several theories about the origin. The most obvious is that the name of the dish derives from parmigiana cheese used in the dish and is produced in northern Italy in the city of Parma. However, eggplant made its first appearance in Sicily and in Italy in the southern regions, not the north. One of the first cookbooks by Vincenzo Corrado published in 1786, mentions that eggplant can be cooked "alla Parmegiana," and in 1837, Ippolito Cavalcanti published a cookbook in Naples that includes a recipe for a dish similar to Eggplant Parmesan.

1 large eggplant, about 1-1/2 pounds
1-1/2 tablespoons salt
1/2 cup all-purpose flour
1/2 cup fine bread crumbs
4 eggs, beaten
1/2 cup olive oil, divided
4 cups pasta sauce
3 cloves garlic, minced
1/2 cup chopped fresh basil
1 tablespoon chopped fresh oregano
1 teaspoon sugar
1/2 cup ricotta cheese
1 cup shredded Parmesan cheese, divided

Preheat oven to 350 degrees.

Peel and slice eggplant 1/2-inch thick slices. Place in colander and salt slices. Place a plate or weight on eggplant to drain for 2 hours. Remove eggplant and pat dry with paper towels. In a flat bowl, combine flour and bread crumbs. In a separate bowl, place beaten eggs. Heat half of the oil in a large skillet to hot. Dip eggplant slices into egg and then into flour mixture. Place in hot oil and cook for 3 minutes. Turn and cook the other side of eggplant until golden, about 5 minutes. Remove from skillet. Heat remaining oil and repeat the coating and frying of the remaining slices of eggplant. Place pasta sauce, garlic, basil, oregano and sugar in a saucepan and heat. Place one cup of sauce in bottom of 12x9-inch baking dish. Place one layer of eggplant on top of sauce. Cover with 2 cups sauce, ricotta cheese and 1/2 cup Parmesan cheese. Add remaining eggplant slices. Cover with remaining sauce and Parmesan cheese. Bake at 350 degrees for 40 minutes until golden on the top.

Yield: 8 servings

Arugula, Shiitake and Goat Cheese Salad, San Lorenzo Market, Orvieto

Arugula is a salad green with a bitter, mustard flavor and a peppery after-taste. It has been popular with Italians for years. The leaves are bright green and resemble the leaves of radishes. The combination of arugula, mushrooms and goat cheese is a taste sensation.

1/2 cup sesame seeds, toasted
1 tablespoon chopped fresh thyme
1 tablespoon coarse cracked black pepper
4 ounces goat cheese log, cut into 8 slices
2 shallots, minced
2 cups sliced shiitake mushrooms
1 cup diced ripe tomatoes (yellow and red)
3 tablespoons plus 1/4 cup vinaigrette
6 cups arugula (one large bunch)
8 slices sourdough bread
1 head garlic,
Salt and pepper to taste
Olive oil for cooking

On a plate, mix together sesame seeds, thyme and coarse black pepper. Dip cheese in seed mixture. Coat non-stick skillet with small amount of olive oil. Pan-sear the cheese until golden brown. Place a small amount of olive oil in a sauté pan. Sauté shallots and shiitakes until soft, about 3 minutes. Add tomatoes and deglaze with 3 tablespoons vinaigrette. Taste for seasoning. In a large bowl, toss the arugula with sautéed vegetables. Add 1/4 cup vinaigrette and toss to coat arugula. Slice the garlic head in half and gently rub the bread. Grill bread until light brown. Arrange greens on 4 serving plates. Top each salad plate with 2 slices of cheese. Serve with grilled bread.

Yield: 4 servings

Vinaigrette

2 tablespoons whole-grain prepared mustard
3 tablespoons red wine vinegar
1/2 cup extra virgin olive oil

In small bowl, whisk together mustard, vinegar and olive oil.

Caprizzi Salad, San Lorenzo Market, Orvieto

It may be the climate, or the soil or the variety or maybe the care given to the tomatoes that arrive at the San Lorenzo Market, Orvieto, that make them the best tasting in the world. They not only taste fantastic, but the colorful displays of red and yellow tomatoes of different shapes make a picture fit to hang in the art gallery. Caprizzi Salad affords the blend of tomatoes, fresh mozzarella and basil flavors. Balsamic vinegar adds a tang to the salad.

4 medium-sized fresh tomatoes; cut each tomato into 3 slices
8 lettuce leaves
8 slices fresh mozzarella cheese
8 leaves fresh basil, chopped
2 tablespoons extra virgin olive oil
2 tablespoons balsamic vinegar
1/2 teaspoon garlic salt

Layer tomatoes on lettuce leaf. Top each tomato slice with a slice of mozzarella cheese. Top with chopped basil. Repeat three times for each salad. Drizzle with olive oil and balsamic vinegar and sprinkle with garlic salt.

Yield: 4 salads

Markets in France

Farmers' markets in France are an integral part of the French love of food. Permanent markets appeared in France in the twelfth century when the king awarded local lords the privilege of setting up markets. Louis VI, known as "Le Gros," was the first to authorize markets in Paris. Small villages and towns held market days once a week and fairs *(foires)* several times a year where local farmers sold their products and tradesmen sold clothes, crafts and farm supplies.

The oldest market in Paris, and perhaps in all of France, was Les Halles. In 1137, Louis VI ordered the establishment of an open-air market near Les Halles. The downtown meat and vegetable market had become too small and congested. The excessive garbage fostered a huge population of rodents that overran the shops and the neighborhood. The new market was located outside the center of the city. Philippe-Auguste, King of France in 1183, is credited with building the permanent structure for the market. As the market grew, more buildings were added. Francis I, the ruler of France in the sixteenth century, recognized the need for remodeling and expanding the market to meet the needs of the fast-growing population of Paris.

The story of the Les Halles Market was described by Emile Zola in the novel *Le Ventre de Paris* (The Belly of Paris) written in 1873. It has been translated into English by Ernest Alfred Vizetelly. The story tells of the farmers arriving with their horse-drawn wagons before dawn. The large dray horses would bring their wagons into a line to enter into the lower levels of the tiered market that housed the butcher shop. The animals that the farmers brought to the market alive were slaughtered and cut into slabs. The blood and guts were washed away in the open sewer. The screeching of the chickens before slaughter could be heard throughout the market.

The farmers with fresh produce drove to an upper level where their stalls were located. The horses were placed in a corral to wait for the close of the market to return home. In the early days, the market was open only three days a week. In the early dawn, after the stalls were set up and the horses taken care of, the vendors would head to the local cafes for the traditional bowl of French Onion Soup.

In 1851, Napoleon III commissioned architect Victor Boltard to construct cast iron umbrellas and ten pavilions with cast iron frames and glass windows. These were built in Les Halles from 1854 to 1912. Napoleon declared, "I want to turn Les Halles into the Louvre of the people." In 1936, two more structures were added. Les Halles contributed to the transformation of Paris into a modern city by creating an organized, controlled location for the distribution of food and goods from the clusters of little stalls, standing cheek by jowl on narrow streets, to the modern iron and glass structures.

Over the next century, the Les Halles Market thrived and continued to grow. In fact, it was outgrowing its location. The city had surrounded the Market. The Market buildings were old and difficult to maintain. Traffic was horrendous. The daily collection of refuse and garbage became overwhelming. Sanitation became a concern of the Paris administration. In 1970, a decision was made to close this historical site and locate the Market outside of Paris at Rungis, near the airport.

Today, an estimated thirty-five thousand farmers' markets in France sell local products. In Paris, there are at least seventy permanent street markets and that many temporary ones. Some are only open for a few hours one day a week while others are in business for three or four days a week. Sunday morning is a good time to find the neighborhood street markets. The vendors will set up one or two tables to display their produce. The more prosperous vendors have stalls in a permanent structure. These markets tend to be open every day of the week except Sunday afternoon and Monday.

Marche Bastille | Paris, France

The Marche Bastille is a permanent Market that is situated on a wide boulevard stretching four long city blocks. The two hundred merchants have stalls along the sides of the walk facing toward the center of the boulevard. A double row of stalls are also located down the center of the boulevard between the outside stalls.

I arrived at the Market around 10 a.m. and found it very busy. All the shoppers, both men and women, were well-dressed. The ladies were wearing dresses or skirts and blouses. Most were middle-aged or older. There were only a few mothers with small children at the Market. The shoppers brought their own shopping bags and some had small carts with wheels to transport their purchases.

The food shops included fruit, vegetables, dried legumes, dried fruits, nuts, fish and shellfish, meats, cheese and breads. The

fruit and vegetable displays at almost every stall were beautifully arranged and a delight to view. They included two types of fresh peaches, pears, apricots, cherries, melons, watermelon, small and large cantaloupe, strawberries, raspberries, fresh figs, currants, papaya and mangos.

Each of the vegetable stalls had a large variety of vegetables. Few markets could compete with the selection available.

There were several types of cabbage, a variety of lettuce in bunches, bib lettuce, red-tipped leaf lettuce, white endive, arugula and many more. Also offered: carrots, cucumbers, radishes, zucchini, yellow summer squash, Hubbard squash, green and white asparagus, tomatoes of various sizes, color and variety, green string beans, wax beans, lava beans, bean sprouts, beets, both fresh and cooked, turnips, fresh green onions, leeks, large white and yellow dried onions, garlic, and fresh green almonds. I had not seen fresh green almonds before. At one stand, the bright red bell peppers and the green bell peppers were placed next to a box with small artichokes.

One merchant sold only mushrooms at his stall. His varieties included oyster, shiitake, button, portobello and porcini.

A variety I did not recognize had a large white cap with green gills.

The vendors of fish and seafood stalls had placed their products on crushed ice arranged according to the species. Several varieties of shrimp were arranged to show the different colors and size of shrimp. The squid, octopus and crab were next in line. The tuna fish were next to the shark, with flounder and salmon next to them. At the far end, the small sardines and anchovies were placed. Other types of fish were available at some stands. A few stalls had eel for sale, one had skinned eel and others had the live eel in

white plastic buckets. Live crab also were kept in buckets, and some of them were attempting to leave the bucket.

I found it interesting that the meat vendors did not always have the meat refrigerated. Here, too, almost every type of meat was sold at the Market. I saw displays of beef, pork, veal, goat and lamb on the counters and enclosed in refrigerated cases. However, only one stall had rabbit or hare available. I did not see offal displayed.

I met James (or Jacques), a friendly butcher who spoke some English and was willing to talk with me. All of the meat he was selling was in large cuts, such as a whole loin of pork or a leg of beef. They were on display on a metal-top table with no refrigeration or ice and no glass screen. I asked James if the meat should be refrigerated, and he said, "It's all right." When a customer requested a cut of meat, James would take the large section of meat to a wooden chopping block where he would cut the desired piece, weigh and wrap it for the shopper.

Poultry was in separate stalls. However, some of the meat vendors did have a limited amount of poultry. The chickens were cleaned, but the heads and feet were left on the bird. Whole ducks were available dressed, and one vendor had duck in sections or quartered. The tiny quail

were also for sale. Two of the stalls had turkey parts available, but I did not see the whole turkey. One vendor was selling the cooked chicken and squab pieces. He was doing a good business.

All the cheese counters had a least one section for refrigeration. The rounds of cheese were often in a glass-enclosed case.

It seemed to me the stalls along the center of the aisle had more of the dried foods. One stand was selling dried legumes, such as peas and beans of all colors and sizes. Another had dried fruits and some dried vegetables. A large variety of nuts from all around the world were also available at the Market.

An enterprising baker was not only selling bread but was baking the bread and rolls right in a small oven in his Market stall. The aroma of the baking bread was a great selling tool. The round, rather flat loaves were made with a variety of grains.

Marche Rue Cler | Paris, France

Marche Rue Cler is on a market street with shops along the boulevard and spilling out into the street. For years, the Marche Rue Cler was a small neighborhood Market. But as word of the great food shopping available spread, more and more customers arrived. Rick Stevens reported on Marche Rue Cler in his Paris Guidebook. This has brought many tourists to the Market. The Market is open Tuesday through Saturday from 10 a.m. to 6 p.m. and on Sunday. Sunday is a very busy day when shoppers come to the Market after Mass to browse, shop and eat foods from the stands along the street. There are not only fresh and raw foods to purchase, but a large number of restaurants, cafes, and coffee shops provide prepared foods. Lenotre is one of the leading patisserie and caterers located in the Market. It is known for excellent quality gourmet food and pastries. Paris has a large, multicultural population, and this is reflected in the restaurants along the street. One can dine on Japanese, African, Moroccan, Indian, Chinese or Arabic food at these local restaurants.

The fromagerie shops along Rue Cler carry four hundred different types of French cheese. There are large wheels, wedges, cylinders, balls and colors from dark burnt orange to creamy white. Each of the cheeses has a notation as

to the region where it was produced. Many of the aged cheeses also list the age of the cheese. The skin from the large, aged wheels is not edible. However, the rind of smaller cheeses, such as Brie and Camembert, are part of the taste. The cheese mongers are happy to discuss the best cheese for your menu and will even determine the right freshness for the day you wish to serve the cheese. The fromagerie shop also may have *frier beurre* and *oeuf* where the shoppers buy butter, eggs and cheese. I do enjoy the taste of cheese, all kinds of cheese. However, I was overwhelmed with the variety of cheeses in this Market. I would need to stay in Paris for a year to taste all of these cheeses.

I saw four butcheries in the neighborhood, so competition is strong for quality and price. Several butchers make their own sausages and are proud of the product. The whole carcass of sheep and goats

were hung on hooks over the work counter. The customers would tell the butcher the cut and quantity of meat they desired, and he would take the carcass down from the hook and fill the shoppers' order. During the Christmas and New Year's holidays, they sell pig's heads and other meat specialties. Shoppers are assured of finding the meat they wish to serve because if one butcher does not have it, another one will.

La Sablaise Poissonnerie is one of the largest and most well-stocked fish shops in all of Paris. The fish and seafood of all types arrive daily, and the fishmongers were happy to tell the shoppers when and where the fish or seafood was caught.

Davoli La Maison du Jambon is an Italian delicatessen and one of the best in Paris. The homemade specialties from sausages and meats to pasta, Italian cheese and great desserts cause long lines of shoppers to queue out into the street.

Several green groceries vie for the customer's attention. Produce is delivered fresh each day from local farmers and the large Rungis Wholesale Market. The variety of brightly colored fresh fruits and vegetables was extensive.

Mouffetard Market | Paris, France

The Mouffetard Market is located on the very old street established centuries ago as a road from Paris to Italy. Historians claim the Market was functioning as early as 1350. The painted wooden buildings along the street are three to four stories tall, with the small shops on the first level. The street is for pedestrian traffic except for delivery carts, vans and small trucks that arrive early in the morning before the Market opens. The Market opens at 8 o'clock every day except Monday.

I arrived around 9 o'clock in the morning and some of the stands were still being dressed for the day. Most of the fruit and vegetable stalls were set up out onto the street in front of the shop. The other permanent shops had their doors open wide to welcome customers.

My first Market experience was at the large fruit and vegetable stand wrapped around a corner. The selection of fresh strawberries and blueberries provided the area with a lovely aroma. The stone fruits were in season, and the peaches and apricots made a bright golden display. At this stand, the variety of vegetables

was limited. However, the tomatoes on their green stems were a bright flaming red color. The busy, middle-aged, strong-appearing vendor was lifting crates of asparagus onto the table. He spoke English and told me that both the green and the white asparagus were organic. He emptied the boxes out onto the counter so the customers would have a big mound of asparagus to choose from for their purchase. The green asparagus stalks were very thin, the size of a lead pencil, and very long, at least eight to ten inches in length.

At a stand across the street was an elderly man of small stature wearing a distinguished gray mustache and dressed in a

dark, well-worn sport coat. I asked if I could take his picture, and he said no, but that I could take pictures of his produce. On a side table, he had fresh herbs. There were large stems of rosemary, bunches of fragrant fresh mint and small clusters of thyme draped on the table. The bundles of basil and parsley ends were wrapped in white parchment paper. Some of the plant roots were still on the stems.

The meat counter of the butcher shop (butcheries) was inside a long, narrow building. The counters were refrigerated. The specialty of the shop was pâtés made with duck, pork, liver and mixed meats. Each product was displayed on a stainless steel tray or in a round ceramic bowl. Cooked, ready-to-eat sausages and salami were also sold. The butcher would slice the sausage if the customer requested to have it cut. I was impressed at the cleanliness of the shop, and the apron of the butcher was pure white, free of any stain from his work.

Two large, well-supplied fish stalls (poissonnerie) were busy with serious shoppers. The fishmonger helped me learn the French names of his fish and seafood. I learned the shark steaks are *esphow*, tuna slices *thon* or *thon rouge*. Squid is *seiche*, sole is called sole, shrimp is *crevettis* (I knew that one), snail is *bulot*, salmon is *saumon*, scallops are *coquilles*, and octopus is *poulpe*. The owner of the shop was very proud of the quality of his products.

The bakery and *patisserie* were located in a corner store. The shelves displaced several types of breads. The baguettes were of varying thickness and shapes. When the bread was purchased, the salesperson would wrap a bag around the center of the bread for carrying and the uncovered bread loaves would stick out of each end of the wrap. The pastries filled a long counter and looked delicious. Many were filled with custard or whipped cream.

The long narrow cheese (*fromagerie*) shop was situated next to the butcher shop. It had many shelves of cheeses. I noticed the small round or tubular-shaped cheeses were displayed on the counter and in glass-enclosed cases, while the hard or firm cheeses were piled on the tables. Several of the cheeses had rind, and some were coated with peppercorns. There were numerous cheeses of all types, making a choice of one or two difficult.

The Market offered a wonderful selection of foods for a great picnic with French baguettes, cheese, fruit, pâté, a jug of wine and thou.

Recipes | French Markets

Fresh Fruit Tart, Bastille Market, Paris

The wide selection of fresh fruit at the large Bastille Market was of top quality. It was at this Market I learned the proper procedure of purchasing fruit in France. The large ripe peaches were a delight to see, so I reached over the well-arranged pile of peaches to pick one up. Immediately, a very excited merchant came rushing over, shaking his head and waving his hand back and forth while saying, "No, no" to me. Although he did not speak much English, and I spoke very little French, I learned one does not pick up the fruit in the Market. When you want a particular fruit, you point at it, and the vendor will package the fruit for you. That really is a good procedure so that all the shoppers do not squeeze the fruit.

The Fresh Fruit Tart recipe calls for berries and stone fruit. This allows one to select the best fresh fruit that is in season for the finished tart.

Crust

1-1/2 cups all-purpose flour
1/2 cup sugar
7 tablespoons cold butter
3 egg yolks
1/2 teaspoon almond extract

Preheat oven to 375 degrees.

Combine flour and sugar in mixing bowl. Cut cold butter into small pieces. Cut butter into flour mixture until small, pea-size crumbs form. Add egg yolks and almond extract, using a fork to incorporate into flour mixture. Press mixture into tart shell. Bake for 15 minutes. Remove from oven and cool on a rack.

Filling

1/2 cup butter
1/3 cup sugar
1 egg
1/2 teaspoon vanilla
1/2 cup ground almonds

In mixing bowl, cream butter and sugar until light, about 2 minutes. Add egg, vanilla and almonds. Beat to blend. Pour onto cool tart crust. Bake at 375 degrees for 30 minutes until slightly golden on top. Remove from oven and cool.

Fruit Topping

2 cups berries (strawberries, raspberries or blueberries)
3 to 4 stone fruit (apricots, peaches or plums)
3/4 cup apricot jam for glaze
2 tablespoons lemon juice
3 tablespoons water

Hull strawberries and slice, if needed. Slice stone fruit. Place jam in saucepan. Add lemon juice and water. Heat to melt jam and form syrup. Brush the top of the tart with apricot syrup. Arrange fruit on top of tart. Brush with remaining jam syrup.

Yield: 8 servings

Bouillabaisse, Bastille Market, Paris

The large selection for fresh fish and seafood at the Bastille Market called out to become a bubbling pot of Bouillabaisse. All the ingredients for this recipe were available in the Market except the wine. Some recipes call for white wine, but this one calls for a sweeter Sauterne wine. This recipe includes seven kinds of fish and seafood. The important part to remember is the order and timing for the addition of each and the close attention to the cooking time. The sauce can be prepared the day before serving, causing the spices to blend into the sauce.

1 cup olive oil
2 sliced onions
1 bunch leeks, sliced
1 stalk celery, sliced
2 cloves garlic, minced
1 green bell pepper, chopped
1 can (16 ounces) diced tomatoes
2 cups vegetable or fish stock
Salt and pepper to taste
Dash sweet paprika, dash cayenne, and dash thyme
Saffron threads
2 pounds clams
1 pound red snapper, cut in cubes
1 pound halibut, cut in cubes
6 prawns, peeled and deveined
1 dozen large scallops
1 Dungeness crab, cracked
1 lobster tail, meat cut in cubes
1 cup Sauterne wine

Sauté first 5 vegetables in oil. Add tomatoes, stock and seasoning. Simmer for 30 minutes to one hour. Add fish according to time each requires to cook. First, the clams for 10 minutes; snapper and halibut 7 to 8 minutes; next the prawns and scallops for 5 minutes; and last the crab and lobster, just long enough to heat through. Add wine. Heat to serve.

Yield: 8 to 10 servings

Cauliflower with Garlic Dressing, Mouffetard Market, Paris

Several fruit and vegetable stands at the Mouffetard Market were selling cauliflower.

The plain, snow-white cauliflower has found some cousins that are yellow, green and purple. The colored ones add a bit of interest compared to the rather plain white cauliflower. A dish containing white, yellow and purple cauliflower is attractive and becomes a conversational piece at the dinner table. The recipe for Cauliflower with a Garlic Dressing welcomes the various colors of cauliflower.

1 head (about 1-1/2 to 2 pounds) cauliflower, any color
1/2 teaspoon sea salt
3 tablespoons extra virgin olive oil
4 cloves garlic, minced
2 tablespoons chopped red onion
2 tablespoons slivered almonds
1 tablespoon thin sliced sweet pimiento
2 tablespoons white wine vinegar
1 tablespoon parsley, chopped

Cut cauliflower into flowerets about 2 inches each. Place the cauliflower into boiling water with sea salt. Cook for 10 minutes until tender crisp. Drain cauliflower and place in bowl to keep warm. Place oil in skillet and heat on medium high. Add garlic, onions and almonds. Cook until golden, approximately 3 to 4 minutes. Remove skillet from heat and add pimiento and vinegar. Pour warm dressing over cauliflower and toss to coat. Sprinkle with parsley.

Yield: 4 to 6 servings

Coq Au Vin, Mouffetard Market, Paris

The whole dressed chickens, as well as the cut pieces of fresh chicken, were available in the Market. Chicken cooked with wine, either red or white, has been a traditional dish in the country homes throughout France. The older hens, when they no longer were laying eggs, ended up in the stew pot with the seasonal vegetables from the garden. Wine helped to tenderize the meat.

1 chicken, 3-1/2 to 4 pounds, cut into serving pieces
Salt and ground black pepper
3 tablespoons olive oil
1/2 cup chopped onions
1/2 cup sliced carrots
4 cloves garlic, chopped
2 tablespoons all-purpose flour
2 cups red wine
1 cup chicken stock
2 tablespoons tomato paste
2 bay leaves
2 sprigs fresh thyme or 1 teaspoon dried thyme
1/2 teaspoon marjoram
1 teaspoon sugar
Salt and pepper to taste

Rinse and pat dry chicken pieces. Heat oil in large, heavy Dutch oven or deep skillet to hot. Rub chicken with salt and pepper. Brown the chicken until golden brown on all sides, about 7 minutes. Do not crowd the chicken in the pan so cook in batches. Remove from heat and keep warm. Add the onions, carrots and garlic to pan and cook until soft, about 10 minutes. Remove from pan and keep warm. Add flour and reduce heat to low. Cook, stirring constantly, until roux just begins to turn light brown. Stir in wine, chicken broth, and tomato paste until well blended. Add bay leaves, thyme, marjoram, sugar and salt and pepper. Return chicken and vegetables to pot. Cover and simmer for 20 to 30 minutes.

Yield: 4 to 6 servings

French Onion Soup, Bastille Market, Paris

French Onion Soup has a fascinating history. However, I do not know how much is fact and how much is myth. The first French Onion Soup was a creation by Louie XIV's chef. The king requested a soup, and the poor chef had no broth to make the soup. He simmered the onions until they were a golden caramel color and added champagne in place of a broth. The king was delighted with the soup. French Onion Soup was also a part of the workingman's diet. A century ago, when the farmers would bring their wagons of produce to the Les Halles Market in Paris, they would always stop at a café near the Market before heading home or even after unloading the wagon. It might have been just before dawn or late at night, but the meal would always include French Onion Soup. Later in the night or into the wee hours of the morning, the people who had been celebrating found a bowl of French Onion Soup helped to reduce any hangover from the beverages they consumed. The soup also has been accredited with eliminating "female problems." The Jewish mother might have served her child chicken broth for a fast recovery from a cold, but French mothers were known to feed their sick children French Onion Soup to make them "all better."

2 tablespoons olive oil
1/2 teaspoon salt
2 large red onions, thinly sliced
2 large sweet yellow onions, thinly sliced
4 cups beef broth
1 can (10.5 ounces) consommé
1/2 cup red wine
1 tablespoon Worcestershire sauce
1 teaspoon sugar
1 bay leaf
4 slices French bread
4 slices Gruyere or Swiss cheese
1 cup shredded Asiago cheese

In a large pot, heat oil to medium high. Add onions and salt. Simmer for 30 minutes, stirring to caramelize the onions. Add broth, consommé, wine, Worcestershire sauce, sugar and bay leaf. Cover and simmer for 20 minutes. Toast bread and cut to fit into soup bowl. Remove bay leaf from soup. Ladle soup into bowls. Top each with a slice of bread, slice of cheese and 1/4 cup shredded Asiago cheese. Place under broiler for 5 minutes until cheese is melted and golden.

Yield: 4 servings

Cheese Stuffed Apples, Marche Rue Cler, Paris

The *fromagerie* shops along Rue Cler carry many types of French cheese. The sharp cheddar cheese used in this recipe can be either white or yellow cheddar. The combination of the sharp cheese and the sweet apple makes a delicious dessert.

4 large baking apples, such as Rome Beauty, Fiji, or Gala
4 ounces shredded sharp cheddar cheese
1/4 cup white wine
4 tablespoons chopped walnuts

Preheat oven to 375 degrees.

Wash and core apples. Cut about 1/4 inch off the top of apples to leave a flat surface. In mixing bowl, combine cheese, wine and nuts. Place apples in baking dish. Fill each apple with cheese mixture. Place extra filling on top of each apple. Bake at 375 degrees for 30 minutes or until apples are tender.

Yield: 4 servings

Brochettes with Red Peppers and Goat Cheese, Mouffetard Market, Paris

French cheese has a world reputation as *excellent.* Several soft cheese such as Gorgonzola, Stilton and goat cheese were available at the Mouffetard Market. Some of the soft cheeses were held in refrigerated cases. The wheels and chunks of hard and semi-hard cheese were displayed on shelves and countertops at the Market.

1 red bell pepper, cut in half and seeds removed
3 tablespoons extra virgin olive oil
2 tablespoons chopped green onions
2 cloves garlic, minced
1 tablespoon chopped fresh basil
1/4 teaspoon salt
1/8 teaspoon black pepper
1 medium tomato, peeled and chopped
1 tablespoon capers, drained
6 thick slices French bread, toasted
3 ounces soft goat cheese

Heat broiler to 500 degrees.

Place red pepper on a baking sheet with cut side down. Place under broiler until black and blistered. Remove from heat and place in paper bag. When pepper is cool, remove skin and most of the char from the pepper. Cut pepper into wide strips. Heat oil in large skillet. Add onions and garlic, sauté for 3 minutes. Add basil, salt, pepper, tomatoes and capers. Cook, stirring until tomatoes are soft and cooked. Toast bread. Cut each slice in half and place on a baking sheet. Top with slice of red pepper. Place a tablespoon of vegetable mixture on top of roasted pepper. Place a rounded teaspoon of soft goat cheese on top of vegetables. Broil until cheese is lightly brown and slightly melted, approximately 2 minutes. Watch closely so toast does not burn on the edge.

Yield: 12 servings

Broiled Lamb Chops, Mouffetard Market, Paris

The meat in the Mouffetard Market was in a refrigerated, glass-covered case. It was the best quality one could buy, according to the French vendor whose name tag said Jacques. He was rather stout, with a thick waist covered in a perfectly white apron. His dark brown eyes were bright and his smile heartwarming. Jacques loved talking about the meat he had for sale. Lamb is a popular meat in France, and all cuts are used. The broiled lamb chops are on the menu at all the restaurants I visited in France.

1/3 cup olive oil
3 cloves garlic, minced
1 teaspoon lemon juice
1 tablespoon crushed rosemary
6 loin lamb chops, about 1 inch thick
Salt and pepper, as desired

Heat oven to broil (500 degrees).

Coat broiling pan with non-stick vegetable spray. Place oil, garlic, lemon juice and rosemary in large plastic bag. Place chops in bag and marinate for 30 minutes, turning occasionally to coat chops. Remove from marinade and shake each chop to remove marinade. Sprinkle salt and pepper on chops if desired. Place under broiler. Broil 4 to 5 inches from the heat for 2 minutes on the first side, turn and cook for 3 minutes on the second side for medium-rare chops.

Yield: 6 servings

Fruit-Stuffed French Toast, Bastille Market, Paris

French toast that is popular in France may have originated in ancient Roman times around the fourth or fifth century. The first French Toast recipe in France was named *Pain a la Romaine* or Roman Bread. In France, the dish is known as *Pain Perdu* or lost bread. The leftover "stale" bread was soaked in milk and eggs and fried for a filling meal. With the addition of honey or jam, it was served for dessert in the homes of the peasants. The recipe book *The Accomplished Cook,* published in 1660, included a recipe for French Toast using toasted bread, wine, orange juice and sugar. There are many recipes for stuffed French Toast using one or more of these ingredients: fruit, ham, cheese or vegetables.

3 large croissants	1-1/2 cups milk
3 ounces cream cheese	1/2 teaspoon vanilla
2 bananas	2 tablespoons sugar
2 cups sliced fresh or frozen strawberries	1/2 teaspoon baking powder
1/4 cup chopped pecans	2 tablespoons brown sugar
6 eggs	1/4 teaspoon cinnamon

Tear croissants into bite-sized pieces. Place half in bottom of greased baking dish. Cut cream cheese into small pieces and place over croissants. Cut bananas into 1/4-inch slices and arrange over croissants in baking dish. Add sliced strawberries. Add nuts over strawberries. Cover top of fruit and nuts with remaining half croissants. In a mixing bowl, combine eggs, milk, vanilla, sugar and baking powder. Beat to blend. Pour egg mixture over croissants. Combine brown sugar and cinnamon and sprinkle over top of casserole. Pat mixture to assure croissants are saturated with egg mixture. Refrigerate for 2 hours or overnight. Bake at 350 degrees for 50 minutes. Let rest for 10 minutes before serving.

Yield: 4 to 6 servings

Prosciutto-Wrapped Roasted Asparagus, Bastille Market, Paris

The vegetables in the Bastille Market were outstanding. Each stall was more colorful than the last. When I visited the Market, it was spring and the vegetables of the season were on display. I found new green, white and purple asparagus. Combine the three types of asparagus with bright red prosciutto for a colorful salad or side dish at a meal.

1/4 cup balsamic vinegar
1 teaspoon honey
8 spears green asparagus
8 spears white asparagus
4 spears purple asparagus
1 tablespoon extra virgin olive oil
1/4 teaspoon salt
1/8 teaspoon black pepper
6 ounces sliced prosciutto
4 ounces crumbled blue cheese

Place vinegar and honey in small saucepan over medium heat. Simmer for 8 to 10 minutes until slightly syrupy. Remove from heat and let cool. Place asparagus in one layer in large baking dish. Drizzle oil over asparagus. Sprinkle with salt and pepper. Toss to coat. Roast asparagus at 425 degrees for 10 minutes. Remove from pan and cool for 10 minutes. Wrap one piece of prosciutto around 2 green, 2 white, and 1 purple asparagus spears. Repeat with remaining asparagus and prosciutto. Place bundles on baking pan and roast for 5 to 6 minutes. Turn once during roasting. Place asparagus bundles on serving dishes. Top with balsamic vinegar syrup and cheese.

Yield: 4 servings

Boeuf Bourguignon, Rue Cler Market, Paris

The beef raised in France is of excellent quality resulting from the breed of cattle and the open pastures and range for the animals. The steaks in the marketplace are well-marbled. In many of the beef dishes, the knuckle bone is included for the flavor of the marrow. Beef Burgundy or Boeuf Bourguignon, as it appears on restaurant menus, is a flavorful entrée.

6 strips honey-smoked bacon, cut into small pieces
1/2 cup all-purpose flour
1/2 teaspoon sea salt
1/4 teaspoon coarse ground black pepper
2 pounds beef round steak, cut into 2-inch cubes
2 tablespoons olive oil
2 tablespoons butter
24 small fresh or frozen pearl onions
24 small button mushrooms
2 tablespoons brandy
2 cups red burgundy wine
1 cup beef broth
1/2 teaspoon thyme
1/2 teaspoon crushed rosemary
1 tablespoon fresh lemon juice
2 teaspoons cornstarch
2 tablespoons water
Salt and pepper, as desired

Sauté bacon in a large, heavy skillet until crisp. Remove from skillet. Reserve bacon fat. Combine flour, salt and pepper. Coat beef cubes in flour mixture. Heat bacon fat in skillet and brown beef, about 5 minutes. Stir to brown on all sides. Remove from skillet and place beef in large baking dish or casserole. Add oil and butter to skillet and heat. Add onions and mushrooms. Sauté until tender; do not brown. Add to beef casserole. Add brandy to skillet to deglaze the drippings. Add wine, broth, thyme, rosemary, and lemon juice. Heat. Dissolve cornstarch in water and add to wine in skillet. Pour over beef in casserole. Cover and simmer for 1 hour. Add onions and mushrooms and continue cooking on top of the stove for 1 additional hour until meat is tender.

Yield: 6 servings

Pommes Anna, Rue Cher Market, Paris

The main starch in a meal in France is the potato, whereas in Italy it is pasta or polenta. *Pommes de Terre* translated means apple of the Earth. The markets in Paris were selling several types and different sizes of potatoes when I had the privilege of visiting them. Pommes Anna is a delicious and simple recipe for potatoes. The dish was created by Adolphe Duglere in honor of Anna DesLions, a "lioness" of the Second Empire.

1-1/2 pounds boiling potatoes (Golden Yukon)
1/2 cup butter
1/2 teaspoon salt

Preheat oven to 400 degrees.

Wash and peel the potatoes. Cut into thin 1/8-inch slices. Clarify butter by heating it in a small skillet to melt. Let cool to lukewarm. Remove froth from the surface of the butter. Pour clear liquid butter into a bowl. Discard milk solids in the bottom of the skillet. Butter the sides and bottom of a 9-inch baking dish. Layer the sliced potatoes into dish. Add salt, if desired. Pour butter over each layer. Cover and bake for 1 hour. Let rest at room temperature for 5 minutes before serving.

Yield: 4 servings

Scallops with Beurre Blanc Sauce, Marche Rue Cler, Paris

Scallops served in their open shell make a beautiful presentation. The Marche Rue Cler in Paris and also the Borough Market in England sold their fresh scallops in the shell. I learned that the scallops in the Marche Rue Cler came from the cold waters off the Normandy coast. The Beurre Blanc Sauce is a reduction of French shallots, wine, vinegar and butter. In some regions of the country, unsalted butter is used for this recipe. In the province of Brittany, it is made with the salted or lightly salted butter that has a subtle taste of iodine and is used with all seafood in that region.

2 pounds large scallops in shells
1/2 teaspoon salt
1/4 teaspoon white pepper
4 French shallots, finely chopped
5 tablespoons dry white wine
3 tablespoons white wine vinegar
1 cup butter, divided
2 tablespoons chopped parsley

Preheat broiler to 500 degrees.

Remove scallops from shells. Place shells on baking sheet and set aside. Rinse scallops and pat dry. Cut each in half horizontally to have 2 round slices. In a saucepan, combine salt, pepper, shallots, wine and vinegar. Simmer to reduce liquid to 1/4 cup. Add 3/4 cup butter to mixture. Whisk vigorously until all the butter is melted. Place the remaining 1/4 cup butter in a non-stick large skillet and heat. Place scallops in hot butter and cook for 1 minute on each side. Divide scallops into 4 scallop shells. Ladle sauce over scallops. Place scallops under hot broiler for 1 minute. Do not overcook. Garnish with parsley. Serve immediately.

Yield: 4 servings

Scrambled Eggs with White Truffles, Marche Rue Cler, Paris

Both white and black truffles are more flavorful when cooked. The white truffle added to eggs makes a gourmet dish. The peak season for truffles is December through February. However, some outlets have them available for additional months. The truffles are expensive because they are found in the wild and are difficult to secure. For years, pigs were used to root out the truffles, and this fungus was known as "food for the wild boar."

4 tablespoons butter
2 tablespoons white truffle oil
8 large eggs
1 ounce white truffles, finely chopped or shaved thin
1/2 teaspoon salt
1/8 teaspoon white pepper

Heat water to simmering in the bottom of a double boiler. Add butter and truffle oil to top of double boiler and heat. In a bowl, whisk together eggs and truffles. Add to top of double boiler and cook, stirring gently until small curds form. Remove eggs from heat Add salt and pepper. Serve immediately. If desired, garnish with a few shaved white truffles.

Yield: 4 servings

Markets in Russia

The history of Russian markets reflects turbulent times of splendor and oppression. By 1705, the Gostiny Dvor, a market for the locals and visiting merchants was established in Troitskaya Square. Peter the Great's architectural plan was to build a market in each part of the rapidly expanding St. Petersburg.

Russian records indicate there were six markets in St. Petersburg in 1782. By the end of the nineteenth century, the number had grown to fifteen. From 1900 to 1913, five private markets opened. World War I caused a shortage of food, and many of the markets closed. The problems for the marketplaces increased with the Civil War from 1918 to 1921. In 1925, the Communist government built the large Kuznechny Market. In the following years, the Market trade died and the few surviving ones, called kolkhoz (collective farm) markets, were selling mainly agricultural products. World War II brought another blow to the existing markets. The recovery of the Soviet-owned markets was slow. New market buildings were constructed, but food supplies were scarce. During the 1970s and 1980s, unauthorized markets called "spontaneous markets" would appear.

The government used every means possible to shut down these markets. The black market flourished.

The dissolution of the Soviet Union in 1991 brought about radical changes in the food markets in Russia. Farmers and craftsmen rushed to open their stands at a city market to supply the small grocery stores and the large, low-income population. By the year 2000, there were eighty-eight markets in St. Petersburg. The farmers' markets have returned to Moscow and many small towns with the blessing of the government. The government's idea is to improve entrepreneurial retail endeavors. There are presently one hundred and twenty-five farmers' markets in Moscow.

Kuznechny Market | St. Petersburg, Russia

I visited the fantastic Kuznechny Market in June 2010. This is the time of celebration in St. Petersburg called "white nights" because the daylight continues all night long.

As I walked into the Market building, I was overwhelmed by the magnitude and scope of the structure. It is well over a block long and fifty or more yards wide, with rows of stalls along the walls and counters and food display cases crisscrossing the center section. It is the largest Market in Russia. The walls are of white tile, and the high ceiling has many lights.

I was at a disadvantage. I do not speak or read Russian, and, in the Market, I did not find an individual who could or would respond to me. Although I smiled and spoke to many of the vendors, telling them how attractive or delicious their products appeared, not one would smile with me. They did not frown or smile; they were just stoic.

To my left as I entered the Market were two high stands selling pickled vegetables. The whole, peeled white and the purple-striped garlic bulb, including two or three inches of the stem, were pickled and piled high in plastic bowls. Beside the garlic, pickled cucumbers, asparagus, carrots, cabbage and peppers were available.

The neat, attractive lady selling the pickles offered me a taste and handed me a whole pickle. The cucumber pickle had a mild salty taste that I found out later is cured in a salt brine with no or very little vinegar. I thanked her and told her I liked the pickle, and she gave me another one. This one was a dill, slightly sweet, with some spice. It, too, was very tasty. The pickles are marinated in rassal, a salty vinegar, with various other ingredients added that might be spices, horseradish, dill, black pepper or hot peppers.

When I asked if I could take her picture, she turned away.

Next to the pickle stands was the only spice stand in the Market. The colorful display of more than sixty different spices, each in a plastic tub, were arranged in rows on a tiered counter. The spices, when ordered by a customer, were measured with a small spoon and placed in a plastic Zip-Lock bag.

Across from the spice stand was the first of many, many stalls selling processed meats. The glass-enclosed counters were filled with cooked meat for slicing as ham, beef, pork, hard sausages and some pâté. On top of the display case were slabs of white pork belly fat. I also saw small rolls of smoked lean and fat pork similar to bacon, only not sliced and in a roll.

I counted fifteen fish stalls along the wall and in the center section. The fish and seafood were in glass-enclosed refrigerated counters. The fish were sold whole, dressed with heads and without heads, fillets, steaks and cutlets. I recognized the salmon, trout, red fish, large and small herring and mackerel. One stall along the fish section had several kinds of smoked fish, both whole and in strips. The selection of seafood, such as squid, octopus, scallops, clams and mussels, was extensive.

All of the dairy products—yogurt, sour cream, a very thick cream called smetana, butter, soft cheese, cream cheese and cottage cheese—were in glass-enclosed cases in the center section of the Market. There

were many stands all run by mature, stern-looking women with kerchiefs on their heads. They did not return my smile when I complimented them on their beautiful yogurts.

Both soft and firm Greek-style yogurts were displayed in large, white plastic buckets. An order of yogurt or sour cream would be placed into a small plastic container and handed to the customer. The fruit-flavored yogurts were cherry, blueberry, orange, peach, strawberry, raspberry and others that I did not recognize.

In another area of the Market, I found deep-fried string cheese. The golden brown bundles were as pretty as a flower bouquet.

The one section of the Market that I was looking forward to seeing was the meat/butcher shop. This large shop stretched completely across the pavilion, and customers could walk around the four sides of the counters to view and select the meat.

This is really a total butcher shop. The beef carcasses arrive whole, skinned and dressed or quartered. The carcasses of sheep, goat, pig and lamb are delivered skinned and dressed. The whole heads of these animals, as well as the heads of beef cattle with the hides removed, are

hung on high hooks in the center of the meat shop for the customers to purchase. I think it would be difficult to carry the head of a cow home from the Market. The shoppers could buy a whole ham, a leg of lamb, a rack of lamb or the entire rib cage, a roast from the round of beef or the whole leg of beef.

The butchers used very large knives and dangerous-looking cleavers. The cleavers appeared to be eighteen inches long and at least ten inches wide. I think they must have weighed thirty to forty pounds. When the butcher would slam the cleaver on a large beef joint, it would shatter.

The wooden cutting blocks appeared to be large tree stumps at least three feet in diameter. Their dark, shiny, burgundy-brown color must have come from the years of use in cutting fresh meat.

I also saw large tubs of animal bones. If the customer ordered some bones, the butcher would break or crush the bones with a whack from his large cleaver.

As I approached the butcher shop, I adjusted my camera to take a picture. Before I could ask if I might take the picture, four or five of the large, muscular butchers clad in bright blue jackets came rushing at me with their arms outstretched in front of them. They

were shouting, "Na, na, na photo!" They looked very angry and fearful. I got the message clearly that they did not want me to take any pictures. Close to the shop I saw two policemen. I immediately put my camera away because the manager at my hotel had told me the police cannot only stop and question me but can confiscate my camera.

I moved out of doors to the numerous high stands of fresh fruits and vegetables. This also was new to me. The front of the stands were all vertical. The first three or more feet were just a flat board. For four or five feet above the base, the fresh produce is arranged on the flat, vertical wall. The products are carefully and artistically arranged on this nearly straight-up wall. The cherries were held in place with a clear plastic tape. All the products fit together snugly. Not all the stands carried vegetables. Fruits were more plentiful, and most of the stands offered a wide selection of good quality fruit. In talking with the hotel manager, I learned that the cherries came from Turkey, the grapes from Chile, the citrus fruit from Spain and the grapes from Italy. I saw small rounds of fresh figs at only one stand. There were no locally grown fruits at the Market at this time of year.

The walls displayed carrots, cauliflower, broccoli, onions, radishes, tomatoes, cabbage, green beans, red and green peppers, celery and greens, such as leaf lettuce parsley, romaine lettuce, iceberg lettuce, red leaf lettuce and dill. I saw bags of potatoes hanging from the upper railing of the stalls.

The customer would point to the product she wished to buy without touching it. The clerk behind the stall, seven feet above the floor, would fill the plastic bag with the correct product from a supply that he had behind the stall. He would lean far over the top of the stall to hand the bag to the customer. I am sure if a customer should accidently remove an

onion or tomato from the display, everything would come tumbling down.

I did find fresh pasta in a stall along with dry packaged pasta. The fresh pasta was very white, and many types were stuffed. Most of the stuffed pasta was round and in various sizes, from marble size to tennis-ball size.

In the center of the Market, taking up a large amount of the space from one end to the other, were glass displays that were several feet tall. Behind the glass were displays of dried fruits, nuts, seeds and some whole spices. The selection of dried fruit was very impressive, including dates, figs, apples, grapes, peaches, mangos, bananas,

apricots, papayas, kiwis, wild cherries, elderberries, blueberries, plums, cranberries, blackberries, raspberries and some I did not recognize.

Outside of the pavilion, I found a flower market. Most of the plants were in small pots or flats to be planted in a home garden. The pure white lilies were large, beautiful and fragrant.

The Kuznechny Market was not very busy on the day I visited. The shoppers looked very serious about what they were buying. I did not hear much conversation and no laughter at the Market.

Recipes | Russian Market

Poached White Fish, Kuznechny Market, St. Petersburg

Poaching fish is a good way to introduce flavors of herbs, citrus or vegetables into the cooked fish. The fish is immersed in the boiling liquid and the temperature of the liquid is quickly reduced to a simmer. Boiling will break the fillet into smaller pieces so the fish is only simmered in the liquid. The fish can be poached in the oven or on top of the stove with a secure cover to keep the steam in the baking dish.

2 pounds boneless whitefish fillets
1 cup dry white wine
1 cup fish stock or bottled clam juice
1/2 teaspoon sea salt
1/4 teaspoon ground white pepper
1/4 cup fresh lemon juice
1/2 teaspoon thyme
2 tablespoons chopped fresh parsley
1 teaspoon cornstarch
3 tablespoons half-and-half cream

Preheat oven to 400 degrees.

Arrange fillets in one layer in a buttered baking dish. Combine wine, fish stock, salt, pepper, lemon juice and thyme in saucepan. Bring to a boil and pour over the fish. Cover the baking dish tightly and bake at 400 degrees for 8 to 10 minutes until fish flakes well with a fork. Transfer fish carefully to a platter. Keep warm. Pour fish liquid into saucepan, add parsley and boil down to about half in volume. Stir cornstarch into cream. Whisk into fish bouillon and cook, while stirring, until thickened. Spoon sauce over fish.

Yield: 6 servings

Russian Black Bread, Kuznechny Market, St. Petersburg

The population of St. Petersburg lived on black rye bread for three-and-one-half years during the siege of Leningrad in 1941 to 1944. The bread was the only food available and was the difference between starvation and life. In times of celebration, black bread is a sign of wealth and health. Russian Black Bread has its own laws, regulations and even price controls established by the government.

2-1/2 cups all-purpose flour plus 1-1/2 cups for kneading
2 cups shredded wheat cereal
2 packages active dry yeast
2 tablespoons sugar
1 tablespoon salt
1 tablespoon instant coffee crystals
1 tablespoon onion powder
2-1/2 cups warm water
1/2 cup molasses
1/4 cup vegetable oil
1 ounce unsweetened chocolate
4 cups rye flour

In large mixing bowl, combine 2-1/2 cups all-purpose flour, wheat cereal, dry yeast, sugar, salt, instant coffee and onion powder. Mix with dough hook. In saucepan or microwave-safe bowl, place water, molasses, oil and chocolate. Heat until very warm (120 to 130 degrees) and chocolate melts. Add water mixture to dry ingredients and mix on medium speed for 3 minutes until well blended. Remove bowl of mixer and gradually add rye flour. Turn dough onto floured surface and knead 1 cup to 1-1/2 cups of the remaining all-purpose flour into dough. Knead for 5 minutes. Dough will be slightly sticky. Place in oiled bowl, coating all sides of dough in the oil. Place in warm, draft-free area. Let dough rise until nearly double, 45 to 60 minutes. Turn dough unto surface to punch down. Divide into two balls. Place in greased 8- or 9-inch round cake pans. Let rise for 40 to 50 minutes. Bake at 375 degrees for 45 to 50 minutes. Coat top of hot loaves with butter. Remove from pans and cool on rack.

Yield: 2 loaves

Borscht, Beet Cabbage Soup, Kuznechny, St. Petersburg

Borsch is a heavy, warm soup for winter and a cold, lighter soup for summer. The ingredients vary from one region to another although southern Russia is credited with publishing the first recipe for borscht. *The Borzoi Cookbook,* translated from Russian by Princess Alexandra Gagarine, was published in London in 1923. It lists several recipes for borscht. All garden vegetables and different meats, such as beef, fowl, mutton and sausages, are included. Beetroot and cabbage are the staples in the recipes.

2 to 3 pounds lean beef pot roast
1 tablespoon salt
2 bay leaves
1/2 teaspoon ground dried basil leaves
1 tablespoon oil
1 medium onion, chopped
4 cloves garlic, minced
2 carrots, peeled and shredded
3 fresh beets, peeled and cubed
4 to 5 cups shredded cabbage
1 can beef consomme
1 cup tomato juice
2 tablespoons tomato paste
2 tablespoons sugar
1/2 teaspoon ground black pepper
Juice of 1 lemon
1/2 cup red wine (optional)
Sour cream for garnish

Place meat in large pot; add water to cover meat, salt, bay leaves and basil. Cover, bring to a boil and reduce heat to simmer. Cook for 1-1/2 to 2 hours until meat is tender. Strain broth and save. Remove beef from pot. Discard bone, fat, and bay leaves. Chop meat into 1 to 2 inch cubes. Set aside. Place oil in pot. Add onions, garlic and carrots. Sauté until vegetables are soft. Add beef broth to vegetables. Place beets in the pot. Cover and bring to a boil. Simmer for 25 to 30 minutes until beets are tender. Add beef cubes, cabbage, consomme, tomato juice, tomato paste, sugar and pepper. If more liquid is needed, add more beef broth. Simmer for 20 minutes until cabbage is tender. Add lemon juice and wine. Stir to blend and simmer for 5 more minutes. Serve in bowls with dollop of sour cream on top.

Yield: 12 servings

White Russian, Kuznechny Market, St. Petersburg

The White Russian cocktail is a sweet drink that is most often served after dinner. It is made with vodka (Russian vodka), Kahlua and cream. The liqueurs are carefully poured into the cocktail glass to allow for different colored layers.

1 ounce Russian vodka
2 ounces Kahlua
1 ounce cream
Ice

Fill the cocktail glass half full with crushed ice. Pour the vodka over the ice. Add the Kahlua by slowly pouring it down the blade of a dinner knife held against the side of the glass. Pour the cream into the glass using the same method as for the Kahlua. There will be a layer of clear ice and vodka, a brown layer of Kahlua and the top layer of cream. Do not stir the drink.

Enjoy!

Yield: 1 serving

Russian Caviar, and Blintzes, Kuznechney Market, St. Petersburg

Caviar is fresh fish eggs, cleaned and preserved carefully with salt. Caviar can be prepared from the eggs of many game fish. Russian caviar from the large sturgeon caught in the Caspian Sea is considered the finest in the world. Unfortunately, the sturgeon population has been about wiped out from overfishing, and Beluga caviar is very rare. Caviar at the fish counters in the Kuznechney Market sold in small jars and as appetizers. Caviar is often served with a small pancake called a blintze, finely chopped onion, chives, hard-cooked eggs and crème fraiche.

4 ounces caviar of choice
1 hard-cooked egg, diced
1/4 cup diced red onion
1/4 cup chopped chives
1/4 cup crème fraiche or sour cream
12 blintzes
1 lemon, cut into wedges

Place the caviar in a glass bowl on a bed of ice. Never place the caviar in sterling silver. The serving spoon is best if made from mother of pearl. Place the diced egg, onion, chives and crème fraiche in separate glass containers. Place the lemon wedges on a small dish. The blintzes should be served warm. Place blintzes in a white cloth napkin on a serving tray. Arrange the dishes of egg, onion, chives, crème fraiche, lemon and blintzes around the bowl of caviar.

Blintzes

1 cup buttermilk
1/2 cup whole milk
2 eggs
1 cup all-purpose flour
1 teaspoon baking soda
1 tablespoon sugar

In a mixing bowl, combine buttermilk, milk and eggs. Stir to blend; do not beat. Add flour, soda and sugar, stirring to form a thin batter. Heat oil in large non-stick skillet to medium hot. Drop batter by the tablespoon to form small pancakes. Cook until light brown on bottom. Turn and continue cooking to brown the other side. Serve warm.

Yield: 12 blintzes

Markets in Greece

It was a bright, sunny, spring day in Athens when Alex, my interpreter, and I were trudging up the walk covered with yellow brown dust to Athens Central Market. I thought of the thousands of people who had followed this same route up to the hills of Acropolis and to the Parthenon. Socrates, Aristotle, St. Paul walked on this path thousands of years ago. Alexander the Great may have driven his chariot along this ancient road.

Trade has been an essential of Greek history. The rocky land and the sandy soil of Greece cannot supply enough of the food crops needed for the population. Records show in 300 B.C. the trade ships brought one hundred fifty thousand tons of wheat to Greece from Egypt, Mesopotamia and other ports. Markets thrived in the port towns. Grains, fish, olive oil and wine were supplied to the markets inland.

By the middle 1800s, the many street markets in Athens were in disarray. The farmers would block the walkways not only with their products but with empty boxes and crates. The areas became unsanitary and unsafe because the farmers left all their garbage, rotten vegetables, broken bottles, broken boxes and over-ripe fruit waste and debris on the site when they would leave for the day.

The main market in the 1840s, if you could call it that, consisted of a group of wooden sheds located in the ruins of the Library of Hadrian. It was a blessing when it burned to the ground in 1884.

In 1875, Panagus Kyriakos, who was the mayor of Athens, decided it was high time to build a thoroughly modern market. Work on the new market buildings was started in 1876 but ran into several problems that delayed the construction. When the old market sheds burned in 1884, work on the new market was intensified. Some of the vendors from the old market actually moved into the unfinished Varvakios Agora, the Central Market (Dimotiki Agora), much to the dismay of the architects and workers.

By 1886, the beautiful glass ceilings were installed, marking the completion of the pavilions. The neoclassical style buildings had several large archways that opened to the streets. Over the centuries, the Market buildings have been upgraded and remodeled. The installation of running water and electricity has aided in maintaining sanitation.

The first organic farming in Greece came about in 1982 by the demand of a Dutch company for organic dried currants. The Dutch certification organization, Skal, worked with a consultant for organic agriculture for the conversion of some Greek farms to commercial organic farming. From 1986, a German firm supported the production of organic olive oil and olives for export. Individual farmers converted to organic farming in the following years. The main products were olive oil, olives, citrus fruit, wine, cereal and cotton. The conversion to organic farming of these products was fairly easy because most were established plants that required less fertilizer or chemicals. Most of the organic products are exported. The Market shoppers have little interest in purchasing organic foods.

Of the arable land in Greece, only 0.6 percent was under organic agriculture in 2009 compared to Norway with 10 percent and Denmark with 25 percent.

Because the price of organically raised food is generally higher than the traditionally produced and processed items, the economy of the area does affect the sales. Recently, Greece has had a severe downturn in its economy, and the higher-priced organic food items are not selling as well as desired.

Dimotiki Agora Market | Athens, Greece

Although there are many street markets throughout the city of Athens, the Varvakeros or Dimotiki Agora is by far the largest and the busiest. Every day around thirty thousand tourists and residents visit the Market, and for the Christmas and Easter holiday foods, the Market is packed with ten times that number. Peter Tsarouchis, of the Greek Embassy, proclaims, "The Market is part of the Athenian lifestyle. Rich and poor, everyone goes there."

The three hundred-plus vendors employ an average of five workers each, making for a large Market population. Lately, many of the employees have migrated from Albania, Bulgaria, Pakistan and Egypt to Athens. Other merchants have family-owned businesses and have been in the Market for generations.

I became aware of the live poultry being sold in the Market by the noise the chickens and ducks were making. A wire cage holding three large red hens with rust- colored feathers were for sale by a serious-looking small man in black, baggy pants and a black, long-sleeved shirt.

I watched while the merchant reached into the cage, grabbed a fighting hen by the legs and pulled her out of the cage. He then carefully tied the feet and legs together, using one hand while holding her upside down with the other. The flopping bird was objecting loudly and kept trying to peck the hand of the man holding her legs. The transaction was completed, and the customer took the hen by her feet and walked down the aisle with the loud, squawking hen clearing his path.

Live ducks with dark green fluorescent feathers, and a black head with white feathers around the eyes looking like white goggles, were kept in several cages out of the sun. In another stall, racks of

baby ducklings were making a ruckus. The wire and plastic cages filled with cute, fluffy, yellow ducklings were stacked one on top of the other. When I was at the Market, it was the Easter season, and I wondered if the ducklings were to be given to the children as pets or if they would be purchased to be raised for dinner on a later day.

Pigeons and doves that were in wire cages were for sale and would soon become someone's dinner. Next to the cages of poultry were bird cages holding song birds. The birds were advertising their singing ability for the potential customers.

Live and butchered rabbits were for sale. In the open Market, I saw a sturdy,

large, older women dressed all in black: black knitted stocking cap, long-sleeved black sweater, an ankle-length, black wool skirt and black leather, well-worn, ankle-high boots. She was the owner of the long-eared, white rabbit that was tied with twine string to one of the cages. She was sitting on a stool waiting for someone to come and buy her rabbit. When Alex, my guide, asked her about the rabbit, she indicated that she did not want to talk with us.

There were two long covered pavilions, one for the fish stalls and the other for meat sales. The fish and seafood pavilion had about one hundred and fifty stalls that were connected to each other. Some fishmongers had more than one stall that was used to display their fish and seafood. The dressed whole fish were laid on a white counter; some were on crushed ice. Some of the fish that I recognized were sea bass, sea bream, mullet, trout, salmon and tilapia. The small, whole, silver sardines, anchovies and smelts were dressed with the heads and tails left on the body. These are generally served fried or grilled

whole. The shellfish, octopus, squid and shrimp were piled in bins on the counter or just spread across the countertop. The variety of shrimp was extensive, from the raw gray and pink heads-on to the shelled and cleaned shrimp. There were several kinds and sizes of squid.

Entire counters were full of pink and black, rather translucent octopus. Grilled octopus is a favorite in Greek cuisine.

Most of the octopuses were the size of a baseball with long tentacles. One stand had a huge octopus the size of a soccer ball placed in the center of its counter. Its eight long arms spread in all directions over the seafood counter.

It was the Easter week when I visited the Market. The large meat pavilion was a busy, noisy place with crowds of shoppers in the aisles. The butchers were chopping the animal bones with large cleavers and cutting the carcasses with loud buzzing saws. Everyone was talking and shouting.

The racks all along the stalls were full of hanging lamb carcasses. Some were so large I was sure they were mature sheep. The animal was either hung whole or split down the middle from the tail through the head. Many of the carcasses had the head still attached. I learned that the lamb is roasted whole, including the head. Lamb is a traditional meat for Easter and is often roasted out of doors on a spit. The whole, skinned, dressed goat carcasses also were hanging from hooks along the stalls.

The meat pavilion is one step beyond the slaughterhouse and was pretty gory. The butchers' white jackets were coated with blood. A young man who was arranging dark red beef livers on the counter had the sleeves of his butcher coat rolled up.

His arms, hands and coat were streaked with animal blood. The hearts, lungs and kidneys also were for sale. Some of the sheep carcasses had the kidneys in the body cavity. The stomachs of the cattle and the sheep were piled on the counters for sale as tripe. It is a light-yellow, fibrous tissue that is used in soups and stews. When I first, last and only time, had tripe, it was in a tomato garlic sauce.

I stopped at two different shops selling only sausages. It was a beautiful, colorful display of sausages of all sizes and shapes. Alex found they used spices from India and Africa in the mixture. They even had the dark, almost black, blood sausage in elongated rings.

In the olive shops, open wooden tubs containing green, rust, brown and black olives in oil or in brine were featured in the Market. Alex told me the tubs were made from the wood of the olive trees. The different batches of olives had many different ingredients, such as orange peel, lemon wedges, oregano, spices, fennel and garlic. The shiny, small black Kalamata olives are from the area around the town of Kalamata in the southern part of Greece. The Kalamata olives are part of every Greek salad. Olives are served every day at mezedes or for snacks in Greece.

I watched an olive merchant, who was a heavyset, middle-aged man with a large black mustache, use his hands to dip the olives from the tubs as the customers would select the ones they desired. The customer and the vendor would carry on a long conservation about the olives. The merchant told them the olives came from his family farm. Alex said the customers like to know where the olives are raised and what is used in treating or curing the olives for the Market.

Where there are olives, there is olive oil. The stalls had bottles, jugs and cans containing gold to green olive oil. Here, too, we were encouraged to taste the product. The taste varied as much as the color from sweet, mild oil that was soothing to the palate to bitter, stringent oil. Oil was also dispensed from a large jug into bottles the shoppers had brought with them.

Cheese is available in every town and village in Greece and can also be purchased from the dairy farmer. In the Athens Central Market, there are several cheese shops and even shops that sell only feta

cheese. Feta cheese is traditionally made in Greece. The feta cheese is cured in salt brine and can be semi-hard to soft and is usually formed into square blocks. It has a slightly grainy texture and a tangy taste.

The cheese shops in the Market sell the cheeses from the different regions of Greece and also imported cheese. Kassseri is a favorite sheep or goat's milk cheese that can be sliced for eating plain or is often baked or deep fried and served with oregano and oil. The kefalotyri is a hard, salty cheese that is sometimes heated, covered with a splash of brandy and flamed.

The Market had many round, white disks of cheese weighing about two to four pounds in piles on the display counter.

We were able to sample cheese at each of the stands.

Legumes and pulses have been eaten for centuries by the people of Greece. Lentils have been found in excavations of Greek ruins dating back five thousand years. Beans, peas, lentils or rice are eaten every day in the Greek home. The assortment of beans and lentils for sale at several stands was varied and colorfully arranged. The whole red lentils, the French green lentils, the split yellow lentils, the black Beluga and the light brown lentils were piled high in metal bins placed next to bins of red kidney beans, black-eyed peas, white chickpeas, garbanzo beans, Flageolets, a pole green bean, and whole white beans. White and brown rice, in the same type of gray metal bins, was often included in the battery of lentils and pulses. The middle-aged owner of one of the stalls was talking all the while he was filling white paper bags with lentils for his customers. It was a delight to watch him. It seemed dried fruit was as popular as fresh fruit. Large bins of golden brown dates would cling to the scoop when the worker would dip them into a plastic bag. The onyx black, shining prunes were in several bins next to the dried apples and dried, sliced orange apricots. The apricot halves were quite large and blemish-free. The figs were loose in bins and also arranged in round trays for gift packages. This entire area had a delightful fruity aroma.

The stands of fresh fruit and vegetables were across the walk from the meat and fish pavilions and did not have a large structure. The stalls were separate from each other.

It was spring, and all the varieties of berries were in the Market. Strawberries reigned supreme, taking up almost all the space at some stalls. The bright red berries had a wonderful aroma that penetrated the whole area. Oranges, lemons, tangerines, grapefruit and limes were the other main fruit offered for sale. Both green striped watermelon and the pale yellow green honeydew melon were available at one stand. I think it was early in the season for the melons.

I noticed many different greens for sale. Artichokes were trimmed to allow about 5 to 6 inches of the stem to remain on the plant. These are attractive when cooked and served with the stem pointing into the air.

Tomatoes and garlic are mainstays in the Greek diet. The stands selling bright red tomatoes were everywhere. I asked the middle-aged lady who was running one stand where the tomatoes were raised. She spoke some English but had difficulty understanding. I decided she said, "In houses." The tomatoes were on the tables next to the large green peppers on one side and cucumbers on the other. White, red and green onions were on display nearby. I thought the stand looked like a large Greek salad.

The bakery shops had fabulous pastries with whip cream filling and custard filling. The small tarts were filled with vanilla custard and topped with a strawberry or pineapple wedge or nuts. Some of the shops were making doughnuts. They were sugar-glazed or frosted with chocolate. The Greek bread was displayed on wooden shelves. All of the loaves were a long oval shape made with different grains. The rolls were shaped in figure eights or as a twisted roll.

One can find everything they would desire at the Market, all types of food, clothing, housewares, tools and more. I found many of the stalls and the foods to be unique. It is a fascinating Market.

Recipes | Greek Markets

Baklava, Dimotiki Agora Market, Athens

Baklava is a national dessert in Greece. The golden, flaky, syrupy-sweet slices were being sold at the pastry and bakery stands in the Market. I noticed that most of the customers were buying only one or two pieces to take home. Honey, an ingredient of the baklava's syrup, was also for sale in the Market. I learned the honey came from several different areas so the flavors varied according to the plants grown in each region.

4 cups finely crushed walnuts
1-1/2 cups sugar
2 teaspoons cinnamon
1 package phyllo dough (40 sheets) (16 ounces)
Butter, melted for brushing phyllo

Preheat oven to 350 degrees.

Combine walnuts, sugar and cinnamon in a mixing bowl. Oil a 9x13-inch baking dish. Place a sheet of phyllo pastry in the baking pan. Brush with melted butter. Repeat this process with 20 sheets of phyllo. Sprinkle with half the walnut mixture. Repeat process with 5 sheets of phyllo, brushing each with butter. Add walnut mixture. Cover with 15 sheets of phyllo, brushing each with butter. Sprinkle drops of water on top of phyllo. Bake for 45 minutes until golden. Remove from oven, cool. Score the top with a sharp knife into diamond design. Pour syrup over phyllo so it runs into the cuts in the phyllo. When cool, cut into diamond pieces using the scored topping as a pattern. Allow to rest for several hours before serving.

Syrup

6 tablespoons honey
1-1/2 cups warm water
1 tablespoon fresh lemon juice

In a saucepan, place honey, water and lemon juice. Simmer for 10 minutes until thick. Pour over baklava. Cool for 2 to 8 hours before serving.

Yield: 16 small servings

Greens, Dates, Pistachio Nuts and Feta Cheese, Dimotiki Agora Market, Athens

Dates, pistachio nuts and feta cheese are found in all the markets in Greece. They are used in cooking or eaten as a snack.

2 cups mixed spring greens
1 cup arugula
1 small head radicchio, cut into 1-inch pieces
1 cup chopped dates
1/2 cup salted pistachios
1/3 cup dried cranberries
3 ounces feta cheese, crumbled
Raspberry walnut dressing, as needed

In large bowl, combine all greens. Add dates, pistachio nuts and cranberries. Add dressing and toss to coat leaves. Dish onto salad plates. Top with feta cheese.

Yield: 4 to 6 servings

Grilled Octopus, Dimotiki Agora Market, Athens

Octopus is a very popular product in the markets of Greece. It is available in all sizes, from the tiny ones weighing only a few ounces to the large ones with tentacles that stretch way across a display counter and weigh eight to ten pounds. It seems every family has its own recipe for octopus. It is used in stews with wine and vegetables, combined with pasta or rice, baked in its own juice, barbecued and pickled. The most common method of preparing octopus is grilling and broiling. The slices of grilled or broiled octopus are eaten as a snack or served with the favorite beverages ouzo or carafakia. The afternoon cocktail hour, called mezedes, features ouzo and snacks. This custom has been going on for centuries in Greece. The ancient Greeks loved their drinks and small dishes of raw shellfish, pickled fish and fried or broiled seafood. I saw several young men cooking octopus on their portable grills at the Market and along the streets. It took a little courage for me to taste the charbroiled pieces, but I found them to be delicious. After that first introduction, I joined the natives in eating octopus at the mezedes during my stay in Greece.

3 pounds octopus, cleaned and trimmed
3 tablespoons fresh lemon juice
1 bay leaf
4 thyme branches
1 tablespoon peppercorns
1/3 cup extra virgin olive oil
1/4 cup finely chopped fresh parsley
3 tablespoons red wine vinegar
1 teaspoon fresh ground black pepper
1 tablespoon dried oregano
1 teaspoon coarse salt
1 lemon, cut into wedges

Preheat grill to hot 450 degrees.

Rub off the red skin of the octopus. Chop the octopus body into quarters, leaving the legs whole. Wash the pieces under running cold water. Place octopus pieces in boiling salted water. Add lemon juice, bay leaf, thyme and peppercorns. Cook for 45 to 90 minutes until tender. Drain and discard all but the octopus. Blot the pieces dry. Smear the grill with oil. Place the octopus pieces and legs on the grill. Close grill cover and cook 4 to 5 minutes. Turn pieces to cook the other side. Continue cooking until tender and dark but not charred. Cut pieces into serving size. Combine olive oil, parsley, vinegar, ground pepper, oregano and salt. Pour mixture over octopus and toss to coat octopus. Marinate for 30 minutes. Serve with lemon wedges.

Yield: 12 to 14 appetizers or 8 entrée servings

Lentil Soup, Dimotiki Agora Market, Athens

The plastic tubs, woven baskets and burlap sacks holding lentils made for an attractive display in the Market. The lentils are color-ful and vary from yellow, red-orange, red, green, brown and black. Some of the lentils were left whole, and others were sold in a split shape. I was impressed with the colors, shapes and textures of the lentils and thought an artist would enjoy painting the display. Some of the stands selling lentils also sold pistachio nuts, walnuts and a seed that looked like soybeans.

1-1/2 cups lentils
2 tablespoons olive oil
1 large onion, chopped
1 teaspoon chopped garlic
3 carrots, chopped
2 stalks celery, chopped
1 bulb fennel, chopped
1 cup diced fresh or canned tomatoes
1/2 teaspoon salt
1/2 teaspoon black pepper
1 teaspoon sweet paprika
3/4 cup white wine
2 bay leaves
7 cups chicken broth
1 cup feta cheese or sour cream
Chopped parsley for garnish

Rinse lentils and soak for 2 hours. Drain. Place the oil in a large, heavy saucepan. Heat oil and sauté onions, garlic, carrots, celery and fennel until tender. Do not brown. Add lentils and remaining ingredients except cheese and parsley. Cover and simmer for 2 hours, stirring occasionally to prevent the lentils from sticking. Remove from heat and in batches puree in a blender until smooth. Return to the saucepan. Cook for 5 minutes to heat. Garnish each bowl of with cheese or sour cream and parsley.

Yield: 10 servings

Greek Salad, Dimotiki Agora Market, Athens

The fresh produce—lettuce, spinach, tomatoes, cucumbers, green and red peppers and red onions—were plentiful in the Market. The various types of olives were sold at several stands. The cheese stands held a wide selection of feta cheese made with sheep's milk and from a mixture of sheep's and goat's milk. The combination of these products can result in an attractive and delicious Greek salad. The simple dressing of lemon juice and olive oil results in a tangy-tart addition to the crisp vegetables.

1 cup iceberg lettuce, torn into bite-sized pieces
1 cup spinach leaves
1 green pepper, cut into cubes
1 red pepper, cut into cubes
1 medium cucumber, cut into cubes
4 slices red onion
1-1/2 cups grape-sized tomatoes (approximately 16 tomatoes)
3/4 cup pitted black olives (Kalamata)
3/4 cup crumbled feta cheese
1/4 cup extra virgin olive oil
2 tablespoons lemon juice
1/4 teaspoon salt

In a large bowl, toss together all vegetables. Divide among 4 salad bowls. Top with olives and feta cheese. Whisk together olive oil, lemon juice, and salt. Drizzle dressing over each salad.

Yield: 4 servings

Spanakopita (Spinach Pie), Dimotiki Agora Market, Athens

Spanakopita is one of the traditional dishes that young Greek girls learn to prepare early in their culinary training. It is a very common dish served mostly as a snack. Spanakopita is made with spinach and herb filling between butter-soaked sheets of phyllo. At the Greek markets, spanakopita was being sold at the bakery shops in different sized pieces and different shapes of slices. Some looked like a flaky turnover.

2 pounds fresh spinach, trimmed and chopped (or 2 pounds frozen spinach, thawed, squeezed dry)
3/4 cup finely chopped green onions
4 garlic cloves, minced
1-1/2 cups crumbled feta cheese
1/2 cup ricotta cheese
3 eggs, beaten
Salt and black pepper, as desired
1 package phyllo pastry (40 sheets)
Butter, melted, for brushing phyllo

Preheat oven to 350 degrees.

Blanch spinach in boiling water. Drain all the liquid from the spinach. Place in colander and allow to cool over the sink. (Or thaw and squeeze dry frozen spinach.) Place in saucepan and add all ingredients except phyllo. Stir to blend. Unwrap phyllo slices and cover with a damp towel. Lightly oil a large baking dish (9x12-inches). Place half the phyllo sheets (20 sheets) in the bottom of the dish, brushing each sheet with melted butter. Add all the filling and spread the remaining phillo sheet (20 sheets) over the top, brushing each one with butter. Sprinkle a small amount of water over the top of the phyllo. Bake at 350 degrees for 45 minutes until golden. Score the top for slicing.

Yield: 20 appetizers or 8 regular servings

Roast Goat or Kid, Dimotiki Agora Market, Athens

In the meat pavilions at the Athens Market, many skinned and dressed carcasses of goats, young goats (kid) and lambs were hung on hooks from the frames of the meat stands. They were not very appetizing to look at. The carcass could be purchased whole or in the desired cut. The whole roast goat or lamb is frequently served at special occasions or for celebrations. They are generally roasted on a rotisserie or over an open flame out of doors. The meat is sometimes marinated or cooked with garlic and herbs to mellow the goat flavor.

2 legs of kid (young goat) about 4 pounds total
1/4 cup wine vinegar
6 garlic cloves, chopped
1/2 teaspoon dried rosemary
1/2 teaspoon dried thyme
1 tablespoon chopped fresh mint
1/4 cup chopped fresh cilantro

1 teaspoon salt
1/2 teaspoon freshly ground black pepper
1/4 cup water
1 tablespoon olive oil
12 small potatoes, peeled
12 small onions, peeled, left whole

In mixing bowl, combine vinegar, garlic, rosemary, thyme, mint, cilantro, salt, pepper and 1/4 cup water. Rub the mixture over the goat meat, covering all sides. Cover and refrigerate for several hours or overnight. Remove from refrigerator and place in a baking pan. Coat with oil. Peel the potatoes and onions and place in salted water in a saucepan. Cook for 12 minutes. Drain and add to meat roasting pan. Add 1 cup water to roasting pan. Place in 400 degree oven and roast for 30 minutes. Reduce heat to 350 degrees and roast for an additional 30 minutes until meat thermometer reaches 170 degrees. Add more water to the roasting pan if the pan becomes dry. Remove from oven and let roast rest for 10 minutes covered with foil. Carve the meat and serve with potatoes and onions.

Yield: 6 to 8 servings

Moussaka with Eggplant, Dimotiki Agora Market, Athens

Moussaka is to the Greeks as lasagna is to the Italians. It is a baked dish layered with potatoes, meat sauce, eggplant and béchamel sauce. (Some recipes call for a mashed potato topping over the ingredients just before baking.) It is not only the large, purple, loaf-shaped eggplant that is available to customers, but also the skinny, long Japanese eggplant, the white, round-as-a-baseball eggplant, and the striped white-and-green or white-and-purple eggplant. Eggplant has had many names since it traveled west from Asia to Europe and beyond. In Greece, it was called melongena. The white eggplant also was known as the "love apple" in Greece.

2 eggplants, about 2 pounds total
4 egg whites, slightly beaten (save the yolks for the béchamel sauce)
2 cups bread crumbs, unseasoned
4 medium white potatoes
1 cup grated kefalotyri or Parmesan cheese (reserve for later assembly of Moussaka)

Peel the eggplant, leaving small strips of peel around the eggplant. Slice in 1/2-inch thick rounds. Place in colander and salt liberally. Place a weight on top of eggplant and place colander in sink for draining. Let rest for 20 minutes. Rinse the eggplant with cold water. Pat dry. Preheat over to 400 degrees. Dip eggplant in beaten egg whites and then in bread crumbs, coating both sides. Place on greased baking sheet and bake for 30 minutes, turning once during the baking. Remove from oven and set aside. Reduce oven temperature to 350 degrees. Peel potatoes and boil in salted water until tender but firm. Drain and cool. Slice into 1/2-inch slices.

Meat Sauce

1 tablespoon vegetable oil
1 large onion, diced
2 cloves garlic, minced
1 pound ground beef or ground lamb
1/3 cup red wine
2 tablespoons chopped fresh parsley
1/2 teaspoon cinnamon
1/8 teaspoon ground allspice
3/4 cup diced and crushed tomatoes
4 tablespoons tomato paste
2 teaspoons sugar
1/2 teaspoon salt
1/8 teaspoon black pepper

In a large skillet, heat oil. Add onions and cook for 3 minutes. Add garlic and cook for an additional minute. Remove from skillet. Add meat to skillet and cook for 5 to 7 minutes, stirring to crumble meat. Return onion and garlic to skillet. Add wine and cook for 4 minutes. Add parsley, cinnamon, allspice, tomatoes, tomato paste, sugar, salt and pepper. Simmer sauce for 15 minutes. Check for seasoning and adjust as needed.

Béchamel Sauce

1/2 cup salted butter
1/2 cup all-purpose flour
2 cups milk, warmed
4 egg yolks, lightly beaten
Pinch ground nutmeg

Melt butter over low heat in a saucepan. Add flour, whisking continuously to make a smooth paste. Allow the flour to cook for a minute but do not brown. Add milk in a steady stream, whisking continuously. Simmer over low heat until thickened but do not boil. Remove from heat and gradually stir in beaten egg yolks. Add nutmeg. Return to heat and stir until thickened. Lightly grease a large baking pan such as a lasagna pan. Sprinkle the bottom with bread crumbs leaving 1/4-inch space around the edges. Place a layer of potatoes on the bread crumbs. Place a layer of eggplant on top of potatoes, using half of the eggplant. Cover with the meat sauce. Sprinkle top with half of the grated cheese. Put the remaining eggplant slices on top of the cheese. Pour the béchamel sauce over the eggplant, allowing sauce to fill edges of pan. Smooth the sauce on top with a spatula. Sprinkle the remaining cheese on top. Bake at 350 degrees for 45 minutes until béchamel sauce is golden. Remove from oven and let rest for 15 to 20 minutes before slicing.

Yield: 4 to 6 servings

Recipe Index

5781

Made in the USA
San Bernardino, CA
06 January 2014